Praise for IRAN'S DEADLY AMBITION

"With Washington fixated on the intricacies of Iran's nuclear
program, Ilan Berman wisely refocuses our attention on
the bigger picture: an Iran with global aspirations and new
international opportunities to advance its radical agenda.
Iran's Deadly Ambition is essential reading for anyone who
wants to understand the next great threat to America's
security and the security of our allies in the Middle East."

—THE HONORABLE JOSEPH LIEBERMAN,
    former senator from Connecticut (1989–2013)

"*Iran's Deadly Ambition* provides a timely look into the true
scope of the many challenges we face from the Islamic
Republic of Iran. Policymakers in Washington and our closest
international partners would do well to read Ilan Berman's
insights beyond the current headlines. They would do even
better to act on his ideas."

—LIEUTENANT GENERAL MICHAEL T. FLYNN (USA, ret.),
    former director of the Defense Intelligence Agency

IRAN'S DEADLY
AMBITION

IRAN'S DEADLY AMBITION

The Islamic Republic's Quest for Global Power

Ilan Berman

Encounter Books
New York • London

First American edition published in 2015 by Encounter Books, an activity of Encounter for Culture and Education, Inc., a nonprofit, tax exempt corporation. Encounter Books website address: www.encounterbooks.com

Manufactured in the United States and printed on acid-free paper. The paper used in this publication meets the minimum requirements of ANSI/NISO z39.48-1992 (R 1997) (*Permanence of Paper*).

First paperback edition published in 2016.
Paperback edition ISBN: 978-1-59403-897-6

THE LIBRARY OF CONGRESS HAS CATALOGUED THE HARDCOVER EDITION AS FOLLOWS:
Berman, Ilan.
Iran's deadly ambition : the Islamic republic's quest for global power / Ilan Berman.
pages cm
Includes bibliographical references and index.
ISBN 978-1-59403-801-3 (hardback) — ISBN 978-1-59403-802-0 (ebook)
1. Iran—Foreign relations—21st century.   2. World politics—21st century.   I. Title.
DS318.83.B47 2015
327.55—dc23
2015010955

PRODUCED BY WILSTED & TAYLOR PUBLISHING SERVICES
Copy editor Lynn Meinhardt
Designer and compositor Nancy Koerner
Proofreader Melody Lacina
Indexer Kevin Milham

For Hillary,
with all my love

Contents

Preface

In Washington, they say, policy debates never truly go away. Instead, they come back, time and time again, albeit occasionally in different forms.

That has certainly been the case with Iran. In 2004, when I wrote my first book on the subject, *Tehran Rising*, few government officials—and even fewer ordinary Americans—were familiar with the ideology animating the Islamic Republic or the true scope of the problems the Iranian regime poses for our foreign partners and for us.

A decade later, quite a few more people are. Yet, by and large, America is as divided as ever about how best to address the strategic challenge that Iran represents. In fact, we have in many ways moved further away from a sober assessment of the scale of Iran's ambitions and its destabilizing potential on the world stage.

So this book is intended, at least in part, to serve as a corrective of sorts. It is not, by any stretch, a comprehensive review of Iran's history, ideology, and activities. Those topics have been covered in countless books already and will assuredly be the subjects of many more. Instead, this work is my humble attempt to outline the true scope of a problem that I am convinced the U.S. government will need to deal with in the years ahead.

That I was able to undertake this project at all is a credit to American Foreign Policy Council President Herman Pirchner, Jr. For nearly fifteen years, he has provided me with an intellectual home, indulged my interests, underwritten my projects, and challenged me to think critically about the state of the world and America's place in it. Through it all, he has been a tireless advocate, a fierce critic, and a true friend.

In putting together this book, I was extremely fortunate to be able to rely on the insights of Michael Doran, Jonathan Schanzer, Joel Rayburn, Matt Levitt, Joseph Humire, Claudia Rosett, Joshua Eisenman, Darin Dutcher, and Larry Haas. They took time out of their busy schedules to provide me with valuable criticism, further refine my thinking, and sharpen my prose. For that, they already have my deepest thanks. But, to the extent that this book helps contribute to the national security debate, they also deserve at least part of the credit. Needless to say, any mistakes that might be contained herein are entirely my own.

As always, I am grateful to Annie Swingen, Jeff Smith, and Rich Harrison, my colleagues at the American Foreign Policy Council, for their support and friendship and for making our work truly a team effort. Thanks go as well to our tireless in-house editor, Liz Wood, for working her magic on this book, the way she has so many times before. Our pool of talented interns, including Cameron Harris, Collin McClure, Jason Czerwiec, and James Williams, also deserves recognition for helping with the research on various aspects of this book, as well as for pitching in on sundry other projects and initiatives.

Most of all, I owe an enormous debt to my family. As any author will tell you, book writing is, by its nature, a lonely and selfish undertaking. It requires the freedom to take long absences from the outside world and depends on the patience of others. My wife, Hillary, and my children, Mark and Lauren, provided me with all that during the months and months that I was preoccupied with this project. But they also gave—and continue to give—me much more: their love, their support, and a reason to keep fighting the good fight.

ILAN BERMAN
Washington, D.C.
January 2015

IRAN'S DEADLY
AMBITION

Introduction

When the hardcover edition of *Iran's Deadly Ambition* went to press in spring 2015, the nuclear deal between Iran and the countries of the P5+1 (the United States, United Kingdom, Russia, China, France, and Germany) had not yet been concluded. Back then, the substance of what was being negotiated behind closed doors in Vienna, Austria, and Lausanne, Switzerland, was the subject of extensive coverage in the media and the topic of even greater speculation in Washington and assorted foreign capitals. But the true extent of the compromise that was eventually reached over Iran's nuclear ambitions wasn't yet known.

Now it is. In July 2015, with great fanfare, the Obama administration formally unveiled the Joint Comprehensive Plan of Action (JCPOA), as the nuclear deal with Iran is formally known. With its release, the American public got its first real glimpse at the extent of the diplomatic bargain struck with Iran.

We have discovered that the agreement is not as bad as it was initially believed. It's actually much worse.

While the JCPOA can be said to include some beneficial elements—short-term constraints on Iranian uranium enrichment, a reduction in the number of centrifuges operated by the Islamic Republic, and a delay of the regime's "plutonium track"—it is materially deficient in at least three key respects.

First, the new nuclear deal does not dismantle Iran's nuclear capability, as originally envisioned by the United States and its negotiating partners. Contrary to the Obama administration's pledges at the outset of talks in November 2013, the JCPOA does not irrevocably reduce Iran's nuclear potential. In fact, it does the opposite: under key provisions of the accord (specifically, those contained in the document's four annexes), the P5+1 nations have actually committed themselves to strengthening and reinforcing Iran's nuclear infrastructure and processes over the next ten years.[1]

As a result, the JCPOA enables a slower but ultimately stronger Iranian nuclear program. And when the agreement expires less than a decade from now, the Islamic Republic will be much closer to a breakout capability than it is today, constituting what some have called a "patient pathway" to the atomic bomb for Iran's ayatollahs.[2]

Second, the new nuclear deal incentivizes further proliferation on the part of Iran and its neighbors. Although President Obama has claimed that the JCPOA closes off all pathways by which Iran can acquire a nuclear capability,[3] the agreement actually focuses on just one of two such routes: indigenous development (the regime's domestic facilities, stockpiles, and nuclear know-how). It does not seriously address the parallel track by which Iran can acquire such a capability: clandestine procurement of components from abroad.

This represents a serious oversight, because Iran maintains active proliferation relationships with a range of suppliers, including the regime of Kim Jong-un in North Korea and private commercial entities in the People's Republic of China. These connections—detailed extensively in Chapter VI— have been essential to Iran's ballistic missile and nuclear advances to date and will enable the Iranian regime to still make progress on its nuclear effort in spite of heightened scrutiny over its domestic activities.

Moreover, Iran's advances have nudged other countries in the Middle East to accelerate their own nuclear plans in response. Most conspicuously, regional rival Saudi Arabia has threatened to pursue its own nuclear option as a strategic counterweight, likely by leveraging its extensive and ongoing strategic relationship with Pakistan.[4] As a result, there is significant potential for a destabilizing cascade of proliferation in the region in coming years, the logical end point of which will be the emergence of multiple nuclear aspirants along Iran's periphery.

Third, and most significant, the nuclear deal has set in motion a fundamental unraveling of the international sanctions regime painstakingly erected over the preceding decade and a half and designed to curtail Iran's global menace. Through both direct and indirect means, the JCPOA has put Iran on the cusp of an economic windfall of unprecedented magnitude.

THE GREAT SANCTIONS GIVEAWAY

In short order, the United States and its partners in the P5+1 released to Iran some $100 billion in previously escrowed oil revenue. As of "implementation day," January 14, 2016, Iran received unfettered access to these funds without limitations on their use.

The scope of this stimulus is enormous. It amounts to roughly a quarter of Iran's annual GDP, which totaled $415 billion in 2014.[5] That sum rivals the entirety of the European Recovery Program (known as the Marshall Plan) launched by the Truman administration in 1948 in the aftermath of World War II—an initiative that disbursed $13 billion ($120 billion in today's dollars) to seventeen countries in Europe over the span of four years. The proportional impact of such relief for Iran is analogous to America's $16.7 trillion economy receiving an infusion of roughly $4.2 trillion—approximately five times the stimulus that stabilized the U.S. financial sector following the 2008 global economic crisis.

The White House has tried to minimize the significance of this concession. Early on, administration officials argued that the Iranian regime would use any windfall overwhelmingly for benign activities, such as improving domestic conditions or strengthening its economy.[6] More recently, they have argued that the economic benefits—while indeed extensive—remain largely unrealized by the Islamic Republic. Thus, in his April 2016 speech before the National Gala dinner of J Street, a liberal political action group that supports the Iran deal, Secretary of State John Kerry noted that Iran had so far received just $3 billion of the overall total.[7]

Both characterizations are deeply misleading. Iran can indeed be expected to utilize a significant portion of the economic relief rendered by the P5+1 for domestic purposes. But the sheer volume of unblocked funds means that the Iranian regime will be able to significantly augment its expenditures on everything from supporting international terrorism to modernizing its military, with detrimental effects for both regional and American security. At the same time, Iran's delay to date in accessing the totality of this aid is a reflection of political choices in Tehran rather than of real-world constraints. Simply put, the Iranian regime can use the entire sum of more than $100 billion. It just has not chosen to do so—at least not yet.

Nor is it accurate to say, as some have argued, that adverse global economic conditions will wipe away any benefit that the Iranian regime might receive from sanctions relief.[8] While Iran's initial windfall is indeed somewhat dampened by the low world price of oil, the Iranian regime is adapting by revising its budget downward, focusing on non-oil exports, and significantly expanding domestic taxation.[9]

Additionally, the stimulus enshrined in the JCPOA will invariably be augmented by the benefits of expanded post-sanctions trade between Iran and countries in Europe and Asia. The agreement will also greatly strengthen the inevitable reintegration of Iran into global institutions from which it was previously proscribed, such as the Society for Worldwide Interbank Financial Telecommunications (SWIFT).[10]

In the meantime, America is proffering still more economic carrots to the Islamic Republic. In the months since the passage of the JCPOA, in response to dissatisfaction in Tehran about its anemic economic recovery so far, the Obama administration has sought to provide the Iranian regime with ever-greater sanctions relief. The justification propounded by top administration officials is that Iran has yet to reap real benefits from the deal, and therefore a further sweetening of the pot is necessary to ensure that Iran continues to abide by the agreement's terms.

In the service of this goal, the White House launched an effort in the spring of 2016 to facilitate Iranian access to the U.S. dollar.[11] The initiative touched off a political firestorm on Capitol Hill, with irate members of Congress protesting that the plan effectively reneged on promises made by the White House last summer in its attempt to sell the nuclear deal to a skeptical Congress. Among those was Treasury Secretary Jack Lew's pledge to the Senate Foreign Relations Committee in July 2015 that, irrespective of the provisions of the new nuclear deal, the administration was committed to keeping existing, and extensive, trade restrictions in place.[12]

Congressional pressure, as well as the risk that direct Iranian access to the U.S. economy would violate provisions of the 2012 National Defense Authorization Act, which mandated that the White House "block and prohibit" Iranian assets if those funds "come within the United States, or are or come within the possession or control of a United States person,"[13] conspired to thwart the administration's initial plan. Nevertheless, the administration appears to be actively examining workarounds that would allow Iran the ability to exploit the strength of the U.S. dollar, possibly through the creation of an offshore clearing facility for facilitating previously prohibited U-turn transactions utilizing the dollar.[14] The White House is doing so, moreover, even though such a step would fundamentally compromise the integrity of the global sanctions regime by allowing Iran's tainted money to permeate U.S. financial institutions.

The Obama administration has even become a direct investor in Iran's nuclear program. As part of an agreement hammered out between Washington and Tehran in late April, the United States has committed to purchasing 32 tons of heavy water—a key byproduct of nuclear development—from Iran. The $8.6 million deal will help Iran fulfill one of the conditions of the JCPOA, which stipulates that Iran gets rid of the substance as a way of ensuring that it is not later used to help create nuclear weapons. But the agreement isn't simply a security measure. It is also intended as an economic signal to other potential economic partners of the Islamic Republic that it is acceptable to invest in the regime's nuclear program. "The idea is: Okay, we tested it, it's perfectly good heavy water. It meets spec. We'll buy a little of this," Energy Secretary Ernest Moniz explained to the *Wall Street Journal*.[15] "That will be a statement to the world: 'You want to buy heavy water from Iran, you can buy heavy water from Iran. It's been done. Even the United States did it.'"

THE LIMITS OF NORMALIZATION

For the moment, relief has yet to kick in in earnest. That is at least partly because Iran's rickety economy suffers from serious structural problems. The International Monetary Fund concluded after a May 2016 visit to the Islamic Republic that the country will need to undertake significant internal reforms on issues such as money laundering and terror financing in order to alleviate investor jitters and facilitate full integration into the global economy.[16] But, over the long term, the cumulative impact of these measures will be nothing short of transformational.

Slowly but surely, Iran's trading partners are beginning to reengage with Iran. In early 2016, Chinese president Xi Jinping visited Tehran and concluded a sweeping 25-year plan to broaden bilateral relations, including a strategy to expand trade between the two countries to $600 billion over the next decade.[17] More decisive still was the May 2016 state visit to Iran of Indian prime minister Narendra Modi, which netted a dozen new pacts on trade, telecommunications, and transportation—including a multiyear, $500 million deal to build and administer two cargo terminals at the southern Iranian port of Chabahar, a project that will effectively make the Islamic Republic a key player in India's future export strategy.[18] And, during a whirlwind spring 2016 trip to Tehran, European Union foreign policy chief Federica Mogherini made clear that Europe, which once ranked as Iran's most substantial trade partner, accounting for 38 percent of Iran's exports and 31 percent of its imports, is eager to reclaim that mantle once again now that sanctions have been lifted.[19]

Eager corporations are starting to do the same. In June 2016, in what represents the first major Western deal with post-sanctions Iran, Boeing concluded a "historic" $25 billion agreement to provide Iran Air, the country's national carrier, with 100 new commercial airplanes.[20] While congressional pressure so far has helped stall implementation of this agreement, it nonetheless represents a sign of the times, as hungry multinational firms begin to dip their toes back into the Iranian market in earnest.

All this has unmistakably placed Iran on the road to sustained recovery. As evidence of this fact, the World Bank now estimates that Iran's GDP—which constricted by nearly 7 percent in 2012 and a further 3 percent in 2013 as a result of Western sanctions—will grow by nearly 6 percent this year alone.[21] Further into the future, Iran's economic horizons look brighter still.

The JCPOA has not, however, yielded a fundamental change in Iran's political outlook. Contrary to the fervent wishes of the Obama administration, the agreement has not fostered a kinder, gentler polity in Iran. While the White House lobbied heavily in favor of the agreement based on the argument that it would help empower moderate forces within Iran, nothing of the sort has happened.

This was evident in Iran's parallel elections in February 2016. The first of these was to appoint representatives to the country's unicameral legislature, commonly known as the Majles. The second was to select officials for the Assembly of Experts, the powerful clerical body that selects and oversees the performance of the country's top religious authority, its supreme leader.

Ahead of the elections, conventional wisdom held that the twin outcomes would be resounding victories for Iran's reformists.[22] In truth, however, the results were far less than met the eye. Mass disqualifications of progressive candidates in the weeks leading up to the vote ensured that those "reformists" who could still stand in the elections were not true moderates—they were overwhelmingly compliant to the regime. In the final calculus, observers were forced to concede that the election results amounted to nothing short of a rout of Iranian president Hassan Rouhani's political allies and a resounding reaffirmation of the conservative status quo in Iranian politics.[23]

The Iranian regime's core anti–American animus, too, remains intact. Iran's supreme leader, Ayatollah Ali Khamenei, recently warned that the United States was using the nuclear deal as a strategic tool in order "to be able to reinstate their previous hegemony" over the Islamic Republic.[24] And in mid-May, Iran's parliament voted overwhelmingly to approve a bill demanding compensation from the United States for "spiritual and material damage" inflicted on Iran over the past six decades as a result of its policies.[25] The message of these and myriad other signals is unmistakable: Iran may have profited handsomely from the nuclear deal, but it has no interest in a more pacific relationship with the country principally responsible for making it possible.

What the JCPOA has succeeded in doing, however, is reinvigorate Iran's global appetite. After laboring for years under international sanctions and with limited means to make its foreign policy vision a reality, the Islamic Republic is now positioned for a landmark global expansion. The pages that follow sketch what that expansion will look like and why a rising Iran represents a major and enduring threat to American interests and the safety and security of U.S. allies abroad.

It is a danger that has only grown more acute since this book was first written.

CHAPTER

I

Iran's Manifest Destiny

What makes Tehran tick? More than three and a half decades after Ayatollah Ruhollah Khomeini swept to power in Tehran on a wave of revolutionary fervor, transforming an erstwhile ally of the United States into a mortal enemy practically overnight, policy makers in Washington still understand precious little about the inner workings of his Islamic Republic. As a result, they consistently misjudge, misunderstand, and misinterpret what the Iranian regime says and does and what its leaders truly believe.

Today, this failure is seen most clearly in the Obama administration's growing calls for normalization with the Iranian regime. During its time in office, the current White House has gravitated steadily toward the notion that Iran is a troublesome yet ultimately benign regional actor. Although President Obama has promised strong action against Iranian rogue behavior, his administration made repeated diplomatic overtures toward the Islamic Republic, propelled by the notion that with the proper mix of diplomatic dialogue and strategic incentives it will be possible to "domesticate" the Iranian regime.[1]

To be fair, the Obama administration is hardly the only

one to harbor this hope. More and more, Western observers have embraced the idea that Iran is a nation with which it is possible to do business. Thus, an extensive special report in a November 2014 edition of the prestigious *Economist* magazine loudly proclaimed that "the revolution is over" in Iran, and that the Islamic Republic is now decisively transitioning beyond "decades of messianic fervour."[2] The unspoken message, reflecting the emerging political consensus on both sides of the Atlantic, is crystal clear: there's no reason to fear the Islamic Republic any longer.

The lure of this idea is undeniable. If it could somehow be rehabilitated, Iran would become a powerful Western ally in the Middle East and a lucrative trading partner for the world. Yet the notion is as misguided as it is appealing. Although the Iranian regime is currently engaged in diplomacy with the West over its nuclear program, there is no indication that it has abandoned the core ideological tenets of Khomeini's revolution, which emphasize antagonism toward the West. Indeed, Iran—like Russia and China—is a revisionist power that actively seeks to remake its immediate region and the world beyond. Thus, as political scientist Walter Russell Mead astutely observed, "Iran wishes to replace the current order in the Middle East—led by Saudi Arabia and dominated by Sunni Arab states—with one centered on Tehran."[3] Iran, in other words, possesses a distinct manifest destiny. And today, even as the international community is preoccupied with its nuclear program, the Islamic Republic is forging ahead with its quest for global influence.

A REVOLUTIONARY PEDIGREE

Iran's contemporary, confrontational worldview dates back to the 1960s and 1970s, when Ayatollah Khomeini languished in exile, first in Iraq and then in France. It was during this time that he codified his ideas about the need for Shiite empowerment and global Islamic revolution. The result, a slender volume entitled *Islamic Government*, went on to serve as the template for Khomeini's Islamic Republic following the successful 1979 revolution.[4]

In short order, after Khomeini's partisans seized power in Tehran, the ideas about domestic governance contained in *Islamic Government* became the foundation for his new religion-based state. Khomeini himself became both the country's political leader and its spiritual model. A sea change took place in foreign policy as well. Iran's new clerical rulers believed fervently that their government marked the start of a global caliphate and that Iran's revolution would augur the dominance of Islam "in all the countries of the world."[5] Accordingly, the country's constitution proclaimed that the Islamic Republic's armed forces "will be responsible not only for guarding and preserving the frontiers of the country, but also for fulfilling the ideological mission of jihad in God's way; that is, extending the sovereignty of God's law throughout the world."[6] Iran's radical vision of Islamic governance, in other words, was intended from the start to be an export commodity.

During the tumultuous decade of the 1980s, as Khomeini's revolutionaries consolidated power at home, the principle of "exporting the revolution" became a cardinal regime priority. Its importance was demonstrated in the fact that, despite the expense of a bloody, grinding eight-year war with Saddam Hussein's Iraq, the fledgling Islamic Republic sunk colossal resources into becoming a hub of "global resistance." In keeping with Khomeini's declaration that "Islam will be victorious in all the countries of the world,"[7] the Iranian regime threw open its borders to a bevy of third-world radicals, from Palestinian resistance fighters to Latin American leftist revolutionaries. These disparate factions (many of which hailed from outside the Muslim world) gravitated to the Islamic Republic, where they obtained military, political, and economic support from an Iranian government eager to demonstrate its revolutionary bona fides and its commitment to a global Islamic order.[8]

Perhaps the most significant development during this period, however, was Iran's creation of a proxy force in Lebanon to help spread its radical global vision. Forged from disparate Shiite militias fighting in Lebanon's chaotic civil war, this "Army of God," or *Hezbollah* in Arabic, became a powerful consolidated militia committed to Iran's worldview. The group's charter, published in 1985, pledged formal allegiance to Ayatollah Khomeini himself and, more broadly, to the *Velayat-e Faqih*, the "rule of the jurisprudent" form of government he institutionalized in Iran.[9]

Ever since, Hezbollah has served as a key prong of Iranian policy. At times working in tandem with—and at others, independent from—Iran's formal revolutionaries in the Islamic Revolutionary Guard Corps (IRGC), the Lebanese militia has sought to further the regime's agenda of "resistance" against Israel and the West, most directly by targeting Israeli and Jewish victims. In exchange, it has been rewarded lavishly, with the Iranian regime bankrolling the militia to the tune of between $100 and $200 million annually for many years.[10] This assistance has given the group global reach and has made it, in the words of former deputy secretary of state Richard Armitage, the "A-team of terrorists."[11]

The death of Khomeini in the late 1980s and a period of sustained economic and political stagnation in the 1990s led many in the West to believe that Iran had entered a "post-revolutionary era."[12] That hope, however, turned out to be fleeting. Over the past dozen years, Iran's revolutionary fervor has returned with a vengeance.

VANGUARD OF THE REVOLUTION

With the exception of Iran's supreme leader, no political actor is more important in shaping Iran's contemporary politics and its place in the world than the regime's feared clerical army, the Islamic Revolutionary Guard Corps (Sepāh-e Pāsdārān-e Enqelāb-e Eslāmi), also known as the IRGC. Originally conceived by Ayatollah Khomeini as a revolutionary vanguard capable of spreading his political model beyond Iran's borders,[13] the IRGC is today far more than simply a national army.

Within Iran, it is nothing short of an economic powerhouse, in control of numerous companies and corporate entities that stretch across broad swathes of the Islamic Republic's economy, from transportation to energy to construction. This power was on display in May 2004, when the Guards shut down Tehran's Imam Khomeini airport rather than allow a Turkish consortium to operate it.[14] The message was unmistakable: the IRGC, rather than the government, was the ultimate arbiter of acceptable commerce within the Islamic Republic.

It was also a testament to the enormous financial power amassed by the IRGC in recent years. In 2007, the *Los Angeles Times* estimated that the Guards had accumulated in excess of $12 billion in business and construction interests and possessed links to more than one hundred companies.[15] That, however, is just the tip of the iceberg. The IRGC, for example, is believed to be in control of practically all of the Islamic Republic's $12-billion-a-year smuggling industry.[16] Its reach extends to virtually every sector of the Iranian economy, from energy to trade to defense-industrial development. But it is in construction where the influence of the Guards is deepest. Khatam al-Anbiya, the IRGC's construction headquarters, is Iran's biggest corporation: a massive, sprawling network of companies, comprising more than 800 affiliates, employing an estimated 40,000 workers, and in control of billions of dollars in assets.[17] All told, the IRGC is believed to command as much as one-third of Iran's entire economy.[18]

This web of activity has alternately been described as a "business conglomerate with guns," a "huge investment company with a complex of business empires and trading companies," and a "de facto foreign ministry" for Iran's revolutionary forces.[19] Yet these descriptions barely scratch the surface of the IRGC's centrality in the Iranian economy and how much power it truly exerts over the Islamic Republic's political direction. The full extent of the IRGC's economic reach is simply not known outside of Iran, hidden as it is behind shell companies, middlemen, and cut-outs, as well as pervasive patronage networks and entrenched political interests. What is clear, however, is that the IRGC has become a state within a state in contemporary Iran.

The IRGC's current prominence is largely the work of one man: Mahmoud Ahmadinejad. His ascendance to the Iranian presidency in 2005 ushered in a golden age of nearly unbridled influence for the Guards in Iranian politics. Ahmadinejad is himself a former Guardsman. He served a stint in the IRGC during the 1980s, working both as an army engineer and as part of the support team for a daring 1987 special forces operation in Kirkuk at the tail end of the Iran-Iraq War.[20] Ahmadinejad maintained his contacts with the Guards following his active duty service, and Iranian military officials and families made up an integral part of his constituent base during his ascent to political power. And once Ahmadinejad assumed the presidency, he wasted no time rewarding his former comrades-in-arms richly.

Within a year, the IRGC racked up an estimated $10 billion in sweetheart deals and no-bid government contracts from the Iranian government.[21] Within two, fully two-thirds of Iran's twenty-one cabinet positions were occupied by members of the IRGC.[22] By then, former Guardsmen and their sympathizers had taken over more than a fifth of the seats in the Majles, Iran's unicameral parliament.[23] By 2010, the situation became even more of a monopoly, with Guardsmen staffing Ahmadinejad's cabinet almost exclusively and occupying roughly a third of all parliamentary posts.[24] Observers likened this takeover to a "creeping coup d'etat," in which Iran's clerical elite slowly became overshadowed by its clerical army.[25]

Over the past several years, Iran watchers have taken note of this trend.[26] So, belatedly, have administration officials. In September 2010, Secretary of State Hillary Clinton acknowledged the changing center of gravity within the Islamic Republic when, in a speech before the Council on Foreign Relations, she described Iran as having transformed into "a military dictatorship with a . . . sort of religious-ideological veneer."[27] But this realization did not contribute to greater clarity in Washington about how to respond to the Iranian regime's rogue behavior.

That behavior, meanwhile, has intensified, commensurate with the IRGC's power. The IRGC today is a global strategic force, and one that is currently active in virtually every region of the world.

The power of the Guards begins with its grip on the regime's strategic capabilities. This includes the Islamic Republic's arsenal of ballistic missiles—an arsenal which is growing rapidly. The centerpiece of that effort is the Shahab-3, a medium-range missile unveiled publicly more than a decade ago. In recent years, the Iranian regime has expanded the range, accuracy, and payload of the Shahab-3 and its variants, and today this class of missiles is estimated to be nuclear-capable and possess a range of between 900 and 1,200 miles, putting all of Israel, the north of India, and parts of Eastern Europe within striking distance. Indeed, Iran is now the most formidable missile power in the Middle East, according to U.S. intelligence-community assessments.[28] And these capabilities are just part of a much larger picture.

In 2005, Iran became the first space-faring nation in the Muslim world when it successfully launched a surveillance satellite into orbit from the missile base in Plesetsk, Russia. Since then, the Iranian regime has racked up a number of additional successful space launches. While these efforts appear to be civilian in nature, the potential military applications cannot be ignored, because the same rocket booster used to place a payload into low Earth orbit can be married to a two-stage ballistic missile to create one of intercontinental range. Iran, in other words, is building the capability to shift rapidly from being a regional missile power to being a global one, with the power to hold at risk Western Europe and beyond.

The control exercised by Iran's clerical army extends to the regime's nuclear program as well. When Ayatollah Khomeini came to power in 1979, he rolled back Shah Mohammad Reza Pahlavi's ambitious plan—sketched out during the 1970s—to make Iran a nuclear power, citing it as un-Islamic in nature. But the Islamic Republic's devastating loss to regional rival Iraq during the subsequent eight-year Iran-Iraq War—and international assistance to the Iraqi war effort during that conflict—helped convince Iran's ayatollahs of the need to revive the country's nascent atomic drive. As a result, by the late 1980s, Iran's nuclear plans were back on track, with the IRGC firmly in charge of their progress.[29]

So it has remained. Today, it is believed that if hostilities arose, the IRGC would "have custody over potentially deployed nuclear weapons, most or all other chemical, biological, radiological, and nuclear weapons," and the ability "to operate Iran's nuclear-armed missile forces if they are deployed."[30] That means, as a practical matter, that no nuclear deal is possible which does not meet with the IRGC's approval—something that represents a complicating, and perhaps insurmountable, obstacle to the nuclear negotiations between Iran and the West.

Iran's clerical army is also a significant naval power. Over the past several years, in keeping with its vision of itself as a global player, the Iranian regime has bolstered its ability to project military power abroad. This has included major upgrades to both its conventional navy, the Islamic Republic of Iran Navy (IRIN), and its clerical counterpart, the Islamic Revolutionary Guard Corps Navy (IRGCN), with significant results.[31] According to intelligence analyst Steven O'Hern, the IRGCN now totals some 18,000 men, making it a "force equal in size to the Iranian Navy," and this force is in operational control of "all of Iran's missile boats and land-based anti-ship missiles."[32]

A decade ago, the U.S. intelligence community assessed that Iran was able to shut off tanker traffic in the Strait of Hormuz, a critical naval waterway through which one-fifth of global oil transits, for brief periods of time.[33] Since then, concerted investments by the Iranian regime have made its maritime forces even more capable. They have also made Iran's clerical army more adventurous on the high seas, something that was demonstrated in dramatic fashion in March 2007, when the IRGCN captured fifteen British sailors off the coast of Iraq. The Iranian regime claimed that the sailors had strayed into Iran's territorial waters—a charge that the British government disputed. But Iran's seizure also put members of the U.S.-led coalition on notice that the Islamic Republic was assuming an increasingly aggressive naval profile in the Persian Gulf, a reality the United States and its allies will inevitably face in the years ahead.

This fact was hammered home in March 2014, when CNN reported that the Islamic Revolutionary Guard Corps was in the process of constructing a large-scale replica of a U.S. naval carrier. Regime officials at first dismissed the construction as simply a movie prop, but the true objective quickly became clear. In a subsequent interview with the official FARS News Agency, Rear Admiral Ali Fadavi, the commander of the IRGCN, confirmed that the mock-up was in fact a military target, and that it was necessary "because sinking and destroying US warships has, is and will be on our agenda."[34]

The IRGC's most visible, and potent, presence, however, is that of its elite paramilitary wing, known as the Quds Force (IRGC-QF). While the larger Guards are preoccupied with everything from territorial defense to economic expansion, the IRGC-QF has been dedicated to a singular aim since its formation in 1990: carrying out the "extra-regional operations of the Islamic Revolutionary Guard Corps."[35] In other words, the IRGC-QF is the vanguard of terrorism and insurgency in the name of the Islamic Republic. And while the size of the force is small—just 10,000 to 15,000 men, less than 10 percent of the IRGC's total forces of more than 125,000[36]—it would be hard to overstate its contributions to global instability. The Quds Force is, quite simply, the purest expression of the Islamic Republic's belief that it "plays a key role in world affairs as the standard bearer of revolutionary Islam and the guardian of oppressed Muslims (and even non-Muslims) everywhere."[37]

PIVOT POINTS

In September 1980, less than two years after the establishment of the Islamic Republic, Ayatollah Khomeini's fledgling regime found itself at war. The cause was an invasion by the neighboring regime of Ba'athist dictator Saddam Hussein, which sought to seize the advantage and strike an early blow against what it saw as an emerging ideological adversary. The resulting conflict lasted for most of the ensuing decade, and when it finally drew to a close in the late summer of 1988, the toll on Iran was enormous.

Officially, Iranian authorities estimated that they suffered close to 300,000 casualties as a result of the hostilities.[38] Western sources, however, put the figure at significantly higher: half a million souls, or more.[39] More than 500,000 others were physically or mentally disabled either during the war or in its aftermath.[40] In all, the conflict may have cost Iran as much as $1 trillion—a devastating economic loss to the fledgling regime in Tehran.[41]

Nearly as significant was the war's psychological impact. Khomeini's revolution gained popularity because its virulent version of insurgent Islam was a compelling alternative to the Shah's secular and stale authoritarianism. Yet in their first military outing, Iran's holy warriors were bested by a secular adversary. The conflict left the Islamic Republic deeply traumatized, but it also helped instill a sense of unity among Iran's populace. Iraq's aggression and the West's support of Saddam Hussein during the conflict bred in Tehran the sense that it was alone against the world.[42]

Nearly in tandem, the Islamic Republic suffered a major ideological crisis. Less than a year after the end of hostilities with Iran, Ayatollah Khomeini unexpectedly died of a heart attack, throwing his regime into partisan chaos. The resulting political tug-of-war led to the rise of a consensus candidate, the country's current supreme leader, Ayatollah Ali Khamenei. It also led many in the West to conclude that Iran's revolutionary fervor had run its course, or that it soon would.[43] For much of the following decade, Western analysis was colored by this vision of a post-revolutionary Iran, one in which practical concerns and economic priorities trumped revolutionary zeal.[44]

The message from Tehran, however, could not have been more different. In the aftermath of Khomeini's passing, Iranian officials took pains to emphasize that the core tenets of Khomeini's revolution—chief among them the ideal of "exporting the revolution"—remained in effect.[45] This priority, however, would be achieved more subtly than it had been in the past. Whereas the heady early days of the Islamic Republic saw the Iranian regime become a locus of global insurgent activities, following the Iran-Iraq War the Iranian regime gravitated toward a new way of war, one characterized by the use of proxies, an economy of violence, and an exceedingly long view of global competition.[46] This remains the strategy pursued by Iran's leaders today.

MISREADING IRAN

Amazingly, most of this context is lost in contemporary political discourse over Iran. Precious few analysts of Iranian politics have bothered to read the formative texts that helped shape the behavior of the Islamic Republic. Fewer still are familiar with the history and strategic culture that continues to animate the Iranian state. As a result, the Beltway policy community is consistently caught off guard by the Iranian regime's foreign adventurism and bankrolling of global terror, as well as by the scope of its international ambitions.

To be fair, not all branches of the U.S. government have been taken by surprise. In its inaugural report to Congress on Iran's military capabilities, released publicly in the spring of 2010, the Pentagon noted that Iran simultaneously is seeking to ensure "the survival of the regime" and to "become the strongest and most influential country in the Middle East and to influence world affairs." The Pentagon also pointed out that the Iranian leadership's long-term "ideological goal is to be able to export its theocratic form of government, its version of Shia Islam, and stand up for the 'oppressed' according to their religious interpretations of the law."[47]

The Pentagon's subsequent 2012 report on the subject said much the same thing. "Iran continues to seek to increase its stature by countering U.S. influence and expanding ties with regional actors while advocating Islamic solidarity," it noted. "Iran also desires to expand economic and security agreements with other nations, particularly members of the Nonaligned Movement in Latin America and Africa."[48]

Yet, as U.S. policy moved steadily toward engagement with Iran's ayatollahs, this assessment was progressively watered down. Thus, in keeping with the Obama administration's change in policy focus, the 2014 edition of the Pentagon's report on Iran's military capabilities was minimalist in nature and said nothing at all about the Islamic Republic's ideological objectives.[49] In that regard, it represents a more or less faithful reflection of the dominant view held by administration officials and supporters—these days, Iran is concerned above all simply with "regime survival."[50]

Iranian leaders, however, are thinking considerably bigger. That was the message Iran's supreme leader, Ayatollah Ali Khamenei, sought to convey to officials in his government as recently as September 2014. In a meeting with members of the Assembly of Experts, the Islamic Republic's premier religious supervisory body, Khamenei asserted that the existing international system is "in the process of change" and a "new order is being formed." These changes, he made clear, are a mortal blow to the West and a boon to Iran. "The power of the West on their two foundations—values and thoughts and the political and military—have become shaky" and can be subverted, Khamenei insisted.[51]

Iran, in other words, is still revolutionary after all these years. And today, very much in line with Khomeini's famous

1980 dictum that his regime must "strive to export our revolution throughout the world,"[52] the Islamic Republic is pursuing a truly global agenda, one that is built around three primary fronts.

The first, and most immediate, is sectarian in nature. The Iranian regime views itself as the vanguard of the so-called Shia Crescent in the Middle East and the ideological champion of the interests of the beleaguered Shia minority in the Sunni-dominated Muslim world.[53] This outlook informs Iran's ongoing sponsorship of Lebanon's Hezbollah militia, its primary—and most important—terrorist proxy, as well as its backing of assorted Shiite insurgent groups in neighboring Iraq and Shia insurgents in Bahrain, Yemen, and elsewhere.

The second front is pan-Islamist. Iran's leaders believe fervently that their regime is the natural ideological leader of the Islamic world and the rightful inheritor of the mantle of the Prophet Mohammed.[54] This conviction underlies Iran's long-standing strategic rivalry with Saudi Arabia, Sunni Islam's most important player—a contest Iran's leaders see as one not only for strategic position, but also for ideological primacy. It is also what animates Iran's repeated efforts over the past decade to goad the countries of the Middle East into a security condominium of its own fashioning, thereby becoming the region's geopolitical center of gravity.

Finally, the Iranian regime has embraced the language of third-world populism, using it in its efforts to enlist countries in Latin America and Africa in a shared revisionist agenda on the global stage. The crux of this message was encapsulated in Mahmoud Ahmadinejad's September 2012 address before the United Nations General Assembly, in which the Iranian president called for the formation of a "new world order" as a substitute for the current domination of the "bullying" West.[55] It is a call that has resonated in many corners of the third world.

Former secretary of state Henry Kissinger once famously remarked that Iran faces a choice of being "a nation or a cause."[56] Today, Iran's leaders believe that their regime can be both. Even as they engage in a dialogue with the West over their nuclear program, they are acting out that conviction.

CHAPTER

II

Subverting the Arab Spring

When a 26-year-old fruit peddler in the rural Tunisian town of Sidi Bouzid set himself on fire in December 2010 to protest government corruption and a lack of economic opportunity, it ignited a regional firestorm. Mohamed Bouazizi's self-immolation touched off escalating protests against the long-serving Tunisian strongman Zine el-Abidine Ben Ali, first in Sidi Bouzid, and subsequently throughout the entire country. Within less than a month, Ben Ali stepped down and fled the country in the face of widespread and sustained opposition to his rule.

Egypt was next. Beginning in January 2011, Hosni Mubarak, Cairo's immutable authoritarian sphinx for more than three decades, also found himself in the public crosshairs. Millions of disgruntled Egyptians took to the streets, congregating in the capital's Tahrir Square to call for release from the political stagnation and economic malaise that had come to characterize Mubarak's rule. In an effort to cling to power, the Egyptian president proffered a number of compromises and power-sharing arrangements. But by then, the crowd was seeking more fundamental change, and Mubarak was forced to resign.

Tunisia and Egypt may be the most dramatic examples of the widespread regional antiestablishment sentiment that became known as the Arab Spring, but they were hardly the only ones. Country after country experienced shockwaves from the political earthquake.

Iran was no different. Publicly, officials in Tehran took an exceedingly optimistic view of the antiregime sentiment sweeping the region. High-ranking Iranian officials repeatedly depicted the regional ferment as an outgrowth of Ayatollah Khomeini's successful 1979 revolution and the start of an "Islamic awakening" in which the Islamic Republic would inevitably play a leading role.[1] Iran's supreme leader, Ayatollah Ali Khamenei, even ordered the creation of a special "secretariat" headed by former foreign minister Ali Akbar Velayati to help bring Islamic movements to the political fore throughout the region.[2]

Privately, however, officials in Tehran were all too aware that they could become the next casualty of the Arab Spring. The controversial June 2009 reelection of Mahmoud Ahmadinejad to the Iranian presidency had brought millions of protesters into the streets of Tehran and other Iranian cities—a groundswell of popular outrage that coalesced into the so-called Green Movement. Months of unrest aimed at the ruling clerical regime followed, presenting the Islamic Republic with its most fundamental political challenge since its 1979 revolution. Although the Iranian government successfully beat back this "green wave," mostly through the use of widespread brutality and repression, officials in Tehran were all too aware that discontent continued to simmer beneath the surface of Iranian society. They therefore worried that popular revolts taking place in Tunis, Cairo, and elsewhere could easily translate into renewed disorder at home. As a result, they determined that, in keeping with the old axiom that "the best defense is a good offense," the surest way to prevent a "Persian Spring" was to harness, co-opt, and exploit these same stirrings abroad.

COURTING CAIRO . . . AND SUBVERTING AL-SISI

Egypt presented Iran with its first opportunity to influence the politics of the Arab Spring. During the three decades before Mubarak's ouster in February 2011, Tehran and Cairo were regional rivals and ideological adversaries. The animus dated back to the early 1980s and stemmed from Iran's opposition to Egypt's initiative, codified at Camp David, to normalize relations with the state of Israel. When Egyptian president Anwar Sadat was subsequently assassinated by a gang of militant army officers, the Islamic Republic openly took the side of the extremists, going so far as to name a street in Tehran after the lead gunman, Khalid Islambouli.[3]

The resulting hostility between the two countries was both deep and enduring. Diplomatic relations, suspended after Sadat's assassination, remained frozen for the following thirty years, as myriad issues—from Iran's sponsorship of the Hamas terrorist group to its nuclear ambitions—created tensions between Tehran and Cairo. But Mubarak's departure and the subsequent rise of a new, Islamist government in Egypt afforded Iran a new strategic opportunity.

Speculation about contacts between Shia Iran and Sunni Islamists, chief among them Egypt's Muslim Brotherhood, had been swirling around for years, encouraged by Iran's cooperation with Hamas and its tactical contacts with al-Qaeda.[4] The rise of the Brotherhood to political prominence in Egypt following Mubarak's ouster brought these connections to the fore. In February 2011, Supreme Leader Ayatollah Ali Khamenei met Kamal al-Halbavi, a senior member of Egypt's Brotherhood, in Tehran, in what was widely seen as an Iranian effort to position itself at the vanguard of the Arab Spring.[5] Thereafter, Tehran became a vocal supporter of the Brotherhood's political agenda and ascent to power in Cairo.

Even before the Brotherhood seized power in 2012, Tehran had already improved its position vis-à-vis the Egyptian state. In mid-February 2011, Iran requested, and Egypt's caretaker government granted, permission for two warships to transit the Suez Canal, which was the first time in more than three decades an Iranian warship passed through those waters.[6] In the weeks that followed, the new government in Cairo also agreed to reestablish long-frozen diplomatic ties.[7] Some Egyptians even went so far as to flirt with the idea of accepting Iran's long-standing offer of nuclear cooperation, something the Egyptian government under Mubarak had categorically rejected.[8] These changes transformed Egypt from a hedge against Iran's regional ambitions into an enabler of them.

The subsequent rise of the Muslim Brotherhood to power in Cairo further deepened this budding alignment. Iranian leaders took pains to praise the "Islamic awakening" that had taken place in Egypt and made concrete political steps to normalize the long-unsettled relationship between Tehran and Cairo.[9]

Iran's ayatollahs found a willing partner in Cairo. In the run-up to his election as president, Mohammed Morsi allegedly conducted an interview with Iran's FARS News Agency, in which he waxed optimistic about the possibility of reactivating bilateral ties. "We must restore normal relations with Iran based on shared interests, and expand areas of political coordination and economic cooperation because this will create a balance of pressure in the region," Morsi is said to have told the news channel.[10] Morsi subsequently denied the interview, perhaps to appease his domestic Sunni constituency. But he said much the same thing in more muted tones in September of that year at the annual summit of the Non-Aligned Movement, coincidentally held in Tehran, when he declared that he was handing over the movement's presidency "to our brothers, the Iranians."[11] (These contacts would come back to haunt Morsi; in February 2014, Egyptian authorities charged the ousted president with espionage and treason, accusing him of conspiring with "foreign powers"—Iran chief among them.[12])

The Iranian-Egyptian détente turned out to be short-lived, however. In June 2013, Morsi's Muslim Brotherhood–dominated government was overthrown and replaced with a military clique dominated by General Abdel Fattah al-Sisi. Initially, al-Sisi struck a conciliatory tone toward the Islamic Republic, making a point of inviting Iran's president-elect, Hassan Rouhani, to attend his swearing-in ceremony—the first time such an offer had been extended since Sadat's assassination.[13] Rouhani demurred, sending an official representative in his place. But the incident was enough to fan speculation that Cairo and Tehran were improving ties.

Indeed, early on, al-Sisi's government appeared genuinely interested in engaging the Islamic Republic. Seeking to fill the void left by the deterioration of the long-standing Egyptian-American strategic relationship, Cairo began courting all manner of new foreign-policy actors—including, most conspicuously, Russia, with which the al-Sisi government signed a multi-billion-dollar deal for arms and defense supplies.[14] Iran figured prominently in this calculus as well; in October 2013, the interim foreign minister Nabil Fahmy said as much when, in an interview with Iran's Press TV, he called the Islamic Republic a "very important" country with which his government is seeking better relations. "The new Iranian president has sent out to the world some positive signals and the world is interested in engaging Iran," Fahmy said.[15] Cairo, moreover, continued to thaw chilly relations despite significant domestic opposition in Egypt over the prospects of détente between the two longtime regional rivals.[16]

Quickly, however, Cairo soured on the possibility of resetting relations with Tehran and came to view Iran once again as a destabilizing force—and for good reason. In January 2014, Egypt's chargé d'affaires to Tehran delivered a communiqué to Iran's foreign ministry formally complaining about Iran's interference in Egypt's internal affairs.[17] Egypt's complaint was a reflection of the Iranian perception that al-Sisi, who launched a very public campaign to clip the political wings of the Muslim Brotherhood in Egypt, was not a worthwhile ally in their "Islamic awakening" and a response to Tehran's consequent attempts to subvert his government.

Iran's efforts in this regard appear to be under way. The Iranian regime reportedly formulated a strategy to train and equip Islamic militants opposed to the Egyptian government.[18] This initiative included training a Libya-based proxy group known as the Free Egyptian Army in northwest Libya and a similar effort by the Islamic Republic's Quds Force paramilitary to train Muslim Brotherhood militants in Sudan, thereby expanding the lethality and sophistication of the insurgent threat facing the Egyptian government.[19]

QUIET SUBVERSION IN BAHRAIN

Egypt was not the only arena in which Iran attempted to improve its regional position. In the Persian Gulf kingdom of Bahrain, Arab Spring–related ferment in 2011 gave Iran a new opening through which to expand its regional influence.

That opening was demographic in nature. The majority (some 70 percent) of Bahrain's 1.3-million-person population was Shia, while the country's ruling al-Khalifa family was Sunni. This was an inversion of the prevailing demographic in the overwhelmingly Sunni Gulf region—and one that provided the Islamic Republic an opportunity for leverage.

Beginning in February 2011, inspired by similar protests in Tunisia and Egypt, Shiite Bahrainis took to the streets to protest systemic inequalities and repression and torture carried out by the al-Khalifa regime.[20] The regime's heavy-handed response, including the imprisonment of opposition activists and large-scale crackdowns on protesters, only generated new momentum for Bahraini activists to advocate the government's overthrow.

They were not alone. Tehran was quick to voice its support of these protests and threw its weight behind the ouster of the al-Khalifa government. "All Islamic countries, as long as they're not themselves involved in the crime, bear responsibility to support the Bahrainis in their fight," Ayatollah Ahmad Jannati, the hard-line imam of Tehran, said in a public sermon that spring.[21] Iran did not content itself with rhetoric alone, launching a covert campaign to destabilize the Gulf kingdom. The extent of this effort was made public in April 2011, when the Bahraini government submitted a confidential report to the United Nations (which was subsequently leaked to the press) in which it accused Iran's terror proxy, Hezbollah, of actively plotting the overthrow of the regime and of training Bahraini militants in both Lebanon and Iran for this purpose.[22] Just three months later, Bahrain's high criminal court sentenced three defendants—one Bahraini and two Iranians—for spying for the Islamic Republic and passing along sensitive information regarding military installations to Iran's Revolutionary Guards.[23] That fall, these developments led Bahrain's foreign minister, Khaled bin Ahmad al-Khalifa, to charge Iran with seeking to subvert Bahrain and make it the "crown jewel" in its larger campaign to penetrate the Persian Gulf.[24]

Iran's efforts at subversion made waves in Washington. "We already have evidence that the Iranians are trying to exploit the situation in Bahrain," Defense Secretary Robert Gates told reporters in April 2011. "We also have evidence that they are talking about what they can do to try to create problems elsewhere as well."[25] For Washington, this was not insignificant, because Bahrain plays an important role in America's military posture in the Middle East, hosting a key naval base for the U.S. Fifth Fleet. As a result, Bahrain's instability had a direct effect upon American plans and raised the possibility that if the al-Khalifa monarchy fell, the United States could find itself shut out of a vital defense arrangement that anchors its regional presence.

Bahrain's Gulf neighbors were even more worried. Understandably, they saw Iran's interference as an existential threat—a challenge to their religious authority and an insurgent effort to revise the geopolitical workings of the Gulf. Or, as the *New York Times* put it in March 2011, Bahrain had become "the latest proxy battle between Iran and Saudi Arabia for regional dominance."[26]

The Gulf monarchies responded accordingly. Using the auspices of the Gulf Cooperation Council (GCC), a six-member security bloc dominated by Saudi Arabia, Gulf states sent approximately 1,000 troops into Bahrain to quell protests.[27] The deployment, ostensibly in response to a "request" by the Bahraini monarchy, was intended to immediately stabilize the government in the capital city of Manama. But just as important was the force's secondary mission: to protect the country from Iran's insurgent fundamentalism, by force if necessary. As the commanding officer told the London-based Saudi daily newspaper *Asharq al-Awsat*, his mission was "to secure Bahrain's vital and strategically important military infrastructure from any foreign interference."[28]

The deployment had its intended effect, blunting Shia protests against the al-Khalifa regime and deterring more significant—and overt—Iranian intervention. In such a way, the GCC succeeded in preventing Iran's attempts to subvert Bahrain at the height of the Arab Spring. And yet, three years later, Iran's destabilizing hand was still evident in the Gulf kingdom. In January 2014, Osama al-Oufi, the country's chief prosecutor, formally charged the Iranian Revolutionary Guards with continuing to provide Bahraini opposition fighters with explosives training. The accusation came on the heels of the Bahraini government's arrest of five suspected militants and intelligence reports of Bahraini fighters based in Iran planning "terrorist bombing operations targeting institutions and places vital to the sovereignty and security of the kingdom."[29] Tehran, it seems, still has designs on Manama.

TIPPING THE SCALES IN SAN'A

In today's Middle East, there is perhaps no more volatile country than Yemen. While Iraq and Syria have captured international headlines of late for their roles as the crucible for the Islamic State's radical jihadist campaign, it is the impoverished southern Gulf state of Yemen that has the potential to become the region's next great flash point. And there, as elsewhere in the region, Iran's destabilizing presence is being felt in dramatic fashion.

Today's Yemen teeters on the brink of being a failed state— home to not one, but three interlocking security challenges. Most prominently, there is al-Qaeda in the Arabian Peninsula (AQAP), al-Qaeda's most capable regional franchise, which has long sought to overthrow the government in San'a and impose a "just" Islamic government and sharia law throughout the country. Secessionist tendencies abound as well, inspired by deep political and socioeconomic inequality, and a broad secessionist movement in the country's impoverished south has tried for years to break free of the Yemeni central government. But perhaps the most well-known—and serious—security challenge confronting the Yemeni regime is the one posed by the Houthi ethnic clan in Yemen's northern province of Saada.

The Houthis, who are Shia Muslims of the Zaydi sect, traditionally enjoyed considerable political and ideological independence, presiding over their own "imamate" from the ninth century until the 1962 officers' coup that forged modern Yemen. Since then, they have periodically pushed back against the traditional authority of the Sunni elite in San'a in an attempt to reassert their autonomy. The recent tensions between the Yemeni government and the Houthis can be traced back to the killing of the clan's leader, Hussein al-Houthi, in June 2004—an event that propelled the clan into open revolt against the Yemeni state.

A decade later, this rebellion is on the march. In 2004, the Houthi movement was modest in size, estimated at just 2,000 fighters.[30] Since then, it has expanded in both size and geographic scope. In late 2011, its leadership claimed to command more than 100,000 members.[31] Today, those numbers are estimated to be larger still.

The Houthi rebellion's resilience and the political and territorial gains it has made despite a massive, sustained crackdown from authorities in San'a have a great deal to do with Iran's assistance. For years, rumors circulated about the clandestine role the Islamic Republic assumed by financing, assisting, and even coordinating Yemen's Houthis in their struggle; however, both Iran and the Houthis denied this connection. In a 2011 interview with Dubai's *The National* newspaper, Houthi leader Mohammed Abdul Salam insisted that "[t]he people of Yemen are supporting us. Our power is through them and not through Iran."[32]

Nonetheless, Iran's covert involvement has been unmistakable. A 2012 expose by the *New York Times* described how Iranian smugglers, backed by the Quds Force, the elite paramilitary unit of Iran's Revolutionary Guards, were shipping AK-47s, rocket-propelled grenades, and other weapons to the Houthis.[33] The following year provided even more concrete proof of Iranian meddling, with the interdiction by Yemeni authorities of an Iranian dhow carrying weapons, including ten Chinese anti-aircraft missiles. Officials in both San'a and Washington confirmed, in the wake of the seizure, that the weapons were intended to aid the Houthi rebels.[34] Iran was also said to be providing sustained logistical, political, and financial support to the rebellion.[35]

So pervasive did Iran's meddling become that, in March 2014, President Hadi took the unprecedented step of publicly pinning the blame on Tehran for Yemen's ongoing instability. "Unfortunately, Iranian interference still exists," Hadi told the pan-Arab newspaper *Al Hayat*. "We asked our Iranian brothers to revise their wrong policies towards Yemen, but our demands have not borne fruit. We have no desire to escalate [the situation] with Tehran but at the same time we hope it will lift its hand off Yemen."[36]

This assistance hardened the political posture of the Houthis, who rebuffed repeated efforts on the part of the Hadi government to reach a political compromise. It also helped tip the scales decisively in the Houthis' favor. The Houthis went on the offensive, seeking to secure key strongholds in Yemen's west, including the strategic port of Midi, close to the country's shared border with Saudi Arabia. Their actions naturally set off alarm bells in Riyadh, with observers describing the Houthi advance as a "grave threat."[37] It culminated in the fall 2014 Houthi takeover of portions of the Yemeni capital, San'a—a move that made the Iranian-supported rebels de facto power brokers in Yemen's future.[38] Today, the Shiite rebels have assumed still greater control and are actively attempting to unseat Yemen's president and government. This has led neighboring Saudi Arabia to intervene militarily in an attempt to beat back their advance.[39]

Tehran, meanwhile, is exploiting other fissures in the Yemeni state as well. As one government official told London's *Asharq al-Awsat* newspaper in July 2012, "Tehran is providing financial and logistical support to the secessionist movement, whilst it is also working to train some armed movements in southern Yemen, in addition to establishing a network of relations with Yemeni parliamentarians, political activists, journalists and writers. Iran is also funding media operations and political parties with the objective of thwarting the transition of power in Yemen."[40]

Iran, in other words, is working hard to penetrate, fragment, and destabilize Yemen, using time-tested methodology perfected on other foreign-policy fronts. As it has done elsewhere in the region, Iran is trying to empower the Shia minority in order to challenge Yemen's established Sunni-dominated status quo. And, by all accounts, Iran has succeeded in doing just that.

A PROXY WAR IN SYRIA

In March 2011, the Arab Spring came to Syria. Prompted by antiestablishment protests in Tunisia and Egypt, opposition activists in the southern city of Deraa began their own low-level civic activism, ranging from street gatherings to spray-painting graffiti. Government forces responded with a spate of detentions, which in turn generated massive street protests and an even wider governmental crackdown. Over the course of some six weeks, dozens of activists were killed by government forces. The deepening repression, however, didn't quell the protests. Rather, it galvanized still greater opposition, which led to the emergence of a constellation of rebel forces and the country's descent into an outright civil war that persists to this day.

Over time, Assad's war became Iran's, too. Syria has long ranked as Iran's most reliable regional partner, and the two countries (with their joint proxy Hezbollah) make up the "axis of resistance" aimed at fighting the United States and Israel.

Not surprisingly, Syria's chaos attracted Iran. Since the start of the fighting, the Iranian regime has become a vital—if undeclared—player in the bloody conflict taking place between the Assad regime and its assorted opponents, both domestic and foreign.

Publicly, Iran has sought to portray a constructive political image through its Syria policy. The Iranian regime, for example, has made a very public show of sending large quantities of humanitarian aid to help alleviate the crisis in Syria, and has been doing so despite significant domestic criticism.[41] In September 2013, Foreign Minister Mohammad Javad Zarif even went so far as to offer the Islamic Republic's help in ridding Syria of chemical weapons.[42] Behind the scenes, however, Iran has pursued a decidedly more assertive—and destructive—role.

Most visibly, Iran's aid has come in the form of foreign fighters. The Iranian regime is thought to have deployed a large contingent of IRGC forces to the Syrian battlefield. Their number includes hundreds of trained snipers, who have reinforced Syrian troops and increased their deadliness against Syria's opposition.[43]

Iran, together with its Lebanese proxy, Hezbollah, has also played a key role by organizing pro-Assad militias among Syria's Alawite and Shia communities, as well as by organizing foreign fighters from Iraq, Yemen, and Lebanon. Iranian officials boast that these "popular committees" now total upward of 50,000 fighters who benefit from training provided in both Iran and Lebanon.[44]

Iran, moreover, is actively seeking to expand its involvement. A May 2014 expose in the *Wall Street Journal* stated that the IRGC has been actively recruiting thousands of refugees from Afghanistan to join the fight in Syria. In exchange, these "volunteers" are offered a monthly salary of $500 and stabilization of their traditionally tenuous residency status in the Islamic Republic.[45]

Iran is assisting the Assad regime by other means, too. The Iranian regime has been complicit in providing significant amounts of arms and war materiel to the Syrian government.[46] This transfer includes sophisticated battlefield hardware. Over the past three years, the Islamic Republic has translated its rapid development of unmanned aerial vehicle (UAV) technology into an export commodity, supplying Syrian regime forces with several variants of its indigenously developed UAVs, including the Pahpad AB-3, the Yasir, and the Shahed 129—equipment that has been used by Assad against his domestic opposition.[47]

Iran's aid to Syria has also taken on an economic dimension. Iran, still under economic pressure from the West, takes part in "sanctions-busting" by providing the Assad regime with monthly lines of credit worth some $500 million with which to purchase crude oil and other products that the United States and Europe have sought to limit.[48] Iran has played a more active role here as well, supplying crude oil to the Syrian regime in Iranian-flagged tankers in spite of Western restrictions, thereby providing Damascus with much-needed economic relief.[49]

Over time, Iran's assistance has helped reshape the contours of the Syrian conflict. Whereas, at the outset, conventional wisdom held that the Assad regime could only cling to power for a short period of time, the contemporary view in both the Middle East and the West is that the Syrian regime has successfully weathered the storm.

The Iranian regime credits itself with this state of affairs. "Thanks to the planning and wisdom of Iran's leaders, Syria's regime could enjoy some stability," a senior commander of the IRGC was cited by the Agence France Presse as saying in the spring of 2014.[50]

For Iran, this represents far more than simply a local victory. Rather, it is perceived to be a direct blow against the nation it calls the Great Satan, the United States. "Since Syria was and continues to be part of the Islamic resistance front and the Islamic Revolution, it provokes the anger of the Americans," IRGC commander Mohammad Ali Jafari explained on Iranian television.[51] Alaeddin Boroujerdi, the chairman of the Iranian parliament's national security and foreign policy committee, put it more succinctly in May 2014. "We have won in Syria," he told reporters. "The regime will stay. The Americans have lost it."[52]

This effort has come at a high cost for Tehran, however. Perhaps more than any other issue, the Iranian regime's support for Assad has put it on the wrong side of the prevailing politics of the Arab Spring. As a result, the Islamic Republic has experienced a massive loss of support in the region and a sharpening of tensions with the Sunni Arab states.

The conflict has exacted a more direct toll as well. A number of high-ranking IRGC officers have been killed in Syria, among them several top paramilitary commanders.[53] But the impact on Hezbollah has been more pronounced still. Although the Lebanese militia was a belated entrant into the hostilities, joining the fight only in mid-2013, it has since become deeply involved in the unfolding civil war on the side of the Assad regime. In the process, it has sustained massive casualties in what has become a bloody, open-ended conflict, leading some analysts to liken the Syrian civil war to "Hezbollah's Vietnam."[54]

Nevertheless, the Islamic Republic persists with what it sees as an important strategic imperative—the perpetuation of Syria as a front line of defense against Western aggression. As Yahya Rahim-Safavi, a senior aide to Supreme Leader

Ayatollah Ali Khamenei, puts it, Iran's "border defense is [now] southern Lebanon with Israel and our deep defensive strategy has reached the Mediterranean above Israel's head."[55]

In other words, Iran sees its Syrian policy as a way of creating strategic depth in regard to, and expanding its range of options against, Israel and the United States. As a result, its leaders equate participation in the war in Syria with Iran's "sacred defense" during the Iran-Iraq War of the 1980s[56] and are prepared, in the words of Major General Qassem Soleimani, head of the IRGC's feared Quds Force, to "support Syria to the end."[57]

REPUBLIC OF FEAR

At home, Iran's response to the ferment taking place elsewhere in the Middle East was to extend and expand domestic restrictions. Already among the world's most repressive regimes, during the past four years the Iranian government has cracked down further on human rights, freedom of expression, and political choice within the Islamic Republic.

This is somewhat surprising. During Hassan Rouhani's bid for the country's presidency in the spring of 2013, he campaigned on a political platform of forty-six mostly domestic promises. This agenda encompassed pledges to reform and improve the Islamic Republic's beleaguered economy, reduce tensions with the West, and, most significant from a local perspective, serve as a champion for the embattled human rights of ordinary Iranians.[58] These promises set Rouhani apart from other presidential hopefuls and allowed him to coast to an easy political victory in Iran's June 2013 election.

But reality has not matched the campaign rhetoric. In the past two years under Rouhani, Iran has experienced a deepening wave of state-directed domestic repression, including, among other things, a significant spike in the rate of public executions. According to the Iran Human Rights Documentation Center, a watchdog organization based in New Haven, Connecticut, the Islamic Republic executed 522 people in 2012, ranking it among the world's most active executioners.[59] In 2013, this figure rose higher still; the Iranian regime is believed to have executed a staggering 665 people, with two-thirds of those killings taking place after Rouhani took office in August.[60] Today, the situation is even worse. According to the International Human Rights Documentation Center, another Iranian watchdog group, 2014 saw a total of 721 official executions by the Iranian regime, with many more likely going unreported.[61]

Iranian officials have embraced their government's role as executioner. The international community should "be grateful for this great service to humanity," Mohammad Javad Larijani, head of the Iranian judiciary's perversely named Human Rights Council, insisted.[62]

Political prisoners abound in Iran as well. In the fall of 2013, before Rouhani's inaugural speech to the U.N. General Assembly in New York, the Iranian regime made a show of freeing a large number of prominent political dissidents. That, however, was simply a cosmetic gesture. The United Nations estimates the number of political prisoners in Iran at 850, while Human Rights Watch and other NGOs believe the number is higher—perhaps considerably so.[63] Among the incarcerated is Iranian-American pastor Saeed Abedini, as well as Mir Hossein Mousavi and Mehdi Karroubi, both of whom served as leaders of Iran's abortive Green Revolution back in 2009. Iran's fractious ethnic politics are reflected in the prison population as well; some 40 percent of political prisoners in Iran are thought to be Kurds.[64]

The ranks of Iranian political prisoners keep growing. Perhaps most prominently, in July 2014, Iranian authorities arrested *Washington Post* Iran reporter Jason Rezaian and his wife, Yeganeh Salehi, a journalist for the Dubai-based

The National newspaper. In the fall of 2014, U.N. secretary-general Ban Ki-moon appealed directly to Iranian president Rouhani to secure their release.[65] Salehi was released from regime custody, but Rezaian remains behind bars and will soon stand trial for "crimes" against the Islamic Republic.[66]

In another repressive move, Iran's regime constricted the country's available media space. Democracy watchdog Freedom House estimates that more than forty newspapers have been shut down by the Iranian government since 2009.[67] Since Rouhani took office in August 2013, the Iranian government has shuttered several more, doing so under various pretexts, including that they were guilty of "spreading lies and insulting the holy precepts of Islam."[68]

This state of affairs has successfully imposed an intellectual orthodoxy on journalism within the Islamic Republic. A spring 2014 survey of the Iranian press by independent journalist Hadi Anvari found that up to 60 percent of all content featured in the country's "reformist" media is pulled from sources affiliated with the Revolutionary Guards.[69] In other words, Iran's hard-liners increasingly control both the conservative and the liberal narrative in the Iranian press.

Perhaps the most far-reaching media change, however, has been the result of the Iranian regime's efforts to complicate access to the World Wide Web. In the aftermath of the 2009 Green Revolution, Iran's leaders have expended extensive time, resources, and effort to isolate the Islamic Republic from the outside world via cyberspace and deny Iran's citizens access to the Internet as a social, political, and cultural meeting place.

In these ways, Iran's leaders have tried to dampen prospects for a "Persian Spring" within their own borders, even as they have tried to harness and exploit the currents of the Arab Spring to their advantage elsewhere in the region.

Iran's Own "War on Terror"

In the spring of 2014, the world woke up to a new and virulent global threat. Over the course of that season, the terrorist group now known as the Islamic State cut a bloody swathe across northern Iraq, routing the Iraqi armed forces in city after city in its merciless drive toward the country's capital, Baghdad.

For the Obama administration, the development was politically unwelcome. In previous years, and particularly since the death of Osama Bin Laden at the hands of U.S. special operators in May 2011, the White House had actively promoted the notion that the struggle known as the *war on terror* had decisively turned a corner. The rise of the Islamic State put the lie to the assertion by administration officials—chief among them President Obama himself—that al-Qaeda and its ilk were "decimated" and on a "path of defeat."[1]

Nevertheless, it should not have come as a surprise. Warning signs of the group's resurgence—then known as al-Qaeda in Iraq, or AQI—were visible as far back as 2012, when it launched a highly successful campaign of bombing attacks and prison breaks.[2] Even so, the speed at which it expanded in Syria and Iraq has been nothing short of meteoric, and its success in capturing both treasure and territory has been startling.

Beginning in early 2012, AQI—also known as the Islamic State in Iraq and the Levant (ISIL) and the Islamic State in Iraq and al-Shams (ISIS)—intervened in the Syrian civil war, mobilizing against the regime of Bashar al-Assad in Damascus. It did so initially in close conjunction with al-Qaeda's local Syrian affiliate, Jabhat al-Nusra. However, infighting over leadership prompted al-Qaeda head Ayman al-Zawahiri to intervene and demand a tactical divorce between the two organizations.[3] Thereafter, an ideological schism formed between them, with al-Zawahiri formally disavowing ISIS in February 2014.[4]

In response, the Islamic State is trying to seize the mantle of global jihadism from al-Qaeda and supplant the Bin Laden network as the ideological center of gravity for Islamic extremists worldwide. To that end, in June 2014, the group's leader, Abu Bakr al-Baghdadi, formally declared the creation of a new "Islamic caliphate" in Iraq and parts of Syria during a high-profile speech in Mosul, Iraq. In the same address, al-Baghdadi anointed himself as the new "caliph" and the "leader for Muslims everywhere."[5] As a result, there is now pitched ideological competition between al-Qaeda and the Islamic State for primacy in the jihadist intellectual narrative, with the two groups trading barbs and proffering competing worldviews in their battle for Islamic "hearts and minds."[6]

The Islamic State is "beyond anything that we've seen," in terms of both its ambitions and its capabilities, the then defense secretary Chuck Hagel warned in August 2014.[7] The statistics bear out his assessment. The U.S. intelligence community estimated that, as of fall 2014, the group could field as many as 31,000 men under arms, making it among the largest terrorist groups on record.[8] (By way of comparison, the State Department's counterterrorism bureau gauged that al-Qaeda's core and its two most potent affiliates, AQAP and AQIM [al-Qaeda in the Islamic Maghreb], number in the low thousands—although, when indirect affiliates such as Indonesia's Jemaah Islamiyah are factored in, that figure is considerably higher.[9]) The Islamic State is also believed to be one of the world's richest groups, with assets valued at around $2 billion.[10] Its rapid advance in both Iraq and Syria, moreover, left the group in control of vast territory. In mid-2014, experts estimated that it held and administered segments of northern Iraq and eastern Syria equivalent to the size of the United Kingdom.[11]

The Islamic State is not just a threat to the West. For Shiite Iran, the rise of the Sunni group poses a grave danger as well—as both a national security threat and a challenge to its ideological legitimacy. This is why the Islamic Republic began a major mobilization against the group. Iran provided both arms and advisors to the Kurdish *peshmerga* guerrillas battling the Islamic State in northern Iraq.[12] It also sent detachments of its Revolutionary Guards to fight against the Islamic State on Iraqi soil.[13] And in a marked departure from normal policy, Iran's supreme leader, Ayatollah Ali Khamenei, reportedly even gave Major General Qassem Soleimani, commander of the elite Quds Force, the green light to coordinate military operations with the United States against the Islamic State.[14]

All this has nudged the United States and Iran into tactical alignment and has fostered the idea that cooperation in countering the Islamic State is, in fact, possible. Secretary of State John Kerry, for example, said publicly that he envisions a role for Iran in the broad coalition that Washington is erecting against the group.[15] Others in the Obama administration have gone even further. In mid-October 2014, President Obama reportedly sent a secret letter to Iran's supreme leader proffering joint coordination in the fight against the Islamic

State, provided Iran could come to terms with the West over its nuclear program.[16]

The idea generated a firestorm of criticism in Washington. "It's sometimes true that very different countries can cooperate against a common enemy, as the United States and Soviet Union did during World War II," noted Michael Doran of the Brookings Institution and Max Boot of the Council on Foreign Relations in the *Washington Post* in the summer of 2014. "But the suggestion of a united U.S.-Iran front is more reminiscent of the wishful thinking among conservatives who argued in the 1930s that Britain and the United States shared a common interest with Nazi Germany in countering communism."[17]

This skepticism is undoubtedly warranted, for Iran's long and sordid history as a sponsor and instigator of international terrorism puts it squarely on the wrong side of today's struggle against radical Islam.

BLOODY ROOTS

Chalk it up to the Islamic Republic's roots in the radical, religious-based protests that coalesced against the secular rule of Shah Mohammad Reza Pahlavi during the 1970s—or to Ayatollah Khomeini's deep-seated belief that, once established, the ideology of his extremist state could become an export commodity and a way to reorder the prevailing geopolitics of the Muslim (and eventually the entire) world. Whatever the reason, since its inception in 1979, Iran's current regime has harnessed terrorism as a key tool of strategic influence and foreign policy.

The formative years of Khomeini's regime saw his government erect an elaborate domestic infrastructure to support and propagate terrorism, spanning multiple ministries and agencies, as well as invest hundreds of millions of dollars in the cause of global Islamic "resistance."[18] In the process, the

Iranian regime created a massive terror machine dedicated to the exportation of its radical ideas.

The United States felt the results of this architecture first-hand in April 1983, when a truck bomb destroyed the U.S. embassy in Beirut, Lebanon, killing 63 people, and then again that October, when a similar explosive device targeted the U.S. marine barracks in Beirut, killing 241. Both attacks were definitively traced back to the Islamic Republic, which—working through proxies such as Hezbollah and the Islamic Jihad Organization—sought to dislodge the American presence in the Levant.[19] In response, the Reagan administration formally designated Iran a state sponsor of terrorism the following year.

So the situation remains. Today, the Islamic Republic still ranks as the world's foremost sponsor of international terrorism—a designation its leaders wear proudly in the name of resistance against the Great Satan (United States) and, more broadly, the West. If anything, the thirteen-plus years since the terrorist attacks of September 11, 2001, and the subsequent start of the war on terror have seen the Islamic Republic continue, and even deepen, its investment in global instability. It has done so through what some scholars have described as an "action network": a web of official and proxy organizations that are "involved in crafting and implementing the covert elements of Iran's foreign policy agenda, from terrorism, political, economic and social subversion; to illicit finance, weapons and narcotics trafficking; and nuclear procurement and proliferation."[20]

The results are striking. In its most recent assessment of global terrorism trends, the U.S. State Department points out that Iran has

- maintained its "support for Palestinian terrorist groups in Gaza," as well as Lebanon's Hezbollah

militia, which it has helped rearm after the latter's
2006 conflict with Israel;

- "increased its presence in Africa and attempted to
  smuggle arms to Houthi separatists in Yemen and
  Shia oppositionists in Bahrain," and;

- used its terror vehicles and proxies to "provide cover
  for intelligence operations, and create instability in
  the Middle East," and has continued "to provide
  arms, financing, training, and the facilitation of Iraqi
  Shia fighters" to reinforce the regime of Bashar al-
  Assad in Syria against its opposition.[21]

The scope of Iran's investment in terrorism is far broader
than could be comfortably covered in these pages. But the
challenge it poses to the United States and its allies is clear.
As scholars Scott Modell and David Asher note, despite years
of economic and political pressure, "Iran seems undeterred
in its mission to confront the 'enemies of Islam' and create new centers of non-Western power around the world."[22]
Today, one such potential center is emerging on Iran's eastern border.

EASTERN PROMISES

For Iran, the start of the war on terror in 2001 was a significant existential challenge. The incursion of the Great Satan,
the United States, and its coalition partners into Afghanistan on their eastern flank worried Iran's ayatollahs, while the
rapid way in which the United States and its allies dismem-
bered the Taliban regime in Kabul raised concerns that the
coalition might soon set its sights on the Islamic Republic.
This sense of siege would only be amplified by the overthrow
of Saddam Hussein's government in Iraq two years later and
the assumption of control over the country by the U.S.-led
Coalition Provisional Authority thereafter.

In response, Iran adopted a two-pronged strategy toward its eastern neighbor. On the one hand, Tehran sought to expand its influence and political clout in post-Taliban Afghanistan, both as a way to prevent a possible tilt toward the West on the part of the central government in Kabul and to carve out a zone of influence that could serve as a strategic buffer. On the other, Tehran worked to counter the presence of foreign forces on Afghan soil and raise the cost for the coalition to remain there.[23]

In pursuit of the first priority, Iran expanded its economic stake in Afghanistan. Over the course of five years, the Islamic Republic invested heavily in various infrastructure, mining, and industrial projects throughout the country. As of 2012, more than 2,000 Iranian companies were estimated to be operating in Afghanistan, and 110 technical-engineering projects totaling some $360 million in business were said to be active.[24] These economic links were cemented by a massive trade deal between the two countries in May 2012 that, among other things, granted Afghanistan access to Iran's port of Chabahar.[25]

Trade between the two countries ballooned. In 2008, Iran's exports to Afghanistan totaled a mere $800 million annually. By 2011, that figure topped $2 billion.[26] And just three years after that, total bilateral trade more than doubled, reaching $5 billion annually and making the Islamic Republic one of Afghanistan's most important trading partners.[27]

Politically, Iran progressively co-opted Afghanistan's fledgling post-Taliban government. Iran had played a key role in organizing Afghanistan's various political factions in support of President Hamid Karzai in the run-up to his election in December 2004.[28] Thereafter, it sought to expand its influence among the country's politicians, using cultural ties, payoffs, and bribes to subvert the independence of Karzai's government, with considerable success. A 2012 assessment by the Institute for the Study of War noted that "Iran's influence permeates the Afghan government at all levels," with many Afghan politicians and government functionaries on Iran's payroll.[29] This rot extended to the very top of Afghanistan's political power structure. In October 2010, President Karzai himself acknowledged accepting $2 million from Iran.[30] Karzai's admission was a telling reminder to Washington of who wielded the real power in Afghanistan.

Simultaneously, Iran forged an alternative center of gravity in Afghanistan's western provinces. In provinces such as Herat and Farah, Iranian influence—in the form of commercial goods, religious sway, and cultural pressure—facilitated a tilt away from Kabul, toward Tehran.[31] And what Iran did not succeed in achieving there by engagement, it did through pressure. In August 2014, Herat's police chief, General Samiullah Qatrah, accused Iran of being partly responsible for a wave of attacks in the province and demanded that "countries friendly with Afghanistan . . . [not] train elements of terror and fear on their soil."[32] Qatrah's comments were proof that in Afghanistan's wild east, the real power broker was not the Afghan central government but Iran's clerical regime.

Expanding its influence is not Iran's only priority, however. Iran also seeks to deny it to others, most prominently the United States and its allies. Over the past several years, Iran carried out a major covert campaign aimed at undermining the U.S.-led coalition in Afghanistan. The extent of this effort was neatly summarized by the U.S. State Department in its 2012 *Country Reports on Terrorism*, which noted that, "[s]ince 2006, Iran has arranged arms shipments to select Taliban members, including small arms and associated ammunition, rocket propelled grenades, mortar rounds, 107mm rockets, and plastic explosives." According to the same assessment, "Iran has shipped a large number of weapons to Kandahar, Afghanistan, aiming to increase its influence in this key province." Iran has also "trained Taliban elements on small unit tactics, small arms, explosives, and indirect fire weapons, such as mortars, artillery, and rockets."[33]

The goal of these efforts wasn't success for the Sunni Taliban, which Shiite Iran saw as both a regional rival and a strategic competitor. Rather, Iran sought to blunt the coalition's political impact and lessen its chances for strategic success. As General David Petraeus, at the time the commander of U.S. Central Command, noted in 2009, Iran does not want "an extremist Sunni regime running their eastern neighbor . . . but they don't want us to succeed too easily either."[34] Nevertheless, Iran's assistance helped bolster the capabilities of Afghan insurgent groups, at significant cost measured in U.S. and Afghan lives.

The Obama administration's announcement in mid-2011 of plans for a formal exit from Afghanistan kicked Iran's efforts into high gear. By the following year, Western observers noted the "soft power" gains made by the Islamic Republic. An October 2012 expose in the *Wall Street Journal* disclosed that Iran was "funding aid projects and expanding intelligence networks across Afghanistan" in anticipation of coalition withdrawal, using proxies such as the Imam Khomeini Relief Committee as agents of influence.[35] The formula employed by Iran was simple and effective. It offered economic aid in the form of loans, stipends, and medical supplies in exchange for loyalty and actionable intelligence on coalition activities.[36]

The fruits of Iran's labor became visible in August 2013, when the two countries signed the Afghanistan-Iran Strategic Cooperation Agreement.[37] The significance of the deal, and the message behind it, was unmistakable: a year and a half before the coalition's exit, Kabul already understood that Tehran, not Washington, was the long-term power broker in Southwest Asia.

So it remains. Afghanistan's tumultuous election in October 2014 may have seen the rise of a new president, Ashraf Ghani Ahmadzai, and a new power-sharing coalition in Kabul, but Iran's influence remains significant, and so does the control it exerts over Afghanistan's political trajectory. Ghani himself said as much in September 2014, when he told visiting Iranian vice president Hossein Shariatmadari that "Afghanistan relations with other countries shall not undermine its relations with Iran," and that "no countries will face any threat from the soil of Afghanistan."[38]

A WAR ON ISRAEL

In the summer of 2014, a new round of hostilities broke out between Israel and the Hamas terrorist movement in the Gaza Strip. Over the course of some fifty days, Hamas rained hundreds of rockets down on Israeli cities and towns, terrorizing the country's population and precipitating a ground invasion of the Gaza Strip by Israel's military forces.

When the dust cleared, the two sides reached what Israeli officials termed a "strategic tie."[39] The Israeli government proved the operational effectiveness of its new Iron Dome missile defense system, which successfully destroyed an estimated 85 percent of incoming projectiles. Israel's subsequent incursion into the Gaza Strip, too, yielded tangible benefits, allowing the Israeli military to identify and eradicate most (although not all) of Hamas's "terror tunnels" and, in the process, foil at least one major planned attack.[40]

But the benefits were arguably greater for Hamas, for whom the conflict was nothing short of a bid for continued relevance. Indeed, before the war, the group was on the ropes, both politically and economically. This was an unexpected development: Hamas's sudden (and surprising) dominance in the late 2006 parliamentary elections in the West Bank and Gaza Strip made the group a power broker in Palestinian politics. This position was cemented several months later, when it successfully undertook a hostile takeover of the Gaza Strip, wresting control of the territory from the Palestinian Authority president, Mahmoud Abbas, and his Fatah faction. Since then, a series of reversals—including Israel's successful Operation Pillar of Defense in 2012 and an ongoing blockade of maritime imports into Gaza—greatly dented the group's legitimacy and mystique. But no event was more damaging to Hamas's political and economic fortunes than falling out with its chief power broker, Iran.

Historically, the Islamic Republic has been a longtime key backer of the Palestinian branch of the Muslim Brotherhood. But, beginning in late 2011, the two underwent what amounted to a strategic divorce over Syria. While Iran assumed a pivotal role as a defender of the Assad regime, Hamas came out vocally against Syria's dictator and in support of the various opposition groups organizing his overthrow. In response, an irate Iran virtually zeroed out its financial support to Hamas and ceased its military cooperation with the group.[41] Adrift, Hamas became critically short on cash, unable to pay salaries for its officials or administer basic governmental functions.[42] And in the acrimonious negotiations with Mahmoud Abbas over the creation of a "unity" government during the spring of 2014, Hamas unexpectedly found itself thrust into the role of junior partner to Abbas's Fatah faction. Against this backdrop, the Gaza war of August–September 2014 can be seen as a last grasp for political relevance on the part of the movement.

By all indications, the ploy worked. In the wake of the conflict, Hamas obtained a new lease on political life, proving to wealthy Gulf donors (like Qatar) that it remains an indispensable part of the resistance against the Jewish state. Perhaps most significantly, it also succeeded in mending fences with Iran.

Even prior to the Gaza war, relations between Hamas and Tehran had begun to move toward rapprochement. In the spring of 2014, negotiations between Hamas and Iran's proxy, Hezbollah, in Lebanon, while failing to bridge differences over Syria, did manage to establish a *modus vivendi* in which Hamas would again garner Iranian support. Thereafter, Iranian parliament speaker Ali Larijani announced that Tehran was poised to resume financial support for Hamas, and Iran's supreme leader, Ayatollah Ali Khamenei, agreed to meet with Khaled Meshaal, the movement's political chief, in Tehran.[43] But the summer 2014 conflict brought the two sides closer still. Hamas had once again proved its worth as a core element of the "axis of resistance" arrayed against Israel. Iran, for its part, saw in a rejuvenated relationship with Hamas "an opportunity to improve its standing in the Islamic world, which had suffered—especially among Sunnis—thanks to its steadfast support of Assad."[44] As a result, the strategic partnership between Iran and Hamas is now back on track—and the likelihood of a future conflict between Israel and an unrepentant, strengthened Hamas is high.[45]

Iran's stake in the Palestinian Territories is far larger than simply Hamas, however. It dates back to the early 1990s, when the Islamic Republic—championing resistance against the "Zionist entity" as an alternative to the Oslo Process then being pursued by the West—took on a leading political role in the West Bank and Gaza Strip.[46] It did so via two primary vehicles. The first was Hamas, with whom Tehran signed a formal accord codifying cooperation in 1992[47]— an arrangement that would endure until the two sides fell out over Syria. The second was the Palestinian Islamic Jihad (PIJ), a smaller yet equally radical Palestinian group that was wholly beholden to Tehran for its existence, depending on the Islamic Republic for its entire budget (some $2 million annually).[48]

By a decade later, that influence gave Iran a major voice in Palestinian politics—and a deciding vote in violence against Israel. In the early 2000s, one Israeli analyst estimated that Iran (via Hezbollah) was responsible for "no less than 80 percent" of terrorism directed against the Jewish state in the Palestinian Second Intifada (2000–2005).[49] Similarly, Israeli officials at the time judged that Iran had succeeded in assuming "control" of terrorism carried out by various Palestinian factions against Israel.[50]

Israeli officials attempted to stem the tide of this support, with some success. In October 2002, Israeli forces seized the ship *Karine A* in the Red Sea, interdicting 50 tons of Iranian arms destined for the Palestinian Authority's dominant Fatah faction, ruled by Yasser Arafat. The incident was the most public of a series of Israeli military successes preventing Iran from playing more deeply in the Palestinian arena. But Arafat's death in 2004 and the subsequent (and somewhat unexpected) parliamentary victory of Hamas in the winter of 2006 provided the Islamic Republic with greater strategic reach throughout the Palestinian Authority.

Yet Iran's predilections clearly rested with the Palestinian Authority's Islamist opposition. Although Tehran had been a historic backer of the Palestine Liberation Organization (PLO), regime officials understood full well that Ramallah's rulers balanced their support against the on-again, off-again Middle East peace process. Thus, when peace talks broke down, as they did in 2000, Arafat's Fatah faction became more than eager for Iranian support in the form of both money and arms. But when peace negotiations resumed, as they did later that year, the Palestinian Authority's relationship with the Islamic Republic cooled considerably. As a result, Iran devoted the lion's share of its attention and support to building a "rejectionist front" of radical groups committed to violent struggle against the Jewish State.

It did so in three principal ways. The first is political support. Iranian officials agitated in favor of Palestinian violence as the most practical way by which to eliminate Israel. Therefore, Supreme Leader Ayatollah Ali Khamenei backed "total armed resistance" to demolish the "Zionist regime," and other regime representatives announced their solidarity with the Palestinian struggle.[51]

The second is funding. Historically, the Iranian regime has been a major source of funding for Hamas. The exact figures remain a point of contention, but Western intelligence services and experts estimate that direct Iranian aid to Hamas ranged from $20 and $50 million annually during the 1990s and anywhere between $3 million and $18 million a year as of the mid-2000s.[52] And while Tehran temporarily slashed its financial assistance to the terror group over Syria, those ties are now on an upswing. According to terrorism expert Avi Jorisch, "Israel's Operation Protective Edge, which began in earnest in early July 2014, has brought Hamas and Iran closer and we are now witnessing a significant re-establishment of bilateral relations."[53]

Finally, Iran helps arm disparate Palestinian factions, increasing their destructive and lethal potential, and thereby their threat to Israel. Not all of Iran's shipments have gotten through defensive measures; for example, in March 2011, Israel's military captured the German-owned vessel *Victoria*, and in March 2014, the Panamanian-flagged *Klos-C* was seized in the Red Sea.[54] Nevertheless, at least some of the Israeli efforts to prevent Iranian arms from finding their way into Palestinian hands have been unsuccessful: the Israel-Gaza War in 2014 showcased a broad array of Hamas-wielded weaponry that had been either developed or delivered by the Islamic Republic.[55]

By these methods, Iran has consistently tried to terrorize, destabilize, and undermine the state of Israel. It is a goal shared broadly by Iran's leaders. Former Iranian president

Mahmoud Ahmadinejad may have generated a firestorm of controversy when, in 2005, he famously called for Israel to be "wiped off the map."[56] But Ahmadinejad's pronouncement was of a piece with Ayatollah Khomeini's original directive that "Israel must be annihilated," and it tracked closely with similar sentiments expressed repeatedly by Iran's current supreme leader. In other words, they were the norm rather than the exception. They reflect the enduring animus that Iran feels for Israel—a hatred that the Islamic Republic has nurtured and perpetuated via the Palestinian arena.

IRAQ'S NEW OWNER

Qassem Soleimani is a quiet, devout man—a humanitarian and populist with a warm smile and a shy demeanor. That, at least, is what the Iranian government would have the world believe. In October 2014, Iranian-regime media initiated, or at least tacitly approved, a social-media campaign aimed at demystifying and popularizing the man heading its campaign against the Islamic State terrorist group in Iraq.[57]

The truth is a good deal more sinister. Soleimani is the long-serving head of the Quds Force, the shadowy elite paramilitary unit of Iran's Islamic Revolutionary Guard Corps. The Quds Force, with an estimated strength of 10,000 to 15,000 soldiers, functions as an asymmetric tool of Iranian influence and strategy. According to the U.S. military, the Iranian government uses the Quds Force "to clandestinely exert military, political, and economic power to advance Iranian national interests abroad." It does so through a wide array of activities, including "gathering tactical intelligence; conducting covert diplomacy; providing training, arms, and financial support to surrogate groups and terrorist organizations; and facilitating some of Iran's provision of humanitarian and economic support to Islamic causes."[58] All this makes Soleimani, in the words of scholar Michael Ledeen, one of Tehran's top "terror masters."

He is also the most powerful strategic operator in today's Middle East. As the *New Yorker*'s Dexter Filkins detailed in a September 2013 expose, during the course of Operation Iraqi Freedom, Soleimani became the man in operational control of a vast covert campaign on behalf of the Iranian government aimed at co-opting Iraq's various political factions and bleeding the U.S.-led coalition.[59] So complete was Soleimani's control that he reportedly put General David Petraeus, the incoming head of U.S. forces in Iraq, on formal notice that he controlled "the policy for Iran with respect to Iraq, Lebanon, Gaza and Afghanistan."[60]

Iran's multipronged strategy, put into motion shortly after the U.S. invasion of Iraq in 2003, was both extensive and intricate. It included, among other things, the co-optation of various Iraqi politicians; political and material support to both Sunni and Shiite militias; massive infiltration of Iranian paramilitary forces and proxies into Iraq; and provision of a wide spectrum of lethal weaponry (including improvised explosive devices) to Iraqi insurgents fighting the coalition.[61] The geopolitical goals of this effort were clear. "Iran has a robust program to exert influence in Iraq in order to limit American power-projection capability in the Middle East, ensure the Iraqi government does not pose a threat to Iran, and build a reliable platform for projecting influence further abroad," a 2008 study by the Combating Terrorism Center at West Point explained.[62]

This need was particularly acute several years ago, when, as a result of military action in both Iraq and Afghanistan, the U.S.-led coalition was ensconced in countries both east and west of Iran. That pressure has abated somewhat in light of America's 2013 withdrawal from Iraq and its unfolding exit from Afghanistan. However, the need for strategic breathing room—akin to the concept of *lebensraum* ("living space") that animated Hitler's Third Reich in its quest for European territory—still animates Tehran's political involvement in Iraq today.

Iran's policy is likewise driven by another factor: spiritual legitimacy. The most important figure in Shia Islam is not Iran's supreme leader, as Iranian officials would have the world believe. In 1989, Iran's current head of state was nothing more than a midlevel ayatollah, and his meteoric rise to power was much more a function of bitter factional infighting between rival power circles in Tehran than of his religious authority.[63] Unlike Ayatollah Khomeini, who wielded unquestioned authority as both Iran's spiritual leader (*marja taqlid*) and its political head (*rahbar*), Khamenei is a leader with a great deal less legitimacy and power. Indeed, in terms of spiritual identification, he is eclipsed by a number of senior clerics within Iran itself. Most notably, former president Mahmoud Ahmadinejad was known to have been a spiritual follower of Ayatollah Mohammad Taqi Mesbah Yazdi, a radical cleric from the Iranian holy city of Qom, rather than of Khamenei.[64]

But no religious figure poses a greater challenge to the legitimacy of Khamenei specifically, and the Islamic Republic more broadly, than Ali al-Sistani, the 84-year-old cleric who serves as the grand marja of seminaries in Najaf, Iraq. Sistani, a grand ayatollah, is unquestionably Iraq's most senior spiritual figure. He also adheres to the traditional, "quietist" worldview that sees Shiites as separate and abstaining from temporal politics. This is fundamentally at variance with the Iranian government's activist political ethos, which views Shiism as an insurgent political strain of Islam and itself as a vanguard of the so-called Shia Revival.[65] Therefore, Iran's consistent attempts to co-opt and subvert the Iraqi state are, at least in part, an effort to weaken alternative religious narratives that might challenge its ideological primacy.

Today, Iran is closer to this goal than ever before. With

Iraq's government in continuing disarray, despite an October 2014 parliamentary election and a change of political leadership, and amid signals from Washington that sustained U.S. boots on the ground are simply out of the question in the fight against the Islamic State, Iran has emerged as what is perhaps the best long-term guarantor of Iraq's security. As a result, Iran is now approaching its desired end state in regard to its western neighbor: a compliant, fractured Iraq that poses no danger to Iran's security and status in the Islamic world.

CHAPTER

IV

Iran's European Enablers

A few years ago, it seemed as if the United States could learn a thing or two from Europe. In the late 2000s, even as the fledgling Obama administration stuck doggedly to its engagement policy toward Tehran, European capitals were rapidly heading in the opposite direction.

In November 2009, in a move that caused nothing short of a political earthquake on the Old Continent, a majority of the Dutch parliament formally voted to place Iran's Islamic Revolutionary Guard Corps on the European Union's terror list. The decision was in part a reaction to the Islamic Republic's brutal crackdown on grassroots protests that followed Mahmoud Ahmadinejad's controversial reelection to the Iranian presidency that summer—a move that sparked outrage among foreign observers. But it was also a policy broadside aimed squarely at the Iranian government's rogue behavior.

The "IRGC is increasingly functioning as the most important instrument of the present regime," the Dutch resolution noted. "[T]his organization has played a leading role during the bloody suppression of the recent popular protests and . . . is increasingly active in facilitating international terrorism, [including] support to Hamas, Hizbullah and anti-Western militias in Iraq." In response, it urged the Dutch government "to advance that the European Union places the Iranian Revolutionary Guards on the European list of terrorist organizations."[1]

The move was a marked departure from prior practice. For years, European diplomats attempted precisely the strategy now being contemplated in Washington as a way of altering the Iranian regime's conduct. To that end, the European Union tried to engage the Islamic Republic in what it termed "critical dialogue" during the 1990s. Between 2003 and 2005, the E.U. 3 (France, Germany, and the United Kingdom) sought in vain to negotiate a compromise with Iran's leaders over nuclear ambitions. Both were manifestations of the continent's extensive trade with the Islamic Republic, which led European leaders to consistently favor engagement over isolation and diplomatic carrots over strategic sticks, with little success.

By November 2009, it seemed, European leaders were talking—and thinking—tougher. And while the Dutch resolution may have been the most prominent sign of this stiffening resolve, it was not the only one. A month earlier, the British government had invoked counterterrorism legislation in order to formally prohibit business ties with Iran's national shipping carrier, Islamic Republic of Iran Shipping Lines (IRISL).[2] The European Commission, meanwhile, was carrying out a preliminary feasibility study of sanctions that could be levied against the Islamic Republic.[3] All this, coupled with sterner rhetoric emanating from Paris, Berlin, and London, led experts to conclude that the European Union was "much closer to backing sanctions in some form than ever before."[4]

Today, a great deal has changed. Over the past two years, and especially since the November 2013 signing of the Joint Plan of Action (JPOA) between the P5+1 nations and Iran,

Europe has moved steadily away from a policy of applying pressure on the Islamic Republic and embraced anew the idea of engagement and outreach.

This reversal is expressed on two fronts, the first of which is legal. Specifically, a series of recent court decisions helped roll back the European Union's sanctions on Iran and its constituent entities. A July 2013 expose by the Reuters news agency outlined how Europe's courts systematically dismantled sanctions previously levied on Iranian individuals and companies.[5] In all, dozens of Iranian companies and individuals previously censured by the European Union saw decisions against them reversed. Those verdicts, made in part on procedural grounds, arguably have transformed the European Union's own judicial system into the biggest obstacle in its effort to maintain pressure on Iran.[6]

But Europe's courts aren't the only area of reversal. On a second front, European businesses have assumed a distinctly unhelpful role. Historically, the countries of the European Union collectively served as Iran's largest trading partner, with billions of dollars in annual two-way trade. That began to change in the late 2000s, as European countries frequently curtailed economic ties to Iran in response to mounting international sanctions. As a result, China surpassed the European Union in 2009 to become Iran's biggest trading partner, with an annual turnover of at least $36.5 billion.[7] Nevertheless, business between Europe and Iran continues to boom and totaled 7.4 billion euros (nearly $9 billion) in 2012.[8] Amid slackening international pressure on Iran, those ties are strengthening anew.

That is because the November 2013 JPOA included a significant easing of restrictions on investment in a number of Iran's economic sectors, including its petrochemical and pharmaceutical industries. This paved the way for European companies, such as Sanofi and Siemens, which had restricted business in the Islamic Republic, to broaden their presence there.[9]

Iran's automotive sector, too, is fast becoming a growth industry. Steady demand had already positioned Iran as the fastest-growing car market in the Middle East, and now the industry is on the cusp of serious expansion. In just one sign of this newfound dynamism, Iran Khodro, the country's largest carmaker, is reportedly looking for international partners, with negotiations said to be under way with French automakers Peugeot and Renault.[10] This scramble for reengagement is animated by the sense that, in the words of one German business executive, investment in Iran has the potential to be the "chance of a century."[11]

For their part, Iranian officials are doing everything they can to encourage foreign interest. To that end, in February 2014, the Iranian regime formally changed the requirements governing international oil contracts in the Islamic Republic. Under the new structure, deals would no longer be buybacks, requiring the host nation to pay the contractor an agreed-upon price for all volumes of hydrocarbons the contractor produces. Instead, they would be fully fledged joint ventures—a more attractive structure that Iranian officials estimate could net the regime as much as $100 billion in new oil deals.[12]

These developments, and many others, have steadily moved the political dial in Europe back toward engagement and normalization with the Iranian regime. That was the message of the first Europe-Iran Forum, which convened in London in October 2014. The high-profile event, which featured presentations by such luminaries as the former British foreign secretary Jack Straw and the former French minister of foreign affairs Hubert Védrine, was held for a singular purpose: to prepare Europe for trade with, and investment in, a post-sanctions Iran.[13]

That process is well under way. Take Germany, which alone accounts for a third or more of Europe's total business with Iran. In 2012, Germany exported $3.4 billion in goods to the Islamic Republic. That year, 136 companies were estimated to be active within the Islamic Republic.[14] And while commercial ties between Berlin and Tehran dipped temporarily as a result of U.S. and European sanctions, they are on the upswing as hungry German businesses position themselves for a post-sanctions economic boom.[15] This momentum, in turn, is augmented by groups, such as the Hamburg-based German-Iranian Chamber of Industry and Commerce, which lobby heavily in favor of trade détente with Tehran.[16]

But Germany is not alone. Throughout the continent, the consensus to isolate and pressure Iran is crumbling, undermined by political considerations and the economic lure of normalized trade. Indeed, even the Netherlands—which championed the idea of pressure on Iran—has begun to go wobbly. Officials in Amsterdam are said to be considering allowing their businesses to reenter the Iranian market.[17]

Thus, in a matter of half a decade, Europe has come full circle, from engagement to isolation and back again, without any real material change having taken place in Tehran. Sadly, this is hardly the first time Europe has done so.

A COSTLY DIALOGUE

It was the fall of 2003, and European diplomats were waxing decidedly optimistic. Only a year before, the world was jolted awake to Iran's nuclear ambitions when a controversial opposition group, the National Council of Resistance of Iran (NCRI), disclosed alarming details about Iran's previously covert nuclear program.[18] The revelations were a highly unwelcome surprise to the United States and Europe, both preoccupied with the opening stages of the global war on terror.

In response, the international community sprang into

action. In February 2003, the International Atomic Energy Agency (IAEA), the United Nations' nuclear watchdog, dispatched a fact-finding mission to the Islamic Republic and found the Iranian government violating its commitments under the 1968 Treaty on the Non-Proliferation of Nuclear Weapons (NPT).[19] The discoveries led to pressure from other quarters, including the Group of Eight (G8) and the European Union, and to rumblings about serious international censure in the form of United Nations Security Council sanctions.

Only eight months later, it looked like Iran was ready to change course. That October, Iran struck a deal with the E.U. 3 countries—France, Germany, and the United Kingdom—to suspend its uranium enrichment activities.[20] For Paris, Berlin, and London, this deal represented a major diplomatic victory. The agreement was also an implicit condemnation of the American approach to Iran, which featured economic pressure as its centerpiece during the final years of the Clinton administration and during President George W. Bush's first years in office.

The euphoria of Europe's leaders turned out to be short-lived, however. By the summer of 2004, just eight months later, Iran reneged on the agreement and was mapping out new plans for centrifuge enrichment.[21] Yet Europe's response wasn't renewed pressure, but still greater engagement. Between the fall of 2004 and the late summer of 2005, the E.U. 3 nations floated no fewer than five separate proposals, ranging from guaranteeing Iran's access to advanced nuclear technology to the possibility of returning spent nuclear fuel to supplier countries.[22] The goal was always the same: to provide the Iranian regime with an opportunity to climb down from confrontation with the West over its nuclear program.

But Iran didn't bite. Officials in Tehran were, indeed, eager to talk to Europe and thereby forestall the possibility of sterner measures from the international community. They were not, however, willing to give up on their nuclear ambitions and substantially scale back the atomic work they saw as their regime's inalienable right.

In this regard, Europe's outreach proved to be nothing short of a godsend. The eagerness of European leaders for some sort of negotiated settlement gave Iran precious time to expand the scope and strength of its nuclear project. As one senior Iranian policy maker candidly explained to a domestic audience in late 2005, in a speech published in the Farsi-language journal *Rahbord*: "While we were talking with the Europeans in Tehran, we were installing equipment in parts of the facility in Isfahan, but we still had a long way to go to complete the project . . . [B]y creating a calm environment, we were able to complete the work on Isfahan."[23] The speaker was none other than the man who served as Iran's chief nuclear negotiator with the E.U. 3 and who is now the Islamic Republic's "moderate" president: Hassan Rouhani.

Today, the situation is much the same. Long-standing hopes for normalization have been rekindled since November 2013, causing European nations to invest heavily in Iranian negotiations. In the process, Europeans have turned a blind eye to a wide range of worrying activity, from parallel work on Iran's ballistic missile arsenal (a key delivery vehicle for any Iranian nuclear device) to unexplained but persistent signs that the Iranian nuclear project has a definite military dimension. European countries have also muted their concerns about Iran's other deformities—including its abysmal track record on the one issue that ostensibly sits at the center of Europe's foreign-policy agenda.

AN UNFULFILLED MANDATE

The summer of 1975 was a rare moment of international harmony at the height of the Cold War. That August, thirty-five world leaders headed to Helsinki. The list of luminaries included U.S. president Gerald Ford and his opposite number in Moscow, Soviet general secretary Leonid Brezhnev. It also encompassed the two faces of a divided Germany: West German chancellor Helmut Schmidt and his East German counterpart, Erich Honecker. They, and thirty-one others, descended on the Finnish capital to conclude the Conference on Security and Cooperation in Europe (CSCE), a three-stage international process first convened in 1973 and aimed at reducing tensions in Europe through greater trade, cooperation, and dialogue.

They were successful. In what Brezhnev at the time called a "triumph of reason," the conferees passed a landmark framework accord, paving the way for greater political and economic cooperation between East and West. But the agreement, which came to be known as the Helsinki Final Act, was much more. It provided a code of conduct for Europe's states to follow in their relations with each other and with nations beyond the CSCE. Among other things, the Helsinki Final Act required that its signatories "recognize the universal significance of human rights and fundamental freedoms, respect for which is an essential factor for the peace, justice and well-being necessary to ensure the development of friendly relations and co-operation among themselves as among all States."[24]

At the time, hopes ran high that this directive would set a new humanitarian standard. Commenting on the accord, President Gerald Ford noted that "history will judge this Conference not by what we say here today, but by what we do tomorrow—not by the promises we make, but by the promises we keep."[25]

By that yardstick, European foreign policy writ large and, in particular, its approach to the Middle East have been abject failures. Today, the directive in the Helsinki Final Act is observed almost entirely in the breach with regard to the continent's relationships with a range of repressive, autocratic regimes.

Iran is prominent among them. The Islamic Republic has long ranked as one of the world's worst human rights abusers, receiving condemnation from a wide array of human rights watchdogs. Moreover, internal conditions have worsened considerably over the past two years. In his March 2014 report on the human rights situation in Iran, U.N. secretary-general Ban Ki-moon noted continued widespread violations of civil and political rights, including political repression and intimidation of journalists and dissidents, a surge in public executions, and significant ongoing instances of torture and arbitrary detention.[26] All of this makes the Iranian regime an exceedingly odd political partner for countries concerned with human rights and freedoms, as European nations profess to be.

For years, this disconnect has drawn the attention of policy makers and experts on both sides of the Atlantic, who have urged Europe to live up to its commitments under the Helsinki Final Act and scale back its collective ties to Iran. They argue that Iran's growing strategic capabilities represent a shared security threat, that Helsinki members have a commitment to the importance of universal human rights, and that Cold War experience suggests that pressuring the Iranian regime on its human rights practices could be an effective way of shaping Iranian behavior.[27]

For the most part, their arguments have fallen on deaf ears. In practice (if not in rhetoric), European nations consistently prioritize economics before human rights in their approach to Iran. As a result, they have failed to take the Islamic Republic to task over its domestic abuses. The bankruptcy of this policy was in full view in 2007, when the Iranian regime carried out a series of public executions while a European parliamentary delegation visited the country.[28] The timing was a very public repudiation of Europe's half-hearted demands for domestic moderation on the part of the Iranian leadership. Tellingly, while that turn of events chilled contacts for a time, it did not lead to a lasting rupture between Tehran and Brussels.

Recent negotiations between Iran and the P5+1 powers emphasize that disconnect. In December 2013, even as human rights abuses within the Islamic Republic continued to worsen, the European Parliament authorized a ten-person delegation to Iran to promote political ties. This time, they did so without preconditions—a clear signal that the European Union was more willing than ever to put its concerns over Iran's internal behavior on the back burner.[29] All of which only confirmed to Iran's leaders that their domestic deformities are, effectively, a cost-free affair. So, too, it seems, is Iran's ongoing support and financing of extremism throughout the eurozone.

TERROR ON THE OLD CONTINENT

Years from now, 2012 is likely to go down in the annals of history as the year of Iranian terror. In an annual report of global terrorist trends released in the spring of 2013, the U.S. State Department noted that 2012 had seen a "resurgence of Iran's state sponsorship of terrorism."[30] During the period in question, the Islamic Republic "was implicated in planned attacks in India, Thailand, Georgia, and Kenya."[31] Yet the most devastating and effective attack carried out during that time by Iranian-linked militants took place in another theater altogether.

That theater was Eastern Europe. In July 2012, a pre-positioned bomb detonated on a passenger bus full of Israeli tourists in the Bulgarian Black Sea resort town of Burgas. The blast killed six people, five Israelis and the driver of the bus, and injured thirty-two others.

In the days following the attack, Israeli prime minister Benjamin Netanyahu linked the Burgas bombing decisively to Hezbollah and its chief sponsor, Iran, calling it part of a "global Iranian terror onslaught" targeting his country's interests and citizens worldwide.[32] That verdict was confirmed seven months later, when the Bulgarian government published its official report. "We have established that the two [suspects in the bombing identified by authorities] were members of the militant wing of Hezbollah," Bulgarian interior minister Tsvetan Tsvetanov confirmed in February 2013, upon the release of his government's formal findings. "There is data showing the financing and connection between Hezbollah and the two suspects."[33]

Hezbollah's presence in Europe was not new, of course. The organization had engaged in a spate of terrorist activity on the continent since the early 1980s, including a plane hijacking in 1984; bombings in Spain, Denmark, and France the following year; and a rash of bombings in Paris between 1985 and 1986.[34] Over time, however, the militia shifted its focus back to the Middle East, and Europe became used primarily as a launching pad for operations elsewhere.[35]

This shift coincided with two developments. The first was a pronounced reversal of political fortune in Tehran brought about by the costly eight-year Iran-Iraq War and the death of Ayatollah Khomeini in 1989—events that conspired to take the wind out of Iran's political sails, at least for a time. The second was the start of the so-called Oslo Process between Israel and the Palestine Liberation Organization, which activated the Palestinian territories as a local theater for Iranian and Hezbollah resistance against the Jewish state.

European officials, once preoccupied with preventing Hezbollah- and Iranian-sponsored terror, breathed a sigh of relief. As Hezbollah shifted to using the continent as a theater for recruitment, fund-raising, and logistical support, officials throughout the eurozone adopted what later became an established laissez-faire attitude. As one European expert described the thinking that eventually dominated Europe's approach toward the terrorist group, "As long as they aren't involved in politics and aren't operating openly, they are tolerated."[36]

Germany emerged as a particular focus in this regard. In the summer of 2002, Germany's Federal Office for the Protection of the Constitution went public with news that Hezbollah was seeking real estate in Berlin to establish a headquarters and "training center for its supporters in the country, then estimated at about 800."[37] The organization's activity expanded significantly thereafter, and by the mid-2000s, German sources estimated that it controlled as many as five Islamic centers in the North Rhine–Westphalia region alone, supported by Iranian funds funneled through the Islamic Republic's German embassy, as well as a nationwide network of as many as 1,000 operatives.[38]

This status quo was altered by Iran, Hezbollah's chief enabler, whose growing activism transformed Europe from a base of operations back into a target. The 2012 Burgas bombing in Bulgaria was in many ways a reversion to type.

In the aftermath of the bombing, European governments belatedly moved against the group. In July 2013, the European Union formally voted to put Hezbollah's military wing on its terrorism blacklist.[39] But the measure was a half-hearted one, taken largely in response to pressure from the United States and Israel. As experts noted at the time, it drew an artificial distinction among the militia's constituent parts, incorrectly identifying Hezbollah's military wing as a separate entity rather than part of a larger whole. That, however, was simply not the case, as even the group's officials themselves admitted. "Hezbollah is a single large organization, we have no wings that are separate from one another," its spokesman, Ibrahim Mussawi, told *Der Spiegel* in the summer of 2013.[40]

As a result, the organization as a whole was able to insulate itself from European pressure.[41]

Although Europe's formal ban on Hezbollah's military wing remains in place, the continent has been loathe to do more against the group, fearing that it might adversely affect Lebanon's fragile economy and political system, of which Hezbollah has become an integral part.[42] Against Hezbollah's chief enabler and sponsor, Iran, Europe has done even less. To date, no comprehensive European legislation has taken significant aim at Iran's ongoing role as a leading sponsor of international terrorism.[43] And because it has not, Europe remains an inviting arena for the destabilizing activities of Iran and its agents.

RUSSIA'S LOSS, IRAN'S GAIN?

In the spring of 2014, European nations suddenly woke up to an uncomfortable reality. Russia annexed Ukraine's Crimean Peninsula that March, and its ongoing covert assistance to Ukrainian separatists raised the specter of a new cold war between Moscow and the West. It was also a wake-up call regarding Europe's precarious energy position.

Europe is deeply—perhaps fatally—dependent on Russian energy. In 2013, the countries of the European Union cumulatively imported 166.3 billion euros (nearly $200 billion) of energy from Russia.[44] As of mid-2014, three Baltic states (Lithuania, Latvia, and Estonia) relied on Russia for 100 percent of their natural gas consumption. Several other countries, including Greece, the Czech Republic, and Slovakia, are in a similar boat, dependent on the Russian Federation for three-quarters or more of their natural gas imports. In all, more than half of the European Union's eighteen countries import 50 percent or more of their natural gas from Moscow.[45] At least four other non-E.U. countries in Europe are also Russian clients: Macedonia, Belarus, Serbia, and Montenegro.[46]

Add to that the personal connections between some of Europe's most prominent politicians and Russia—for example, former German chancellor Gerhard Schröder, who sat for years on the board of the Russian state-run energy giant Gazprom—and it's easy to see why some observers liken Russia to "Europe's gas station."[47]

For years, experts sounded warnings about Europe's unhealthy energy dependency on Russia and the outsized political influence wielded by the Kremlin in European politics as a result.[48] But it was not until the most recent crisis in Ukraine that the dangers of Europe's reliance became apparent. As a result, there is new momentum among European states to reduce their reliance on an increasingly aggressive, expansionist Kremlin.[49]

Moscow's loss could end up being Tehran's gain. Savvy Iranian officials have seized the moment, and they emphatically claim that Iran is ready to replace Russia as Europe's natural gas supplier.[50] In May 2014, Iran's oil minister, Bijan Zangeneh, confirmed that the Islamic Republic was prepared to provide "large volumes" of gas to Europe "via pipeline or in the form of liquefied natural gas (LNG)."[51] Other official statements make clear that Iran's leaders are eager to exploit the opportunity presented by European-Russian tensions to improve their economic and energy position.

But can they do it? According to industry experts, Tehran faces numerous challenges to becoming Europe's energy supplier. For one thing, Iran's energy infrastructure—long neglected as a result of Western sanctions—requires major upgrades in order to make it capable of sustained energy exports of the type needed by European nations. Such a face-lift would require massive foreign investment, since government projections of needed expenditures are in the neighborhood of $300 billion over the next several years.[52] For another, Tehran is expanding its political ties to Moscow, with a number of new accords inked over the past year. This deepening cooperation is likely to make the Iranian government loathe to work at cross-purposes with the Kremlin.

Nevertheless, Iran's interest is telling. Officials in Tehran understand that if they can provide at least some of the roughly 160 billion cubic meters of gas Europe currently obtains from Russia, it would be a massive shot in the arm for the still rickety Iranian economy. It would be an even bigger boon to the Iranian regime's international standing, making Europe a key stakeholder in ending Iran's global isolation.

Europe appears inclined to become just that. Its leaders are eager to return to the good old days of the 1990s, when— under the auspices of their "critical dialogue" with Tehran— they managed to forge deep economic and political bonds with the Islamic Republic. As Danish Foreign Minister Martin Lidegaard put it in a September 2014 interview with the *Tehran Times*, "All the EU countries feel the same way . . . that Iran could be a very important ally."[53] That is precisely what the Iranian government is banking on.

CHAPTER V

Eurasia Calling

It was an odd choice for a maiden foreign-policy outing. On September 12, 2013, less than a month after being sworn in as Iran's president, Hassan Rouhani embarked upon his first trip abroad. His destination wasn't Beijing, which had steadily risen in importance over the preceding year as a trading partner for a sanctions-stricken Islamic Republic. Nor was it Europe, where the Iranian regime still enjoyed a wellspring of commercial support, despite mounting economic pressure levied on Tehran by the European Union. Rather, the focus of Rouhani's attention was the tiny Central Asian republic of Kyrgyzstan, which was playing host to the annual meeting of the most important security alliance to emerge since the end of the Cold War: the Shanghai Cooperation Organization (SCO).

Established in June 2001, the SCO is an expansion of the Shanghai Five, a regional group begun in 1996 with the purpose of strengthening the common security of its member states: Russia, China, Kazakhstan, Kyrgyzstan, and Tajikistan. By contrast, both the membership and the mission of the SCO are substantially broader than those of its root group. Ostensibly, the goal of the new bloc, which now also encompasses

Uzbekistan as a full member and Mongolia, Pakistan, India, and Iran as observer nations, is to expand regional economic, cultural, and counterterrorism cooperation.[1] Iran's involvement underscores the bloc's unstated purpose: the diminution of American influence in the post-Soviet space. It is an objective that Tehran shares with Beijing and Moscow, the SCO's principal strategic players.

Iran has been a part of the bloc since 2005, and its role has been both active and vocal. At the SCO's June 2006 summit, Iranian president Mahmoud Ahmadinejad was a guest of honor, delivering a public address that called upon the group to play a greater role against "the threats of domineering powers"—a thinly veiled reference to the United States.[2] The speech was a clear indication of how Iran truly saw the SCO: as an energy-rich geopolitical alliance stretching from the Taiwan Strait to the Strait of Hormuz. This led some Western experts to warn that an SCO incorporating Iran would be essentially "an OPEC with bombs."[3]

For years, however, the bloc held Iran at arm's length, worried over its fraught relations with the West, one of several problems Tehran could bring into the fold.[4] Cognizant of this fact, Rouhani used his September 2013 visit to Bishkek, Kyrgyzstan's capital, to marshal support among SCO members for his country's nuclear program, to back Russia's stance on Syria, and to call for the ouster of the U.S.-led coalition from Afghanistan.[5]

The charm offensive had the desired effect. By the following year, SCO members were singing a decidedly different tune. In September 2014, at the organization's summit in Dushanbe, Tajikistan, the bloc finalized the mechanism for including new members, paving the way for Iran, as well as Pakistan and India, to finally be brought formally into the fold.[6]

The reasons for the move were practical. The impending U.S. withdrawal from Afghanistan created an opening for both Beijing and Moscow to play a greater role there. At the same time, SCO members were painfully aware of the possibility that, without greater counterterrorism cooperation among regional states, America's exit could lead to the resurgence of the Taliban and other Islamist forces in the geopolitical periphery of Russia and China. The resulting consensus in Beijing, as elsewhere, was that an expansion of the bloc had "become absolutely necessary."[7]

All this, naturally, is music to the ears of Iranian policy makers, who have made clear that full membership in the bloc remains a strategic objective for the Islamic Republic.[8] But such hopes have been put on hold—at least temporarily. Just days after the September 2014 summit, SCO officials declared that Iran's bid to join the organization as a full member could not be considered at the present time on account of the bloc's stipulation that "countries under international sanctions cannot get membership."[9]

Yet that state of affairs is exceedingly temporary. Should Iran hammer out a deal with the West over its nuclear program, there is little doubt that it will gain SCO membership in short order. Indeed, officials in Moscow are banking on it and are actively attempting to establish a link between the two issues. According to Russian foreign minister Sergei Lavrov, membership for the Islamic Republic in the SCO is "becoming more actual in order to settle Iran's nuclear issue."[10] In other words, Moscow sees Tehran's inclusion in the bloc as a sweetener for Iranian good behavior.

Others, however, worry that Iranian membership in the SCO could, at the very least, make the Islamic Republic more geopolitically adventurous. At worst, given the size of China's economy and the combined energy potential of the SCO's Central Asian members, it could crush any chance for the West to isolate the Islamic Republic in a meaningful way.

Yet Iran's courtship of the SCO is just part of a larger

story. The past two decades have seen a concerted effort by the Iranian government to expand its footprint throughout the territory once occupied by the Soviet Union. It has done so by leveraging its historical, linguistic, and cultural ties to the "Stans" of Central Asia (Kazakhstan, Kyrgyzstan, Tajikistan, Turkmenistan, and Uzbekistan), by exploiting the countries of the South Caucasus as conduits for its illicit nuclear trade, and by aligning itself with the region's emerging security architectures, like the SCO. But nowhere in the region is Tehran's footprint more significant than in Moscow, where the Islamic Republic now enjoys a deep—and growing—strategic partnership with a fellow rogue state: Vladimir Putin's Russia.

FROM RUSSIA, WITH LOVE

On August 5, 2014, as the planned November deadline for nuclear talks between Iran and the P5+1 powers approached, Russia's energy ministry announced a most unwelcome development. While meeting in Moscow, Iran's oil czar, Bijan Zangeneh, and his Russian counterpart, Alexander Novak, had signed a five-year memorandum of understanding worth an estimated $20 billion, laying the groundwork for a deeper economic relationship between the two countries, including an oil-for-goods swap that could see Russia purchase as much as 500,000 barrels of Iranian oil daily, approximately a fifth of the Islamic Republic's total output.[11]

The deal stunned Western policy makers. It had been in the works for months, even as Western diplomats worked feverishly to pressure Iran over its nuclear program. And if fully implemented, it held the power to blunt the effect of U.S. and European sanctions against the Islamic Republic. As such, it was a telling reminder of the strategic bonds between Iran and Russia, and how that relationship could undermine Western efforts to bring Iran's nuclear program to heel.

The contemporary strategic bonds between Moscow and Tehran date back to the early 1990s, when Russia, reeling from the collapse of the Soviet Union, sought—and acquired—a new strategic partner in Iran. To be sure, close diplomatic ties between the two countries had existed during the latter part of the Cold War, when the Soviet Union supported the Islamist opposition to Iran's shah and subsequently made common cause with Khomeini's newly minted revolution. But it was in the post–Cold War era that bilateral cooperation truly flourished.

For Moscow, partnership with Iran was driven by three primary interests. Commercially, Russia's once-robust defense industry was reeling from the Soviet collapse and in dire need of new clients. Iran, then coming out of its costly eight-year conflict with Saddam Hussein's Iraq, fit that bill perfectly and became nothing short of an economic lifeline for the struggling Russian state.[12] Ideologically, Moscow was eager to secure Tehran's good behavior in the post-Soviet space. The breakup of the USSR had untethered five majority-Muslim states (the so-called Stans) from Russia. Officials in Moscow also worried that the wave of Islamic radicalism then sweeping the region could lead to a further fragmentation of Russia itself, and that Iran, which had a long history of fomenting instability abroad, could play a hand in it if it was not properly mollified. Finally, Moscow was also searching for allies to augment its diminished post–Cold War status and help it to challenge America's perceived hegemony in world affairs. Iran's radical regime, with its long-standing hatred of the Great Satan, seemed like a logical partner.

Iran's motivations dovetailed with those of Russia. In the early, heady days after the USSR's collapse, Iran's leaders hoped for expanded influence in the post-Soviet space.[13] But years of grinding war with neighboring Iraq left the Islamic Republic demoralized, militarily diminished, and in need of a patron. As a result, Iran's leaders abandoned their grandiose hopes for a "Union of Islamic Republics" on the territory of the former Soviet Union in favor of partnership with the Kremlin.

At first, it would be fair to say that the resulting strategic alignment was a marriage of convenience; it was a way for Moscow to play in Mideast politics in the wake of the Soviet collapse as an external ally for a struggling Tehran. Over time, however, it became much more.

The Kremlin, for instance, emerged as a key enabler of Iran's nuclear ambitions. In the mid-1990s, despite U.S. and European concerns, Russia signed an agreement to build a plutonium plant in the southern Iranian port city of Bushehr.[14] It also committed to providing the Islamic Republic with nuclear training and know-how, which helped Iran build the critical knowledge base necessary to eventually cross the nuclear threshold.[15] In other words, much of our contemporary problem with Iran's nuclear program is of Russian manufacture.

Over the years, that assistance has continued, even as Western powers have tried to convince Iran to curtail its nuclear activities. As recently as November 2014, Russia inked an agreement to build two additional reactors in the Islamic Republic as supplements to Bushehr.[16] That, however, may be just the beginning. Construction of the two new plants could be "possibly followed by another six," news coverage of the arrangement made clear, making Moscow a major stakeholder in Iran's nuclear future.[17]

Over the years, Moscow has also provided Tehran with much-needed armaments for its ongoing military modernization. In 2000, as a reflection of their burgeoning strategic ties, Iran ranked as Russia's third-largest arms client.[18] This assistance has allowed Iran to launch a full-spectrum modernization of its military capabilities.[19] In September 2013, Russia announced an $800-million deal under which it would, among other things, provide Iran with new S-300 anti-aircraft missiles.[20] The move represented a significant reversal; back in 2007, the two countries had signed a deal for Iran to acquire the S-300, but the arrangement was cancelled three years later as a result of U.N. pressure and Russian jitters over potential Israeli military action against Iran.

Today, the relationship is even more significant. Over the past year, as a result of the ongoing crisis in Ukraine, Moscow has reverted to its traditional adversarial role vis-à-vis the West. As a result, Russia's relationship with Iran has become more important than ever before.

In November 2013, Ukrainian strongman Viktor Yanukovych blinked in the face of Russian pressure and reversed political course, turning away from the European Union. Up until then, Kyiv had been on track to sign an association agreement with the European Union that would have put it on a solidly Euro-Atlantic path. But Russian political pressure and the Kremlin's promise of a $15-billion bailout for Ukraine's struggling economy led Yanukovych to scrap plans for integration with Europe in favor of a supporting role in Russian President Vladimir Putin's premier economic project, the Eurasian Union.

That decision prompted widespread protests in Kyiv and other Ukrainian cities—a wave of popular discontent that became known as the Euromaidan. Weeks of unrest succeeded in removing Yanukovych from power, but they also precipitated a massive Russian response. Moscow stage-managed a referendum in Ukraine's heavily pro-Russian Crimean Peninsula and then annexed the territory into the Russian Federation. It also launched a sustained campaign of subversion in Ukraine's south and east, assisting pro-Russian rebels to establish, and then hold, their own separatist enclaves in Donetsk and Luhansk.

Russia's strategy, which relies on irregular detachments, covert influence, and low-intensity conflict, has been dubbed a "hybrid war" by U.S. and European officials.[21] It has also engendered a significant Western response; to date, the United States and European Union have applied multiple rounds of sanctions on the Russian Federation and worked to exclude Russia from multilateral fora, such as the Organisation for Economic Co-operation and Development (OECD) and G8. So strained are relations between Russia and the West that observers actively talk about a new cold war with Moscow.[22]

Yet there is little doubt that the Western response to Russian aggression has been constrained, at least in part, by a harsh reality. With its permanent seat on the U.N. Security Council, its nuclear arsenal, and its ubiquitous presence in world affairs, Moscow remains a key player on a multitude of international issues—and perhaps none is more important than Iran's nuclear capability. Russia is a core member of the P5+1, and its alignment is essential to the diplomatic consensus aimed at limiting Iran's nuclear ambitions. All this, Roger Cohen of the *New York Times* astutely points out, is bound to influence and constrain White House policy toward the Kremlin, lest a forceful response make it more difficult to secure a deal with Iran's ayatollahs.[23]

If Moscow has any say in the matter, its role could become more important still. Current plans reportedly under discussion between Iran and the P5+1 envision a nuclear compromise in which the Islamic Republic would send its spent uranium to Russia for safekeeping.[24] Such a move would effectively make the Kremlin, now hewing to an increasingly anti-Western line, the custodian of Iran's nuclear breakout potential, with all of the security implications this connotes.

COURTING THE SOUTH CAUCASUS

The Republic of Georgia is far and away the most pro-American nation in Eurasia. The country's 2003 Rose Revolution, which saw the ouster of pro-Kremlin strongman Eduard Shevardnadze and his replacement with Western-oriented Mikheil Saakashvili, made it an early adopter of the Bush administration's "freedom agenda." That placed Tbilisi on a Euro-Atlantic trajectory, reversing decades of subservience to Moscow. Policy makers in Washington took notice, and when Georgia found itself in Russia's military crosshairs in August 2008, the Bush administration quickly provided both humanitarian aid and public political support.[25] In a testament to its gratitude, the bustling four-lane thoroughfare that stretches from the country's main airport through the nation's capital is named the George W. Bush Highway.

Yet Georgia is also a major hub of Iranian activity. A fall 2014 investigation by the Foundation for Defense of Democracies, a Washington-based think tank, found that Iranian proxies and middlemen have used Georgia—itself once a part of the Persian Empire—extensively "to facilitate banking transactions for sanctioned Iranian entities" and to insinuate themselves into the local economy through the acquisition of local businesses and companies. These businesses, according to the study, include shipping, trading, and transportation companies.[26]

Iran's presence is particularly significant in Georgia's Poti Free Industrial Zone, a tax-free area on the Black Sea that has been in operation since 2010. "Of the 166 companies currently registered, Iranian nationals own 84, or 52.5 percent," the study notes. "Together, over 60 percent of Poti Free Zone registered entities can be traced back to Iranian ownership."[27] It is a situation that Georgia's government, now headed by academic and politician Giorgi Margvelashvili, has not yet begun to address in earnest.

Iran's penetration of Georgia is only part of a larger push into the region known as the South Caucasus. Nor is it the most important one. That honor belongs to Iran's strong relationship with Armenia, for whom the Islamic Republic has become "one of the main and most dependable allies" during the past two decades.[28]

The ties between Tehran and Yerevan date back to the Soviet collapse, when Iran became an early investor in Armenia's defense industry and came to rely extensively on the newly independent state as a source for high-tech arms.[29] In return, Tehran turned into a backer of Armenia in its claims against rival Azerbaijan for sovereignty over the disputed region of Nagorno-Karabakh.

Iran's backing of Armenia had another, more immediate, cause as well. Azeris constitute Iran's largest ethnic minority, making up nearly a fifth of the total Iranian population. At some 13 million souls today, that is significantly more than the entire population of the nation of Azerbaijan.[30] As a result, the Iranian regime has been perennially haunted by the specter of Azeri separatism and has waged a persistent clandestine campaign aimed at destabilizing its northern neighbor, with the goal of ensuring that Azeri separatism never gains enough traction to pose a threat to Iran's territorial integrity.[31] This consideration, coupled with Azerbaijan's pronounced tilt toward both Israel and the United States over the past decade, has only reinforced the importance for Iran's leaders of backing Armenia, irrespective of the deep religious differences between Shiite Tehran and Christian Yerevan.

Armenia, for its part, has come to see Iran as a strategic lifeline, and for good reason. Yerevan, after all, has strained relations with three out of four of its neighbors. To the west, Armenia's common border with Turkey remains sealed, a product of political disagreements stemming from Ankara's long-standing refusal to recognize the 1919 Armenian genocide. To Armenia's east lies regional rival Azerbaijan, which contests ownership of the Nagorno-Karabakh enclave in what has turned into the region's most prominent frozen conflict. And to the north lies pro-Western Georgia—a country with which ties have been problematic at best since the Russian-Georgian War in 2008, owing to Armenia's warming relations with the Kremlin.[32]

All this makes Iran—which lies to the south—an indispensable trade and political partner and a gateway through which isolated Armenia can reach the world. "For Armenia," explains Richard Giragosian of Yerevan's Regional Studies Center, "Iran offers an important alternative to closed borders and unresolved conflict and tension with its other neighbors, and offers an opportunity to overcome Armenia's geographic isolation as a small landlocked state."[33]

Ties between the two countries reflect this reality. Over the past two decades, Yerevan and Tehran have forged a robust economic and military relationship, encapsulating multiple defense cooperation pacts, as well as a joint natural gas pipeline which, since its inauguration in 2007, has made Armenia a major energy client of the Islamic Republic.[34] Trade between the two countries is robust, totaling $1 billion in 2010.[35] In 2012, Iran ranked as Armenia's fifth-largest trading partner in terms of both imports and exports.[36] Military contacts between Tehran and Yerevan have ballooned over the past decade, with new accords on a range of strategic issues, from counterterrorism to military exchanges.[37]

Even Iran's traditionally strained ties to Azerbaijan are on the upswing. Political ties between the two countries have improved markedly, with Iranian president Hassan Rouhani and his Azeri counterpart, Ilham Aliyev, meeting four times in 2014 alone.[38] Recent months have seen better economic

ties between the two sides as well, with new cooperation being considered on joint energy projects and border-security,
customs, and legal issues. As an indication of this unfolding
reality, in December 2014, the Azeri parliament approved a
joint declaration of friendship and cooperation with the Islamic Republic.[39] These steps threaten, among other things,
to adversely affect the unfolding strategic bonds between
Azerbaijan and Israel.

Yet Iran has found even more pliable partners in the post-
Soviet space.

IRAN IN THE STANS

In the spring of 2013, the U.S. government took aim at a
little-known Iranian businessman named Babak Zanjani.
That April, the Treasury Department blacklisted Zanjani and
several front companies he controlled for moving "billions
of dollars on behalf of the Iranian regime" and for helping
the Iranian government to conduct energy trade globally in
violation of U.S. and Western sanctions.[40] A key hub of this
network was the tiny Central Asian nation of Tajikistan.[41]

The Treasury action was not entirely unprecedented. Zanjani had been sanctioned by the European Union for expe-
diting Iranian oil deals and laundering the revenue for Iran
in Dushanbe.[42] (Since then, the Iranian businessman has received an unexpected reprieve; in the summer of 2014, the
European Union rolled back its 2012 sanctions against him,
citing a lack of evidence.[43])

That Zanjani chose Tajikistan as a base for his activities
is not surprising. The Central Asian republic is known to
be a notorious hub for illicit finance. The Basel Institute on
Governance, a Swiss policy institute, ranked Tajikistan the
fourth-most-at-risk nation in the world for corrupt financial
practices in its 2013 AML (Anti-Money Laundering) Index.[44]
Moreover, Iran maintains deep cultural, linguistic, and his-

torical roots in the country dating back centuries. Indeed, of all the Persian Empire's former holdings, Tajikistan, where the language remains Farsi written in Cyrillic characters, has the strongest Iranian influence.

Those bonds were on display in the immediate post-Soviet period, when Tehran assumed an outsized role in Tajikistan's simmering civil war, which stretched from May 1992 until the summer of 1997. During that period, Iran played a distinctly disruptive part, supporting—and radicalizing—the country's various Islamist political factions, insinuating itself into Tajik schools and culture, and fomenting pro-Iranian grassroots sentiment.[45] Concerns over this growing influence led many U.S. politicians to ignore, or even tacitly approve of, Russia's reengagement with Dushanbe in the late 1990s.[46] The belief, clearly, was that a Tajikistan under Moscow's sway was more desirable than one under Tehran's.

But Iran's outreach continued. A slew of commercial activity, both private and public, led to a notable uptick in trade, and the Iranian government ended the decade of the 2000s as one of Tajikistan's main trading partners. Iran continued to proffer attractive economic projects to Dushanbe, as it did in 2012, when President Mahmoud Ahmadinejad, visiting Tajikistan to celebrate the Persian New Year (Nowruz), pledged greater economic cooperation in the form of new gas and water pipelines—projects that would be game changers for Tajikistan and allow the country to break its dependency on China and neighboring Uzbekistan for energy.[47]

All this has helped push Tajikistan decisively into Iran's orbit. Tajik foreign minister Hamrokhon Zarifi acknowledged his country's orientation in July 2013, when he called the Islamic Republic a "strategic partner" of his government.[48]

Iran's ties with the other Central Asian states have followed the same upward trajectory. The past decade has seen Iran make notable inroads in Uzbekistan, Kazakhstan,

Turkmenistan, and Kyrgyzstan. These contacts are measured less in economic ties—Iran's trade with the region remains largely peripheral[49]—and more in political acceptance and pragmatic engagement.[50]

Tehran's interest is very much a modern phenomenon. "Despite centuries of cultural, commercial and political interchange," scholars Sebastien Peyrouse and Sadykzhan Ibraimov have noted, "Central Asia is a region that contemporary Iran has largely ignored."[51] As a sign of this neglect, it was not until 2001 that Iran's foreign minister, Kamal Kharrazi, articulated anything resembling a coherent strategy toward Eurasia.[52]

That is decidedly not the case today. For much of the past decade, Iran has viewed the region in tactical terms. In the words of one observer, "Iran's closer cooperation with the Central Asian countries, in particular with Tajikistan, decrease[s] the impact of the sanctions, imposed by the international community against the country."[53] Today, however, as a function of its expanding foreign-policy horizons, Iran is thinking bigger and seeking to reclaim its historic geopolitical role in Eurasia.[54] And while this effort is still far from being realized, two things are already clear. The first is that Iran's ayatollahs are angling for a more prominent role in the post-Soviet space. The second is that they are succeeding.

Iran's Asian Lifeline

O n January 26, 2012, Secretary of Defense Leon Panetta and General Martin Dempsey, chairman of the Joint Chiefs of Staff of the U.S. Armed Forces, convened a major press conference at the Pentagon. The objective was to outline the policies and programs prioritized by the Pentagon as part of an effort to build a "smaller and leaner, but agile, flexible, ready and technologically advanced" military.[1] The centerpiece of the event was, without a doubt, the unveiling of a new strategic priority: to rebalance American resources and pay more attention to Asia.

"U.S. economic and security interests are inextricably linked to developments in the arc extending from the Western Pacific and East Asia into the Indian Ocean region and South Asia, creating a mix of evolving challenges and opportunities," the accompanying military policy-planning document outlined. "Accordingly, while the U.S. military will continue to contribute to security globally, we will of necessity rebalance toward the Asia-Pacific region."[2]

The rationale behind the move was understandable. The preceding three years had been difficult ones for the Obama administration, punctuated as they were by the turmoil of the Arab Spring, the outbreak of the Syrian civil war, and numerous other crises in the Middle East for which the White House did not seem to have a ready response. America's relations with Europe, too, had soured significantly, as Team Obama progressively walked away from NATO defense and security commitments in pursuit of a better relationship with Russia. Against this backdrop, a pivot toward Asia was widely seen as a quest for greener foreign-policy pastures.

It was also opportunistic. China's so-called peaceful rise to regional prominence, and the increasingly adventurist foreign policy pursued by Beijing as a result, had created widespread unease among Asian nations. The Obama administration was eager to exploit opportunities created by these jitters and by the willingness of regional states to cooperate more fully with Washington on security and political issues.

But America was not alone. Other nations tilted toward Asia as well, viewing it as an arena of economic opportunity and strategic engagement. The list includes Russia, which embarked on its own pivot toward Asia years ago, and Turkey, whose prime minister, Recep Tayyip Erdogan, has stressed the country's distinct Asian ambitions on many occasions. But it was Iran's focus on the Asia–Pacific that was perhaps the most interesting.

For Iran's pivot, although undoubtedly more rudimentary than that of the United States, nonetheless held enormous strategic significance. Over the past several years, Asia has emerged as an economic lifeline for the Islamic Republic and is an arena where regional partners have helped lessen the economic pain caused by widening American and European sanctions. But Asia is much more than that; it is a theater in which Tehran has begun to successfully put its global vision into action.

A HELPING HAND FROM CHINA

In Iran's Asia strategy, no country matters more than China. In the three and a half decades since Iran's 1979 Islamic Revolution, Tehran and Beijing have forged a vibrant strategic partnership—one animated by mutual commercial and military benefit and a shared interest in diluting perceived Western (specifically, American) hegemony. Today, ties between Tehran and Beijing are driven, above all, by one thing: energy.

Over the past fifteen years, China's rapid economic growth, averaging some 8 percent annually, has generated a voracious appetite for energy. China's oil consumption is now estimated to be growing at a rate of 7.5 percent per year—seven times faster than that of the United States.[3] In September 2013, China surpassed the United States as the world's leading importer of oil. And by the end of the decade, it will spend a projected $500 billion annually on the purchase of crude oil from foreign sources.[4] Even so, China faces a looming energy deficit—one that could top nine million barrels of crude daily by the end of this decade, according to some projections.[5]

All this has made Iran—a bona fide energy powerhouse that holds the world's second-largest reserves of natural gas and some 10 percent of the planet's proven oil reserves—an indispensable partner for the People's Republic of China (PRC). Sino-Iranian ties reflect this realization: in 2004, the countries inked two massive accords, worth an estimated $100 billion over twenty-five years, that gave Chinese firms the rights to develop Iranian petroleum and natural gas reserves.[6] In 2005, their bilateral energy partnership was estimated to be worth in excess of $120 billion.[7]

These contacts reflect a deep and enduring Chinese dependency on the Islamic Republic. Simply put, the Iranian regime has become a major engine of China's economic growth, with all that this implies. When calculated in 2011,

Iran was estimated to have provided China with nearly 12 percent of its total annual foreign crude, making it roughly as significant for China, in energy terms, as Saudi Arabia is for the United States.[8] Despite China's minor success in diversifying its energy sources over the past two years, the country's energy picture today is largely the same; as of the summer of 2014, the PRC relied on Iran for a tenth of its foreign energy imports.[9]

China's energy needs, in turn, have become an economic lifeline for Iran. Over the past several years, as its economic fortunes in the West dimmed as a result of U.S. and European sanctions, Iran began to turn more and more to Asia. By 2013, Asian nations (among them Japan, India, and South Korea) made up the lion's share of Iran's energy trade. But it was China that assumed the most prominent role. When tallied in early 2013 by the Economist Intelligence Unit, China accounted for approximately 50 percent of Iran's total crude oil exports (roughly 500,000 barrels per day).[10] And these energy ties have only grown since Iran's negotiations with the West have begun to warm.

As part of its confidence-building measures toward Tehran, the Obama administration announced the suspension—at least temporarily—of the Comprehensive Iran Sanctions, Accountability, and Divestment Act of 2010, which required major Iranian energy clients, including China, to steadily reduce imports of crude from the Islamic Republic in order to avoid sanctions from the United States.[11] Predictably, the energy flow from Iran to China has surged since then. In the first half of 2014, China imported 50 percent more oil from Iran than during the same period a year earlier.[12]

The burgeoning energy ties between Tehran and Beijing, in turn, have fueled a deeper strategic alignment. To be sure, China has long played an important role as a supplier of arms and technology to Iran. As early as 1992, China committed to supplying the Islamic Republic with a 300-megawatt nuclear power reactor, and subsequent years saw additional agreements related to weapons of mass destruction (WMDs) that made the PRC, in the words of one U.S. intelligence assessment, a "principal supplier of nuclear technology to Iran."[13] Arms trade also flourished, with the value of Chinese arms transfers to the Islamic Republic reaching $600 million by the year 2000.[14]

Today's cooperation between Tehran and Beijing is deeper still—and more strategically significant. China, for example, has become a financial conduit for the global activities of Iran's Revolutionary Guards. According to a Western intelligence report leaked to the media in the fall of 2014, several Chinese firms are helping to finance the global activities of the IRGC's elite paramilitary unit, the Quds Force, using funds transferred from the Central Bank of Iran to the Bank of Kunlun, a Chinese financial institution. "The money transfers from accounts held by the CBI with Bank Kunlun are initiated by the Quds Force and transferred to Chinese companies connected to the Quds Force in order to meet its financial needs," the study reports. The exact sums transferred via this financial channel have not been disclosed, but they are believed to be in the hundreds of millions of dollars annually.[15]

Iran is also emerging as a military partner for the PRC. In October 2014, China's chief naval officer, Admiral Wu Shengli, hosted his Iranian counterpart, Rear Admiral Habibollah Sayyari, in Beijing. Their summit produced a commitment to "further pragmatic cooperation and the uninterrupted development of ties between the two militaries."[16] That alliance is already taking shape, punctuated by the fall 2014 visit of two Chinese warships to the southern Iranian port of Bandar Abbas and indications that the two navies are building a "'blue water' friendship" in tandem with China's expanding maritime activities beyond the Asia-Pacific the-ater.[17]

The symbiotic nature of this relationship is clear. China provides Iran with a necessary energy lifeline in Asia—one that has withstood, and even expanded in the face of, Western sanctions. And Iran is a means by which China can broaden its influence in the Middle East, even as it dilutes the strength of the Obama administration's Asia pivot.[18]

A STRATEGIC PARTNERSHIP WITH PYONGYANG

North Korea is the world's last remaining Stalinist state. A wildly repressive, brutal dynastic dictatorship, it is a historical anachronism: a country trapped in time, with a population almost entirely cordoned off from the outside world. It's not for nothing that the Democratic People's Republic of Korea (DPRK) is known as the Hermit Kingdom.

Yet, in at least one way, North Korea is a major player in contemporary geopolitics. Beyond being a purveyor of regular bombastic threats against the United States and a de-stabilizing force in its immediate neighborhood, its most sig-nificant—and adverse—role might just be as the chief Asian enabler for the Middle East's emerging hegemon: Iran.

For those who care to look, signs of this partnership are evident throughout Asia. But nowhere is it more visible than in North Korea's capital of Pyongyang, which plays host to Iran's embassy—a sprawling, seven-building compound, complete with the first mosque in North Korea that is one of only five places of worship formally allowed in the city.[19] The estate is a tangible manifestation of the close ties between Tehran and Pyongyang that have developed over the past three decades.

The Iran-DPRK partnership has roots in the immediate af-termath of the 1979 Islamic Revolution, which transformed a onetime ally of the West into a dangerous adversary virtually overnight. In order to evade the weapons embargo imposed by a skittish Carter administration in the Iranian revolution's heady early days, the country's clerical army, the Revolutionary Guards, put a premium on erecting its own weapons infrastructure. It did so by acquiring arms from a number of foreign states, most prominently, China and the USSR. The regime of Kim Il-sung of North Korea figured prominently in this regard as well. By the early 1980s, the U.S. government estimated that, together, China and North Korea were providing the Islamic Republic with 40 percent of its arms. By the late 1980s, that figure rose to 70 percent.[20]

The centerpiece of this budding relationship quickly became cooperation on strategic capabilities. The two are said to have established collaborative missile development back in 1985, under an agreement through which Iran helped to underwrite North Korea's production of 300-kilometer-range Scud-B missiles in exchange for new technology and the option to purchase the completed Scuds. Iran exercised that option two years later, when it reportedly purchased 100 Scud-Bs to use in the closing battles of its long-running war with Iraq.[21]

Iran and North Korea's cooperation expanded in the 1990s, when they jointly developed Iran's Shahab missile series, which—not coincidentally—is closely based on North Korea's nuclear-capable Nodong missile. Indeed, according to ballistic missile experts, the Nodong, Taepodong-1, and Taepodong-2 missiles were the basis for Iran's Shahab-3 and Shahab-4, now in service, and Shahab-5 and Shahab-6, currently in development. The two states are now thought to be collaborating on the development of a nuclear-capable intercontinental ballistic missile.[22]

Iran has also looked to the DPRK for help with its nuclear program. A January 2006 article in *Jane's Defense Weekly* noted that the IRGC initiated procurement contracts with North

Korea to bolster fortifications for nuclear facilities in anticipation of possible preemptive strikes. As part of this effort,
a group affiliated with the North Korean government was
involved in designing and constructing tunnels and underground facilities around the Isfahan and Natanz sites.[23]

Not surprisingly, Iran and North Korea's strategic capabilities have evolved in tandem, and the two countries have
collaborated extensively. Iranian scientists and technicians,
for example, have a front-row seat to the DPRK's ballistic missile development and have regularly attended missile
launches in North Korea since at least the early 1990s. Iran is
known to have dispatched delegations to attend the DPRK's
Nodong tests in July 2006 and March 2009.[24] And in the fall
of 2013, the *Washington Free Beacon* reported that a delegation of Iranian technical experts visited Pyongyang as part of
ongoing collaboration on the development of a new rocket
booster that uses technology that could significantly advance
Iran's long-range missile effort. U.S. intelligence sources described the 80-ton booster in question as a potential thruster
for a "super ICBM" or "heavy lift space launcher"—in other
words, something that could allow Iran, currently a regional
missile power, to become a global one.[25]

Compelling evidence also exists that Pyongyang and Tehran have collaborated on the Iranian nuclear front. During
the early 1990s, much of that interaction was secret, due
to U.S. pressure on North Korea over its own nuclear development. Even so, press reports from the time strongly
suggest that some level of cooperation was under way.[26]
Later, cooperation became more active—and public. Both
countries benefited from the nuclear know-how of Pakistani scientist Abdul Qadeer Khan. And North Korea is said
to have dispatched hundreds of nuclear experts to work in
the Islamic Republic and to have provided it with key nuclear software.[27] During North Korea's February 2013 nuclear

test, some unusual spectators were in attendance: a delegation of Iranian scientists who offered to pay tens of millions of dollars to the DPRK for permission to witness it.[28] All this leads Western experts to speculate that North Korea may have served as an atomic proxy for the Islamic Republic, and that one or more of the nuclear tests carried out by the DPRK over the past decade were to assess Iranian, not North Korean, capabilities.[29]

Clearly, Iran has learned valuable lessons from North Korea's nuclear playbook. Over the past two decades, the DPRK "has cut a series of nuclear freeze deals, collecting security guarantees, diplomatic concessions and material benefits along the way," notes Claudia Rosett, a leading North Korea watcher at the Foundation for Defense of Democracies. "North Korea has cheated and reneged on every deal. Today, the Kim regime has uranium enrichment facilities, has restarted (again) its plutonium-producing nuclear reactor at Yongbyon, has conducted a series of increasingly successful long-range missile tests, and has carried out three nuclear tests, in 2006, 2009 and 2013."[30] For Iran, now engaged in nuclear diplomacy with the West, the North Korean model of obfuscation, delay, and deception presents an attractive way of doing business.

North Korea's partnership with Iran does not end with nuclear collusion, however. The DPRK also extends support to Iran's terror proxy of choice: Lebanon's Hezbollah militia. A number of top Hezbollah officials received military training in North Korea, including the group's secretary-general, Hassan Nasrallah; intelligence and security chief, Ibrahim Akil; and counter-espionage czar, Mustapha Badreddine.[31] The DPRK is also believed to have helped Hezbollah construct elaborate underground tunnels in southern Lebanon, which were uncovered in the aftermath of the 2006 war between Hezbollah and Israel.[32]

Iran's collusion with North Korea has been more than a simple bilateral affair. Other rogues have benefited from the Iranian-DPRK alliance. Chief among these has been the regime of Bashar al-Assad in Syria. According to Ali Reza Asghari, a high-level Iranian defector, Iran helped finance North Korea's participation in Syria's nuclear weapons program.[33] This allegation is lent credence by the fact that Syria's al-Khibar nuclear reactor, which was successfully destroyed by Israel in a covert bombing campaign in 2007, turned out to be of a design analogous to the DPRK's own plant at Yongbyon.[34]

The depth of the strategic bonds between Iran and North Korea was on full display in September 2012, when the two countries signed a pact on scientific-technical cooperation.[35] The signing of the agreement, which closely resembled agreements signed by North Korea and Syria roughly a decade earlier, took place in Tehran and was presided over by President Mahmoud Ahmadinejad and Kim Yong-nam, the powerful chairman of the Presidium of the Supreme People's Assembly. The stature of the participants is telling: Kim Yong-nam is the titular head of state of the DPRK; and while real power resides with North Korea's current leader, Kim Jong-un, it is Kim Yong-nam who usually represents North Korea abroad for high affairs of state. He led the delegation to the signing of the Syria agreement in 2002, and his presence at the Tehran deal in 2012 was indicative of the importance that North Korea placed on its ties with Iran.

But the summit was also much more than that. "The Islamic Republic of Iran and North Korea have common enemies since the arrogant powers can't bear independent governments," Iran's supreme leader, Ayatollah Ali Khamenei, is said to have told Kim during his visit.[36] Khamenei's message was unmistakable: Iran sees North Korea as an ally in its efforts to increase its global power and influence and dilute that of the West.

The feeling is definitely mutual. Today, North Korea's partnership with the Islamic Republic remains as vibrant as ever, despite the recent changing of the guard in Pyongyang. In December 2011, North Korea's long-serving "Dear Leader," Kim Jong-il, died of what is believed to have been a heart attack and was succeeded by his 28-year-old son, Kim Jong-un. The three years since have seen North Korea's "Young Leader" systematically attempt to consolidate his hold on power at home. He has done so in brutal fashion, complete with the disappearance of political adversaries and the grisly execution of competitors.[37]

North Korean foreign conduct has also worsened. An accelerating staccato of provocations has defined the younger Kim's attempts to demonstrate his political bona fides on the world stage.[38] As a result, it is reasonable to expect that Pyongyang's relationships with a slew of nefarious international actors will intensify.

That, in turn, could be a boon to Pyongyang's allies in Tehran. In his October 2014 testimony before the Senate Select Committee on Intelligence, Director of National Intelligence James Clapper made note of "North Korea's export of ballistic missiles and associated materials to several countries, including Iran and Syria."[39] That continuing commerce, experts caution, could provide Iran with an alternative pathway to the atomic bomb—one that could allow the Islamic Republic to go nuclear even if a diplomatic deal with the West is concluded.[40]

A COVERT THEATER

In April 2014, police in Bangkok swooped down on two men: a French-Lebanese national named Daoud Farhat, and Youssef Ayad, a Lebanese citizen of the Philippines. The two men had arrived in the Thai capital a week earlier, and their presence was flagged by Thai authorities, who had been alerted by the Israeli government that the pair, both members of Lebanon's Hezbollah militia, were heading to the South Asian state. During interrogation, Ayad confessed to Thai police that "his group entered Thailand to carry out a bomb attack against Israeli tourists and other Israeli groups" during the Jewish holiday of Passover.[41]

The foiled plot was far from unique. Two years earlier, a suspected member of Hezbollah was apprehended by Thai police on a tip from the Israeli embassy in Bangkok.[42] Israeli officials in the Thai capital, as elsewhere, were on high alert because Iran had blamed the Jewish state and the United States of jointly masterminding the assassination of a nuclear scientist, Mostafa Ahmadi Roshan, in Tehran, on January 11, 2012.[43]

A month later, in February 2012, terrorists linked to both Iran and Hezbollah successfully bombed an Israeli diplomatic vehicle in New Delhi, injuring a member of the Israeli embassy.[44] That attack coincided with the fourth anniversary of the death of Hezbollah military leader Imad Mughniyeh, who was killed in Beirut, Lebanon, in 2009, in an assassination widely attributed to Israel. It was also unexpected. B. Raman, a leading Indian security specialist, said that "Hezbollah has neither operated in New Delhi in the past nor is it known to have sleeper cells in India."[45]

Hezbollah's Asian penetration has gradually taken shape over the past two decades. In his definitive book on Hezbollah's global activities, counterterrorism specialist Matthew Levitt notes that the militia's presence in Asia was a practical outgrowth of Iran's desire to "export its version of Shia Islam beyond its natural borders."[46] That initiative entailed, in part, recruiting and training Asian militants, creating active cells throughout Southeast and South Asia, and orchestrating repeated acts of terror throughout the Pacific Rim.[47]

Hezbollah is not the only sign of Iran's presence in Asia,

however. The Iranian regime itself relies heavily upon the region as a significant hub for procurement and logistical support relating to the country's strategic programs. Over the past five years, a slew of Iranian companies and corporate entities were blacklisted by the U.S. government for their role in procuring WMD-related materiel to assist Iran's nuclear and ballistic missile efforts.[48] A great many of those actors, it turns out, were active in Asia, where vast territorial expanses, lax regulatory environments, and thriving black markets made such illicit purchases easy.

This activity continues, despite ongoing nuclear talks between Iran and the P5+1 powers. A May 2014 report by the U.N. Panel of Experts reported "a decrease in the number of detected attempts by Iran to procure items for prohibited programs, and related seizures, since mid-2013." Yet the U.N. study was quick to point out that this trend "may be a function of more sophisticated procurement strategies on the part of Iran, which has developed methods of concealing procurement, while expanding prohibited activities."[49] Indeed, just four months later, the Institute for Science and International Security, a Washington-based think tank, published an analysis focusing on the pervasive and ongoing nature of Iran's "illicit procurements" relating to its nuclear program and counseled that any nuclear deal struck with the Islamic Republic will need to include "an architecture that prevents Iran from importing goods for banned or covert nuclear programs."[50]

Asia has also emerged as a significant financial hub for Iran's clerical army. In May 2014, details of the IRGC's illicit economic activities in the region began to emerge when Asian news sources disclosed a web of suspicious financial activity, encompassing more than $1 billion of funds squirreled away in a major South Korean bank by Petro Sina Arya, an IRGC-linked company, and active accounts for branches of

Khatam al-Anbiya, the IRGC's construction headquarters, in Malaysia.[51] The financial activity, news reports concluded, was a systematic effort by the Iranian regime aimed at "dodging internationally coordinated economic sanctions."[52]

These machinations highlight just how much the Islamic Republic has come to exploit Asia as a covert theater for clandestine and illegal activities. But Iran's ayatollahs are thinking bigger still.

FUELING ASIA'S FUTURE?

In late January 2013, the government of Asif Ali Zardari in Pakistan unveiled an unusual new initiative: the creation of a 1,300-kilometer natural gas pipeline stretching from eastern Iran through Afghanistan and into western Pakistan. The idea was one that had been discussed for some time, and a framework deal for the project had even been signed by Zardari and Iranian president Mahmoud Ahmadinejad back in May 2009. But worries in Islamabad over an unfavorable American response had so far prevented Pakistani officials from going through with the project. That was no longer the case, it seemed. As one Pakistani official told the *Financial Times*, "A decision has been made that we can't delay this project for any longer. This is Pakistan's essential lifeline. We are going ahead with this project."[53]

However, those plans remain mostly unrealized. In December 2013, the Islamic Republic cancelled its plans to loan Islamabad $500 million to build the Pakistani portion of the pipeline, leaving the future of the project in limbo.[54]

Yet the project is far from stillborn. Iran is estimated to have already sunk more than $2 billion of its own money into the "peace pipeline," making its continuation—finances permitting—a major priority for the Iranian government.[55] Moreover, Tehran can rely on a compliant partner in Islamabad, because of Pakistan's massive debt to the Islamic Republic. As of September 2014, Pakistan owed Iran on the order of $100 million in unpaid electricity bills, but still relies heavily on Iranian energy to power its western provinces.[56] All this gives the Islamic Republic significant leverage by which to bring Pakistan in line with its regional vision.

If it does, it could be a game changer for both Iran and Asia. As energy expert Gal Luft noted, the pipeline is not a "standard energy project" or simply a way to avoid international isolation in the face of Western economic pressure. Rather, it is a potential conduit for the Iranian regime to make itself an indispensable strategic player in Asia. For Iran, the energy route constitutes "an opportunity, should the pipeline be extended to either India or China, to create an unbreakable long term political and economic dependence of billions of Chinese and Indian customers on its gas."[57]

In the meantime, Iran is busy making other plans. Slackening international pressure on the Islamic Republic has allowed it to revive energy diplomacy in the region, and the Iranian regime now actively talks to both India and Afghanistan. The objective is the creation of an alternative energy route stretching into Asia that would link Afghanistan with India via Pakistan and make Iran a major player in South Asia.[58]

These plans, and many others being explored by Iranian officials, are a testament to the inroads Iran has successfully made into Asia in recent years. But Iran's foothold there pales in comparison with the systematic way in which it has penetrated America's own geopolitical backyard over the past decade.

VII

A Foothold in Latin America

S anta Cruz de la Sierra is a bustling city of some 1.1 million people situated in Bolivia's eastern lowlands. As the country's industrial capital, it holds national pride of place as a hub for business, investment, energy, and industry—and as a harbor for pockets of political opposition to Bolivia's wildly popular leftist strongman, Evo Morales.

But Santa Cruz is also something more. For just a few kilometers away from the city, set back on the side of a dusty highway, lies one of the most dangerous places in the Western Hemisphere. That place is the regional defense school of the Bolivarian Alliance of the Americas, the radical leftist political and economic bloc established by Cuba's Fidel Castro and Venezuela's Hugo Chávez in the early 2000s.

Inaugurated in Havana in 2004, the alliance—known as ALBA—has grown exponentially in both size and political influence over the past decade. "ALBA currently has close to 70 million members, an economy of almost $700 billion and a territory of 2.5 million square kilometers," notes Latin America expert Joel Hirst. "If Argentina is included in this mix, ALBA becomes larger than Mexico."[1] And Iran has been involved in ALBA's activities almost from its inception.

A formal observer nation of the bloc, the Islamic Republic is believed to have provided nearly $2 million in seed money for the establishment of the academy, and no less senior a figure than Defense Minister Ahmad Vahidi presided over the facility's formal inauguration in May 2011.[2] Today, the facility remains shrouded in mystery, but at least some facts have come to light. Covering over 5,500 square meters and with the capacity to garrison over 200 students at once, the school states that its goal is to "shape civilian and military leadership that will define the role of the armed forces for the study of defense, security and development in Latin America."[3] Its curriculum stresses what is commonly known as fourth-generation warfare—asymmetric tactics and ideological indoctrination.[4]

Iran's involvement in the ALBA school serves as a microcosm of its activities in the Americas. Over the past decade, the Islamic Republic's presence in the region has expanded dramatically, and it is still growing. So, too, is the potential threat that Iran poses to the U.S. homeland.

IRAN AND VENEZUELA: BIRDS OF A FEATHER

Understanding Iran's presence in Latin America today begins with Venezuela. Since the Islamic Republic first exhibited activity in the Western Hemisphere in the mid-1980s, when it helped its chief terrorist proxy, Hezbollah, become entrenched in the lawless Tri-Border Area at the intersection of Argentina, Brazil, and Paraguay, the Iranian regime's formal outreach to the region has grown significantly. Its roots lie in December 1998, when Hugo Rafael Chávez Frías was elected president of Venezuela.

Chávez's ascent to power was a long-sought-after political victory for Venezuela's radical left. In 1992, Chávez—at that time, a military officer—attempted to orchestrate a coup to unseat the country's president, Carlos Andrés Pérez Rodríguez. The attempt failed, and Chávez was imprisoned, even as Venezuela descended into a protracted period of political upheaval. Upon his release a little over a year later, Chávez rose to lead the country's leftist political opposition, ultimately running for—and securing—the presidency in Venezuela's 1998 elections.

Once installed in office, Chávez commenced a dramatic change in Venezuela's political direction. Between April and July of 1999, he stage-managed the passage of a referendum authorizing the drafting of a new national constitution—one encapsulating the radical, revolutionary worldview the new strongman had come to embrace.[5] That vision was built upon the nineteenth-century Spanish explorer Simón de Bolívar's concept for "Gran Colombia": a united Latin American federation of states free of external influence. In Chávez's hands, however, Bolívar's ideas took on a distinctly anti-American, antiestablishment bent. They also launched Venezuela's new leader on a quest for allies who shared his radical vision.

Iran, with its long pedigree of revolutionary fervor, emerged as a natural potential partner. Accordingly, Chávez took his first trip to the Islamic Republic in the spring of 2001, hoping to jump-start a fraternal anti-American alliance.[6] His goal was a high-minded one: in his words, it was to "prepare the road for peace, justice, stability, and progress in the 21st century."[7] But the reception Chávez received was chilly; the Iranian regime, preoccupied with the coalition presence in neighboring Afghanistan and Iraq and in the throes of significant domestic ferment, was hesitant to forge ties to Venezuela, at least initially.[8]

All this changed, however, with the election of Mahmoud Ahmadinejad to the Iranian presidency in 2005. From the start, the firebrand former mayor of Tehran shared a warm personal rapport with the Venezuelan president. There was also a common vision: despite the tactical differences,

Chávez's dream of an anti-American axis in the Western Hemisphere jibed well with Iran's brand of insurgent, revolutionary political Islam.

Practical considerations also abounded. By the mid-2000s, Western economic sanctions—levied against the Islamic Republic by the United States and its allies in Europe—had begun to bite. The economic dislocation caused by this pressure prompted the Iranian regime to pursue a peripheral strategy and engage potential allies beyond its immediate geopolitical neighborhood in a bid to rally international support and blunt the impact of sanctions. And Latin America, with its sympathetic leftist governments and vast ungoverned spaces, seemed like a target of opportunity.

The result was an ideological meeting of the minds. As Chávez himself described it in 2006, "two revolutions are now joining hands." The two sides, according to the Venezuelan strongman, were "the Persian people, warriors of the Middle East" and "the sons of Simon Bolivar, warriors of the Caribbean."[9] A year later, in a public affirmation of their alignment, Chávez and Ahmadinejad jointly declared the formation of an "axis of unity" between Venezuela and Iran. The goal of this partnership was clear: "to defeat the imperialism of North America."[10]

The synergy was more than simply rhetorical. By the late 2000s, the two had forged a formidable strategic partnership—one that included cooperation on an array of licit and illicit ventures.

Venezuela, for instance, assumed a key role in Iran's efforts to circumvent the international sanctions levied against it over its nuclear activities. In 2009, the two sides inaugurated a binational investment bank to facilitate their economic cooperation. This was followed by the establishment of a wholly Iranian-owned financial institution, the Banco Internacional de Desarrollo, in Venezuela, where it operated largely beyond the reach of U.S. sanctions. Through this vehicle, Tehran could "circumvent financial sanctions imposed by the United States, the European Union and the United Nations through the use of the Venezuelan financial system," according to one expert.[11]

The Chávez regime likewise became a military partner for the Islamic Republic. Pursuant to an April 2008 Memorandum of Understanding on military cooperation, the two established numerous joint defense-industrial projects on Venezuelan soil. These efforts included collaboration between Venezuela's official weapons maker, the Compañía Anónima Venezolana de Industrias Militares (CAVIM), and various Iranian entities.[12] Caracas and Tehran joined hands and helped other rogues as well. In 2008, Western intelligence sources determined that Venezuela helped Iran supply missile components to the regime of Bashar al-Assad in Syria.[13]

Iran, for its part, became an exporter of drone technology to Venezuela, boosting Chávez's efforts to create an indigenous unmanned aerial vehicle (UAV) program.[14] It also expanded its paramilitary presence in Venezuela: the Pentagon's 2010 report on Iranian military power noted that the IRGC's Quds Force exhibited "an increased presence in Latin America, particularly Venezuela."[15] This took the form of Iranian military advisors, who were embedded with the Venezuelan military, and a training camp run by the IRGC near Venezuela's border with Colombia, which served as a platform to train assorted Mideast radicals.[16] Iran's influence, in turn, rubbed off on Venezuela's military, which was restructured along asymmetric lines.[17]

As a corollary, Venezuela also became a major hub for Iran's chief terrorist proxy, Hezbollah. In 2008, the Bush administration directly accused the Chávez regime of serving as a safe haven for and financial supporter of the Lebanese militia. That year, the Treasury Department's Office of Foreign

Assets Control (OFAC) formally listed two people, one of them a Venezuelan diplomat, as Specially Designated Individuals for assisting the group. In making the designations, Adam Szubin, OFAC's director of political affairs, specifically referred to "the government of Venezuela employing and providing safe harbor for Hezbollah facilitators and fundraisers."[18] Indeed, Hezbollah is known to use Venezuela's free trade zone of Margarita Island as a major financing and fundraising center and to base support cells there.[19] The organization has also been accused of training Venezuelan militants in south Lebanon for possible attacks on American soil and operating training camps inside Venezuela itself, with the collusion of sympathetic government officials.[20]

Economic ties also ballooned, underpinned by hundreds of bilateral cooperation accords and joint projects. Many of these ventures were bizarre, wasteful, or downright suspicious, ranging from tractor plants to bicycle factories to milk-processing facilities—leading many analysts in the West to conclude, with some merit, that they were simply cover for more covert and nefarious strategic cooperation.

But perhaps Venezuela's most significant contribution to the Iranian cause was its role as a gateway, providing the Islamic Republic with both legitimacy and entry into the Americas.

BEYOND CARACAS

On March 5, 2013, Hugo Chávez finally succumbed to an aggressive form of cancer. Chávez had been sick for years, and Latin America watchers in Washington and elsewhere had closely watched his deteriorating health and medical care, complete with treatments in foreign locales such as Havana, Cuba. But the extent of Chávez's illness, and its impact on the Venezuelan strongman's ability to govern, was a closely guarded secret in Caracas, known only to his inner circle and to a select few allies of his "Bolivarian revolution."

Iran was among them. Almost certainly, the Islamic Republic had a better awareness and understanding of the health of Venezuela's leader than did Western intelligence agencies. And as a result, Iran moved early and robustly to broaden its footprint in Latin America.

Practically from the start of contacts between Caracas and Tehran, Iran viewed its relationship with Venezuela as a vehicle by which to expand its geopolitical presence in the Americas. And, thanks to active assistance from Chávez, Iran succeeded in creating "an extensive regional network of economic, diplomatic, industrial and commercial activities" in Central and South America before Chávez's death.[21] To date, the Iranian regime is estimated to have signed approximately 500 cooperative agreements with regional governments, many of them economic in nature. But, with the notable exception of those concluded with Venezuela, the vast majority of these commitments have yet to materialize. Nevertheless, Iran's overall trade with the region has grown considerably. Between 2000 and 2005, it averaged approximately $1.33 billion annually. As of 2012, the figure had more than doubled, to $3.67 billion.[22] Today, that figure is estimated to be significantly lower, owing to Venezuela's economic implosion under the reign of Nicolás Maduro, but Iran's trade is expected to rebound as Venezuela's fortunes improve.

Politically, in the past decade, Iran's diplomatic footprint in the Americas has significantly broadened. In 2005, Iran had only five embassies in all of Central and South America. By 2012, that number had more than doubled, to eleven.[23] Today, Iran boasts an official diplomatic presence in Argentina, Bolivia, Brazil, Chile, Colombia, Cuba, Ecuador, Mexico, Nicaragua, Uruguay, and Venezuela.

Iran has also launched a major public diplomacy offensive designed to win the "hearts and minds" of the regional populace. In early 2012, on the heels of what became known as Mahmoud Ahmadinejad's "tour of tyrants," during which the Iranian firebrand visited Venezuela, Nicaragua, Cuba, and Ecuador, the Islamic Republic launched a dedicated Spanish-language television channel known as HispanTV.[24] Funded by the Iranian government's official corporation Islamic Republic of Iran Broadcasting (IRIB), it broadcasts out of Tehran to fourteen countries in the region.[25] The goal, according to Iranian officials, is to broaden the Iranian regime's "ideological legitimacy" among friendly governments in the region—and to diminish the influence of "dominance seekers," a thinly veiled reference to the United States.[26]

Perhaps most significantly, Iran has engaged in extensive cultural contacts throughout the region. It has done so via more than a dozen formal cultural centers throughout South and Central America, as well as through outreach to the various indigenous populations that represent important bases of political support for regional leaders, such as Bolivia's Evo Morales, Ecuador's Rafael Correa, and Peru's Ollanta Humala.[27] These contacts, and concurrent proselytization activities (known as *dawah*), are carried out through a network of informal ambassadors operating in the region—a network that was trained and nurtured by Mohsen Rabbani, a former Iranian cultural attaché to Argentina who is known to have masterminded the 1994 attack by the Asociación Mutual Israelita Argentina (AMIA).[28] This activity was mapped out in detail by the Pentagon in its 2010 report to Congress on Iran's military power, which noted that the Quds Force, the elite paramilitary unit of Iran's Revolutionary Guards, was now deeply involved in the Americas, stationing "operatives in foreign embassies, charities and religious/cultural institutions to foster relationships with people, often building on existing socio-economic ties with the well-established Shia Diaspora," and even carrying out "para-

military operations to support extremists and destabilize un-
friendly regimes."[29]

Yet it is with two of Venezuela's fellow "Bolivarian" nations that Tehran has made the most substantial inroads.

COURTING LA PAZ AND QUITO

Iranian president Mahmoud Ahmadinejad made his inaugural
trek to Bolivia's remote capital, La Paz, in September 2007,
activating contacts made possible by Venezuela's patronage.
On that occasion, Ahmadinejad and Bolivian president Evo
Morales signed a cooperation agreement worth an estimated
$1.1 billion, under which Iran pledged a half-decade of in-
vestment in Bolivian natural gas facilities, agriculture, and
humanitarian programs.[30] This was followed, a year later, by
Iran's formal opening of an embassy in La Paz and Bolivia's
highly symbolic transfer of its Middle Eastern diplomatic mission from Egypt to Iran.[31]

Since that time, contacts between Tehran and La Paz have
deepened dramatically. Bolivia appears to be a significant
source of strategic resources for the Islamic Republic. As of
2012, Iran was believed to have begun uranium exploration
in no fewer than eleven locations in the east of the country.[32]
Iran has also become a partner in developing Bolivia's reserves
of lithium, a key strategic mineral with applications for nuclear weapons development, pursuant to a formal agreement
signed with the Morales government in 2010.[33] Iran is seeking at least two other minerals utilized in nuclear work and
the production of ballistic missiles: tantalum and thorium.[34]
In September 2012, for example, Bolivian police seized two
tons of what was suspected to be uranium ore destined for
Iran's nuclear program.[35] The shipment was later ascertained
to be tantalite, the primary source of tantalum.

Iran likewise is exploiting Bolivia's largely unregulated political climate, leveraging quiet official support from the gov-

ernment of Evo Morales, to establish a significant asymmetric presence in the country. The ALBA regional defense school outside Santa Cruz, Bolivia, may be the most striking example of this paramilitary presence, but it is hardly the only one. Indeed, as of 2012, regional officials were estimating between 50 and 300 Iranian trainers were present in Bolivia alone.[36]

Commercially, Iran's interest in Bolivia is reflected by surging bilateral trade. Iran has also offered hundreds of millions of dollars in loans to the Bolivian government[37] and potential sales of warplanes and helicopters to the Bolivian military.[38] And while none of these ventures have yet materialized, it is clear that Tehran sees Bolivia and its populist leader, Evo Morales, as an indispensable regional partner and ally against the injustice of "colonial governments," chief among them, the United States.[39]

In tandem with its outreach to Bolivia, Tehran has also set its sights on Ecuador. Like its contacts with the government of Evo Morales, Iran's ties to the Ecuadorian government are comparatively new, dating back only to the election of Rafael Correa to the Ecuadorian presidency in 2007. However, in the short time since, Correa's regime has begun to emerge as an important regional partner for the Islamic Republic, and for good reason. Ecuador's membership in OPEC, participation in the ALBA bloc, dollarized economy, and lax immigration controls all make it an attractive partner. So, too, does the prominent role Correa hopes to play in the region—particularly in the wake of Chávez's passing.

Cooperation between the two countries remains largely aspirational, however. Despite warm diplomatic ties and a slew of bilateral agreements signed in recent years, Tehran and Quito have not meaningfully expanded their formal relationship over the past ten years. Trade, too, remains minimal.[40] Yet, political interest in a broader partnership is clearly present.

Such cooperation is likely to be buoyed by the state of political debate in Ecuador itself. Correa, who handily won reelection in the spring of 2013, enjoys tremendous domestic popularity because of his efforts to alleviate poverty and improve the standard of living, particularly among the poor, through subsidies and social programs. These initiatives have earned him both the goodwill of the Ecuadorian masses and a great deal of latitude on the foreign-policy front—freedom that could allow Correa to rapidly operationalize his country's relationship with Iran, using the legal infrastructure that already is being laid via bilateral agreements in various sectors, particularly banking and mining.

Of these developments, the most worrisome are the tacit military ties that have been erected between Quito and Tehran. A number of secret military cooperation agreements are known to have been signed between the two countries in recent years, and at least some level of Iranian activity is believed to be present in the port city of Manta—a key strategic point because of its proximity to narco-trafficking routes and the Panama Canal, the object of surveillance. However, meaningful military-to-military cooperation between Iran and Ecuador may be difficult to achieve, since the Ecuadorian military is strongly tied to the United States after years of deep and institutionalized cooperation between the Pentagon and the Ecuadorian Ministry of Defense.

But even if the formal relationship between Ecuador and Iran remains tentative, Iran's asymmetric presence in the country is advancing rapidly. Iran's presence, according to local experts, is "deep and profound but secret" and includes troubling links between Iran and organized criminal groups.[41] The Iranian regime is also believed to be carrying out illicit financial activities in Ecuador, using banking agreements and bilateral commerce as cover. Perhaps the best example of this activity is the notorious COFIEC Bank affair, in which the

Iranian government established commercial links with a state-owned bank as a means of skirting international sanctions.[42]

The Islamic Republic also has become an active recruiter and proselytizer in Ecuador. A 2012 investigation by the news magazine *Vistazo* found that at an Iranian-backed cultural center in Quito was being used as a base to recruit disaffected Ecuadorians for conversion and to provide ideological training and indoctrination.[43]

These gains are notable, both for their intensity and for what they indicate about Iran's position as an integral part of ongoing leftist anti-American resistance in the region. But Tehran is thinking bigger still.

REGAINING GROUND IN BRAZIL

When he touched down in Brazil on June 20, 2012, Mahmoud Ahmadinejad was a man on a mission. Publicly, the purpose of the Iranian president's visit—his first to the South American nation since 2009—was to join the more than one hundred other dignitaries attending the United Nations Conference on Sustainable Development taking place in Rio de Janeiro. The real reason for Ahmadinejad's trip, however, was more urgent. Iran's president hoped to use his personal touch to reinvigorate the once-robust ties between Tehran and Brasília.

Ahmadinejad had his work cut out for him. During the administration of Luiz Inácio Lula da Silva, who served as Brazil's president from 2003 to 2011, Brasília was one of Tehran's strongest partners in Latin America. Under Lula's leftist government, Brazil turned into a major diplomatic backer of the Islamic Republic's will to nuclear power, with Brazilian officials rejecting the sanctions they believed were being unjustly imposed upon Tehran.[44] Bilateral trade—which had been at low levels throughout the 1980s and 1990s—soared, hitting $2.9 billion annually in 2008.[45]

But political ties took a marked turn for the worse with the ascension of Dilma Rousseff to the Brazilian presidency in January 2011. Rousseff, a former women's rights activist who spent time in prison, made a point of distancing herself from Iran, repeatedly rebuffing Iran's diplomatic overtures and signaling her displeasure at Iran's troubling human rights record. For Iran, the reversal was both sudden and surprising, and officials in Tehran saw it as nothing short of a betrayal. Iranian government spokesman Ali Akbar Javanfekr said as much in an interview with São Paulo's influential *Folha de São Paulo* newspaper, in which he blamed Rousseff for abandoning Lula's legacy and having "destroyed years of good relations."[46]

If Ahmadinejad hoped his 2012 visit would help thaw these icy political bilateral ties, he was sorely mistaken. On that occasion, Iran's head of state failed to even secure an audience with Brazil's president, and he left the country shortly after the U.N. summit concluded without much access to key Brazilian decision makers. Even so, Iran has reasons to be optimistic that its relationship with South America's most important geopolitical player will eventually get back on track.

For one thing, the change in political tenor that accompanied Rousseff's ascension did not lead to a complete rupture between the two countries. Trade ties between the two countries remain robust—at least from Iran's perspective. In 2012, Brazil did more than $2.1 billion in business with Iran, making it far and away the Islamic Republic's largest trading partner in the region.[47] Diplomatic contacts, too, have continued. The institutional and bureaucratic infrastructure that enabled close ties between Tehran and Brasília during Lula's tenure remain in effect, complete with regular meetings between Iran's envoy and Brazil's foreign-policy establishment. As one local observer put it, "there has been a change in the retail, but not in the wholesale."[48]

For another, Iran's informal presence in the country is significant—and getting stronger. According to regional experts, there are signs of active recruitment and proselytization among Brazil's poor by Muslim elements, including representatives of Iran.[49] The network of Mohsen Rabbani, the Islamic Republic's informal ambassador to Latin America, is also known to be active in Brazil, as is Hezbollah, which maintains a significant presence in the triple frontier at the intersection of Brazil, Paraguay, and Argentina. In Brazil, as elsewhere in the region, Iran's proselytization—and the growing appeal of Islam in general—is assisted by a lack of economic opportunity and by a lingering political atomization among segments of the population. This trend is reflected in the growing number of converts and mosques now visible in São Paulo and other Brazilian cities.

Iran's interest is understandable. Brazil ranks as Latin America's largest economy and the world's seventh largest, according to both the World Bank and the International Monetary Fund. By dint of this global economic stature, Brazil represents a major geopolitical prize for Iran—the cooperation of which would greatly hamper any future Western efforts to economically isolate the Islamic Republic. And today, as the West continues to normalize its relationship with the Iranian regime, Brazil is beginning to show an interest in revisiting its once-robust ties to Tehran.[50]

TEHRAN'S TANGO WITH ARGENTINA

In March 1992, Argentina became the first Latin American victim of Islamist terror when Hezbollah, Iran's Lebanese proxy, carried out a suicide bombing against Israel's embassy in Buenos Aires, killing 29 and injuring 242 others. Two years later, in July 1994, the group struck again in even more devastating fashion, bombing the Argentine-Israeli Mutual Association (AMIA) in Buenos Aires. That attack claimed the lives of 85 civilians and injured more than 300 others, making it the most devastating incident of Islam-inspired violence in Latin American history. A subsequent investigation by Argentine state prosecutors found that the attack had been "ordered by the highest authorities of the Islamic Republic of Iran in conjunction with Hezbollah."[51]

All of this makes Argentina an exceedingly odd candidate for Iranian outreach. Yet, contrary to all conventional wisdom, recent years have seen a marked improvement in ties between the two countries. Since 2011, Argentina's leftist president, Cristina Fernández de Kirchner, has broken with tradition and hewed to a more conciliatory line toward Iran.

Signs of a reorientation first appeared in the fall of 2011, when Argentina's U.N. envoy, Jorge Argüello, broke with historic practice and remained seated during Iranian president Mahmoud Ahmadinejad's address before the General Assembly. The move was a very public statement that Buenos Aires was ready to turn the diplomatic page in its relationship with Tehran.

The about-face was surprising, to say the least. During his time as president from 2003 to 2007, the late Néstor Kirchner had hewed to a consistently anti-Iranian line, demanding greater accountability from Iran for its involvement in the 1994 AMIA attack. But Kirchner's widow and successor as president, Cristina Kirchner, gradually took a different tack.

The reasons for the reversal were both practical and ideological. Economically, Argentina was in steep decline as a result of Kirchner's populist policies, from higher taxes to greater regulation. Argentina's financial books became so speculative and manipulated that, in February 2012, the prestigious *Economist* magazine took the unprecedented step of removing the country from its indicators page.[52] This left the Kirchner government economically isolated, and over time it provided the "incentive for the Argentine government to reverse its policy toward Iran."[53]

Iran was quick to exploit the opening. In 2012, Argentina's wily foreign minister, Héctor Timerman, met with his Iranian counterpart, Ali Akbar Salehi, in what was widely seen as an effort to engineer a more public rapprochement between Tehran and Buenos Aires.[54] The initiative bore fruit: by early 2013, Iran and Argentina managed to create a "truth commission" to investigate the 1994 AMIA bombing.[55] The arrangement was absurd, insofar as it effectively allowed Iran to investigate a crime that it itself was accused of committing. Nevertheless, it was a concrete sign that Kirchner was willing to allow Iran to rewrite its sordid history with her country.

The thaw had a distinctly economic component as well. Minimal as it was for years on account of frayed relations, Iranian-Argentine trade surged, increasing by more than 500 percent over 2005 levels. By 2013, thanks to the burgeoning contacts between the two countries, economic ties rested at $1.2 billion annually.[56]

Since then, relations have soured somewhat. A predictable failure by Iran to seriously investigate the events surrounding the AMIA bombing led to a drop in public support for the arrangement, culminating in the annulment of the deal by an Argentine court in May 2014 on the grounds that it was unconstitutional.[57] More recently, the Iranian-Argentine relationship has come under renewed scrutiny by the international community following the suspected murder of Argentine state prosecutor Alberto Nisman, the principal investigator into the AMIA bombing, just hours before his scheduled appearance before the Argentine Congress to present his findings of collusion between the Kirchner government and the Islamic Republic.

Nevertheless, a real, lasting restoration of relations between

Argentina and Iran remains possible—if not probable—for a host of domestic reasons. As scholars Julián Obligio and Diego Naveira noted, "President Fernández de Kirchner's populist economic policies, including: massive public spending, increased regulation, higher taxes, trade barriers, and poor monetary policy have led to chaos, a dwindling economic growth rate, high levels of inflation and unemployment, and a drop in foreign reserves that have thrown Argentina into economic free fall."[58] Amid this deterioration, Cristina Kirchner's government has become desperate for foreign allies and more willing to forgive the Iranian regime for its rogue behavior.

Argentina's loss may be Iran's gain—and a serious national security problem for the United States. This is because Argentina ranks as Latin America's most advanced weapons state. From the 1960s through the 1990s, successive governments in Buenos Aires developed the country's nuclear program and ballistic missile capabilities. While it has progressively turned away from developing weapons of mass destruction over the past two decades, Argentina today still boasts a robust nuclear energy program. And because it does, nonproliferation experts have warned, the possibility that a cash-strapped Kirchner regime could become a "proliferation turntable," transferring vital nuclear-related know-how to the Islamic Republic, cannot be ruled out.[59]

IRAN'S OBJECTIVES

What, exactly, does Iran want in the Americas? Over the past decade and a half, Iran's engagement with Central and South America has taken the form of a bewildering array of activities. At first blush, these efforts appear disorganized and only marginally effective, leading some analysts to dismiss Iran's regional presence as little more than an "axis of annoyance."[60] Others have minimized the long-term strategic significance of Iran's regional inroads, seeing them as defensive in nature—a simple reaction to Western sanctions that is aimed at shoring up support for the regime's nuclear effort and broadening international sympathies for Tehran.

Upon closer examination, however, it becomes clear that Iran's activities in Latin America amount to far more than that. A 2009 dossier prepared by Israel's Ministry of Foreign Affairs noted that "since Ahmadinejad's rise to power, Tehran has been promoting an aggressive policy aimed at bolstering its ties with Latin American countries with the declared goal of 'bringing America to its knees.' "[61] Three years later, the Pentagon came to much the same conclusion. "Iran continues to seek to increase its stature by countering U.S. influence and expanding ties with regional actors while advocating Islamic solidarity," it noted in its April 2012 *Annual Report on Military Power of Iran.*[62] Iran, in other words, is pursuing what military planners might call an "anti-access strategy" in Latin America—promoting its own ideology and influence at the expense of the United States. Or, as former Iranian president Mahmoud Ahmadinejad himself put it some time ago, "when the Western countries were trying to isolate Iran, we went to the U.S. backyard."[63]

The goal of this multipronged outreach is clear. Iran seeks to improve its regional position and do so at the expense of the United States. It is an objective that remains in effect today, despite the fact that Latin America, and therefore Iran's standing in the region, is in a state of profound political flux. The April 2013 death of Venezuelan president Hugo Chávez removed one half of the Iranian regime's most-vibrant personal relationship in the region, and ensuing domestic instability has called into question whether his successor, Nicolás Maduro, can be a serious regional partner for Iran in the near future. The end of Mahmoud Ahmadinejad's tenure as Iran's president in June 2013 removed the other half of the favorable relationship. But it did not spell an end to Iran's activities and presence in the Americas.

Ahmadinejad's successor, Hassan Rouhani, has declared his government's commitment to expanding ties to Latin America.[64] And, increasingly, Iranian officials are putting their money where their mouths are. In May 2014, a high-level parliamentary delegation from Iran embarked upon a Latin American tour—an exercise that involved public affirmations of the close bonds and continued strategic convergence between Iran and the ALBA bloc of nations.[65] That same month, the Rouhani government announced a plan to nearly triple the number of its commercial attachés abroad—including those in Latin America.[66] The message to Latin America's political leaders was unmistakable: the Islamic Republic isn't going away.

GATHERING THREAT, LAGGING RESPONSE

For years, and despite mounting evidence to the contrary, policy experts within the Washington Beltway have minimized the importance of Iran's infiltration into the Americas. Such a view is distinctly shortsighted, because the Islamic Republic has directly targeted the United States from Latin America on at least three occasions in the past decade.

The first was an unsuccessful 2007 plot involving a Guyanese national to blow up fuel tanks underneath New York's John F. Kennedy Airport. According to the late Argentine state prosecutor Alberto Nisman, the perpetrator, Abdul Kadir, was a disciple and agent of Iranian cleric Mohsen Rabbani, the alleged mastermind of the 1994 terrorist attack on the AMIA cultural center in Buenos Aires, Argentina, and had previously "carried out the Iranian infiltration in Guyana" under Rabbani's direction.[67] Kadir was sentenced in 2010 to life in prison in the Eastern District of New York for his role in the plot. Had it succeeded, the attempt would have caused

"extensive damage to the airport and to the New York economy, as well as the loss of numerous lives," the FBI assessed.[68]

The second was an elaborate October 2011 attempt by
Iran's Revolutionary Guards to assassinate Saudi Arabia's ambassador to the United States, Adel al-Jubeir, at a Washington,
D.C., restaurant, using members of Mexico's notorious Los
Zetas drug cartel to carry out the hit. The plot also involved
plans to bankroll cartel bombings at the Israeli embassy in
Washington and the Israeli and Saudi embassies in Buenos
Aires. In a press conference divulging details of the failed
scheme, Attorney General Eric Holder noted that it was "di-
rected and approved by elements of the Iranian government
and, specifically, senior members of the Quds Force," the
IRGC's elite paramilitary unit.[69]

The third was a plan by Venezuelan and Iranian diplomats
to use Mexican hackers to penetrate U.S. defense and intelligence facilities and launch widespread cyber attacks in the
United States. The effort was described in a December 2011
investigative documentary by the Spanish-language television network Univision, which featured secret recordings of
the plotters.[70] In the wake of the documentary's airing, Venezuela's consul general to Miami was declared persona non
grata and expelled from the country.[71]

But the U.S. government has been slow to wake up to the
Iranian threat south of the border. It was not until the October 2011 attempt on the life of Saudi envoy Adel al-Jubeir
became public knowledge that lawmakers finally began to
focus in earnest on the intrusion of the Islamic Republic into
the Western Hemisphere.

Revelations surrounding the foiled plot sparked a flurry
of activity in Congress, culminating in the passage of the
Countering Iran in the Western Hemisphere Act of 2012.[72]
Introduced in January 2012 by South Carolina congress-
man Jeff Duncan (R–SC-3), the bill was intended to compel

the U.S. government to formulate a strategic response to Iranian activity in Central and South America. Its central provision was the requirement that the U.S. Department of State draft "an assessment of the threats posed to the United States by Iran's growing presence and activity in the Western Hemisphere."[73]

In a rare instance of bipartisan consensus, the act passed both houses of Congress easily and was signed into law by President Obama in December 2012. But, when it finally materialized in the summer of 2013, the resulting "comprehensive strategy" left a great deal to be desired. Much to the chagrin of congressional lawmakers, the State Department's assessment systematically downplayed Iran's presence in the Americas and offered little by way of serious strategic guidance on the issue. A September 2014 study by the U.S. Government Accountability Office concluded as much when it found the State Department's strategy woefully deficient on a number of fronts, including fully mapping Iran's soft-power initiatives in the region, exploring connections between the Iranian regime and its proxies and transnational criminal groups in the Americas, and laying out a plan to partner with regional nations to better isolate Iran and its agents.[74]

In the face of pressure from Congress, the State Department committed to a reevaluation of its findings.[75] But no such revision has been forthcoming, and in the meantime, momentum toward a real, comprehensive assessment of, and response to, Iran's activities in the Americas has faltered. As a result, the U.S. government remains woefully behind the curve in identifying, contesting, and weakening Iran's regional influence.

Iran, meanwhile, is forging ahead with its activities in the Americas, irrespective of its unfolding rapprochement with the United States and Europe.

"Iran is now encountering a new Latin America, one that

is increasingly anti–U.S. and anti–Israel in its composition, and one that provides Tehran with numerous opportunities to expand its influence," notes Joseph Humire of the Center for a Secure Free Society, a Latin America and counterterrorism policy think tank in Washington.[76] It is an arena where Iran may soon gain additional local partners and even greater geopolitical freedom of action.

VIII

Inroads in Africa

L ate on the evening of October 23, 2012, the Sudanese capital of Khartoum was rocked by a spectacular blast. The cause was not a military clash, although the war-torn city had seen its share of fighting during Sudan's multiple, protracted civil wars, which had raged from 1955 to 1972, and again from 1983 until 2005. Rather, it was the product of a very different kind of conflict: a shadow war between Iran and Israel.

The blast took place at the city's Yarmouk Industrial Complex, a military depot that had been flagged by Western governments for its involvement in Iran's weapons-of-mass-destruction programs.[1] Within days, Sudan's information minister, Ahmed Belal Osman, confirmed that the explosion was the result of an Israeli airstrike aimed at destroying stockpiles of Iranian arms.[2] Sudanese opposition groups drew an even more direct connection to the Islamic Republic, identifying the facility as belonging to Iran's Revolutionary Guards.[3] Israeli officials, for their part, tacitly acknowledged their involvement in what they described as an effort to dislodge the terrorist infrastructure constructed by enemies of the Jewish state.[4]

Weeks later, the context became clearer still. In mid-November, Israel launched Pillar of Defense, a major military operation aimed at degrading the strategic capabilities of the Hamas terrorist group that dominated the Gaza Strip. Hamas was a major client and proxy of the Islamic Republic, and the armaments destroyed at the Yarmouk facility were of precisely the type that Israel was seeking to prevent the group from possessing. The Yarmouk attack had another purpose as well; according to Israeli analysts and intelligence sources, Sudan had been identified as a critical node in the pipeline Iran used to transfer armaments to Hamas and other militants and the place "where the parts for Iranian weapons are assembled."[5]

That Sudan figured so prominently in Israel's calculus was a testament to the strategic bonds forged between Iran's ayatollahs and the country's corrupt and brutal dictatorship. Those ties date back to 1991, when Iranian president Ali Akbar Hashemi Rafsanjani visited Khartoum to formally establish contacts with Sudanese strongman Omar al-Bashir, who had taken power in a coup two years earlier. Al-Bashir's ascent to power had been fueled by Islamist fervor, and once in power he quickly imposed strict sharia law throughout the country, complete with mandated Islamic dress for women and harsh Quranic punishments for crimes.[6] The Iranian regime came to see al-Bashir's Sudan as a kindred spirit. "The Islamic Revolution of Sudan," Rafsanjani announced during his inaugural visit to Khartoum, "alongside Iran's pioneer revolution, can doubtless be the source of movement and revolution throughout the Islamic world."[7]

In the years that followed, Iran translated this sentiment into concrete action. It established a beachhead for its Revolutionary Guards in Sudan, deploying a detachment of Guardsmen to create and then advise a militia for the country's ruling National Islamic Front (NIF) and creating multiple training camps for Islamic militants in the country's south.[8] Concomitantly, the IRGC's Quds Force established a strategic alliance with the NIF and its spiritual head, Hassan al-Turabi.[9] Iran's government, meanwhile, made concrete investments in al-Bashir's regime, and by the mid-1990s, it had extended hundreds of millions of dollars in military aid to Khartoum.[10]

Those investments were strategic, because Sudan's location on the African continent made it a major prize. "Sudan at the time bordered nine nations, some of which were Muslim," notes analyst Steven O'Hern, "making it ideally situated for use by the Revolutionary Guard as a base and transit point for other operations in Africa."[11] Moreover, Sudan's protracted, multidecade civil strife made its ruling regime eager for international allies and dependent on foreign sources of weaponry, while its Islamist outlook made it a suitable—and pliable—partner for the Islamic Republic.

Over the past dozen years, Tehran has armed Sudan to the teeth, providing an estimated $12 billion in heavy weaponry to the al-Bashir regime between 2004 and 2006 alone.[12] It has also run political interference for Sudan's repressive rulers, opposing international efforts to indict al-Bashir[13] and seeking a united economic front with Khartoum as a way of confronting sanctions on both governments levied by the West.[14] In a demonstration of this solidarity, just days after the International Criminal Court charged the Sudanese leader with no fewer than five counts of crimes against humanity and two counts of war crimes for his role in the humanitarian disaster in Darfur, the head of the Iranian parliament and former nuclear negotiator, Ali Larijani, visited Sudan and publicly embraced al-Bashir.[15]

Sudan, meanwhile, has thrown its weight behind Iran's steady progress toward nuclear capability, terming it a "great victory for the Islamic world."[16] And it has wagered heavily on the strategic partnership built with Tehran. That was one of the major take-aways from the leaked minutes of an August 2014 closed-door meeting of Sudan's top leadership. "We will not sacrifice our relations with the Islamists and Iran for a relationship with the Saudis and the Gulf states," Sudan's defense minister, Yehya Mohammed Kheir, declared at the gathering. "What is possible is a relationship that serves our mutual economic interests in terms of investment and employment."[17]

Yet that partnership is just one part of a larger Iranian strategy in Africa—one designed to build influence, forge new political bonds, acquire strategic resources for its nuclear program, and establish a foothold for its terrorist networks. As in other parts of the third world (most prominently, Latin America), Iran has done so by exploiting the region's vast ungoverned spaces, sympathetic regimes, and economic privation. And over the past decade, it has charted some notable successes. Although its African outreach remains relatively rudimentary and haphazard, observers say that the Islamic Republic has nonetheless succeeded in exploiting the region "to accumulate asymmetrical victories for its aggressive, anti-western agenda."[18]

AFRICA'S ALLY

By the end of his tenure, Mahmoud Ahmadinejad was a man on the ropes. Political reversals abounded during the once-popular president's second term, from 2009 through 2013. There was widespread and growing anger at the country's deepening domestic economic malaise, something that was attributed nearly as much to Ahmadinejad's flawed stewardship of the Iranian economy as it was to Western sanctions.[19] Ahmadinejad's political power, moreover, was unmistakably on the wane following an acrimonious political tug-of-war with his one-time protector, Iranian supreme leader

Ayatollah Ali Khamenei—a contest that Iran's chief cleric won handily.[20]

Yet Iran's president was still thinking big. And on one of his last foreign trips as the Islamic Republic's political head of state, Ahmadinejad went to a very particular place. Ahmadinejad's three-country tour of Africa in January 2013, during which he visited Benin, Ghana, and Burkina Faso, was "not a surprising choice of destination," observers noted.[21] It was, rather, a reflection of the Islamic Republic's major political and economic investment in forging new bonds with regimes throughout the continent. Those ties are extensive, and encompass a significant portion of the continent's fifty-four countries.

As Michael Rubin of the American Enterprise Institute noted, Iran's approach to Africa is rooted in multiple objectives.[22] Foremost among them is diplomatic outreach. Iran's foreign policy has focused heavily on the African continent in recent years, with Iranian officials identifying sympathetic regional regimes as particular targets of opportunity. Iran today boasts official embassies in nearly 24 of Africa's 54 nations—significantly more than it did just a few years ago, and no mean feat for a country that the West has systematically attempted to isolate over the better part of the past two decades.[23]

Tellingly, Iran has prioritized engagement with a number of regional states that occupy strategic positions in multilateral fora, such as the United Nations Security Council and the International Atomic Energy Agency, the U.N.'s nuclear watchdog. That list includes Gabon and Togo, as well as Rwanda and Uganda—all of which have occupied rotating slots as nonpermanent members of the Security Council in recent years. Iran's outreach has also extended to Kenya, Niger, and Tanzania, all countries that sit on the board of the IAEA. In this way, notes Rubin, Iran seeks to undermine

Western strategy "by paralyzing international organizations."[24] Through its engagement with these nations, Iran has attempted to fracture the international consensus surrounding its international isolation in the very venue where it matters the most: the United Nations.

Of all the targets of Iranian outreach, no country has received a greater share of attention than South Africa. Tehran reestablished ties to Pretoria in the early 1990s, after fifteen years of diplomatic silence to protest South Africa's apartheid policies. Since then, political and economic ties have ballooned. During the 1990s, bilateral trade hit $4 billion annually, as the two countries signed a series of energy and commercial agreements.[25] By the late 2000s, that figure topped $21 billion, fueled by South Africa's extensive energy purchases from the Islamic Republic. As of 2010, Iran was estimated to account for fully a quarter of South Africa's energy imports.[26] And while energy ties between the two countries have dwindled since as South Africa has fallen into line behind Western prohibitions and cut its oil imports from Iran, other aspects of their economic relationship remain strong. In October 2013, for example, Iranian and South African officials negotiated a new agreement facilitating "greater trade, skills transfer, technology research and development."[27]

All this has bred no small amount of sympathy on the part of South Africa for Iran's international outlook. In February 2012, for example, Pretoria used its position at the IAEA to run interference for the Islamic Republic when the body was poised to condemn Iran for irregularities in its nuclear activities.[28] Moreover, the country's telecom giant, MTN, was implicated in coordinating clandestine arms deals between Tehran and Pretoria and helping the Iranian regime to bust Western sanctions.[29] In fact, according to counterterrorism expert Avi Jorisch, MTN—which derives fully a fifth of its multi-billion-dollar annual business from Iran—is so deeply

involved in commercial activities within the Islamic Republic that it has waded into the country's internal politics and
"played a critical role in helping the Iranian regime to hunt
down its opposition."[30]

Amid Iran's ongoing negotiations with the West, the regime's
diplomatic fortunes in Africa have brightened still further. A
case in point is Tehran's ties to the Kingdom of Morocco.
That North African nation has long had an acrimonious relationship with the Islamic Republic, with King Mohammed
VI publicly denouncing President Mahmoud Ahmadinejad's
Holocaust denial and even going so far as to formally cut off
diplomatic contacts in 2009.[31] Yet, as Iran's interaction with
the West has begun to rehabilitate the Islamic Republic in
the eyes of the world, Rabat has softened its stance toward
Tehran, so much so that as of this writing, the two countries
are poised to fully normalize their diplomatic relations.[32]

Simultaneously, Iran is beginning to exploit Africa as a
strategic base of operations. This consideration has informed
Iran's systematic outreach to Sudan over the past two decades. It is also in evidence in the Horn of Africa, where
Iran has taken advantage of Eritrea's political vulnerability
and its ongoing conflict with neighboring Ethiopia to establish a strategic foothold in the country.[33] This includes a significant naval presence off of Eritrea's southern coast, where
Iranian warships have docked since at least 2008. This activity
is logical: "Eritrea offers the Iranian navy a friendly port of
call to support extended deployments in the Gulf of Aden/
Red Sea," notes Jeffrey Lefebvre of the University of Connecticut. "Eritrea also provides a maritime link between Iran
and Syria by supporting Iranian naval forces moving from the
Indian Ocean through the Red Sea and Suez Canal to the
Mediterranean."[34]

This is significant in and of itself as an indicator of Iran's
widening strategic horizons. Indeed, it makes up part of a

larger Iranian effort to extend the power projection and reach of its naval forces, in keeping with the Islamic Republic's vision of itself as a global power.[35] But it is also supremely pragmatic; for Iran, a military presence in Africa is part of a flanking strategy by which it can outmaneuver the United States and its regional allies on the continent.[36]

Yet it is the final area of Iran's regional involvement that is perhaps the most significant. In recent years, the Islamic Republic has homed in on the African continent as a critical source of fuel for its nuclear program—and, by extension, its global ambitions.

A RESOURCE QUEST

Since the start of the international crisis over Iran's nuclear program more than a decade ago, the international community has steadily gravitated toward the notion that Iran's atomic program is by now largely self-sufficient and that, as a result, its progress toward nuclear status is now largely unstoppable. Indeed, that perception has permeated the ongoing nuclear negotiations between Iran and the West, during which the United States and the other P5+1 powers have progressively rolled back their demands for "zero enrichment" from the Islamic Republic and, in doing so, have implicitly accepted the permanence of Iran's nuclear program. This view has been encouraged by Iran's leaders, who have intoned time and again the Islamic Republic's "inalienable" right to nuclear status. And yet, Iran's nuclear program suffers from a major—perhaps fatal—deficiency: a significant deficit of uranium ore, the critical raw material needed to fuel its atomic effort. That shortage, moreover, has grown parallel to the maturity and sophistication of Iran's nuclear effort.

According to nonproliferation experts, Iran's indigenous uranium ore reserves are known to be both "limited and mostly of poor quality."[37] Thus, when Iran's shah mapped out an ambitious national plan for nuclear power in the 1970s, his government was forced to procure significant quantities of the mineral from South Africa. Four decades later, this aging stockpile has been mostly depleted.[38] Indeed, according to a 2013 analysis by the Carnegie Endowment for International Peace, Iran is compelled by "the scarcity, and low quality, of its domestic uranium resources . . . to rely on external sources of natural or processed uranium."[39]

Accordingly, Iran embarked in recent years on a widening quest to acquire supplies of uranium ore from abroad. In 2009, for example, it attempted to purchase more than 1,000 tons of uranium ore from the Central Asian republic of Kazakhstan at a cost of nearly half-a-billion dollars.[40] In that particular case, deft diplomacy on the part of the United States and its European allies helped stymie Iranian efforts—at least temporarily. But Iran's quest has continued. In February 2011, the Associated Press obtained an intelligence assessment of Iran's nuclear program compiled by a member state of the International Atomic Energy Agency, which highlighted that the Islamic Republic is engaged in an extensive worldwide search for new and stable sources of uranium to fuel its nuclear program.[41]

This quest naturally brought Iran to Africa. A significant percentage of Africa's fifty-four nations either contain major uranium deposits or already serve as exporters of the strategic mineral. All told, Africa is estimated to be home to more than a tenth of the world's proven uranium reserves.[42] And the World Nuclear Association estimated that as of 2010, just four African nations—Namibia, Niger, Malawi, and South Africa—accounted for nearly a fifth of all uranium produced globally.[43] All of which makes the continent a major strategic prize for the Islamic Republic, spurring Iranian efforts to enlist African nations as suppliers for its nuclear effort.

Most conspicuously, this includes the regime of Robert

Mugabe in Zimbabwe, which has emerged as a key enabler of Iran's quest for the bomb. Back in March 2012, as part of meetings between the Iranian defense minister, Ahmad Vahidi, and his Zimbabwean counterpart, Emmerson Mnangagwa, Iran formally pledged to modernize and reinforce Zimbabwe's military as part of the "consolidating and deepening" political ties between the two countries.[44] The news fueled speculation that Mugabe's Zimbabwe, short on cash but flush with uranium ore, could become a significant source of nuclear assistance for the Islamic Republic. That speculation was borne out the following year, when the two countries are believed to have signed a memorandum of understanding paving the way for the eventual exportation of uranium to the Islamic Republic.[45] The U.S. government took the news seriously enough to issue a warning to Harare to refrain from uranium sales that might benefit the Iranian nuclear effort.[46]

The Democratic People's Republic of Congo has been another target of opportunity. A 2006 United Nations report noted that at least one significant shipment of uranium left the Congo en route to Iran.[47] In 2009, in a diplomatic cable later published by WikiLeaks, the U.S. embassy in Tanzania's capital, Dar es Salaam, warned Washington that lax security at Congolese mines and nuclear sites made them attractive sources of uranium for Iran and that Tanzania could become a significant transshipment point for nuclear-related materials headed to Iran.[48]

Niger's resource wealth, too, has received its share of attention from Iran. In April 2013, Iranian president Mahmoud Ahmadinejad embarked upon a very public, three-country tour of the region, stopping in both Niger—the world's fifth-largest producer of uranium—and neighboring Benin.[49] The destinations were not coincidental; given Niger's landlocked status in West Africa, any export of its resources requires ports and transshipment facilities, which Benin has in abundance.

Similarly, contacts between Iran and Guinea have surged over the past decade, in parallel with the development and maturation of Guinea's uranium deposits. In 2010, for example, Iranian foreign minister Manouchehr Mottaki announced a 140-percent increase in trade ties between the two countries, underpinned by a number of new mining agreements giving Tehran greater access to Guinea's extractive industries.[50] In much the same way, Iran has attempted to build bonds to other resource-rich nations on the continent. "Recent Iranian outreach to Gambia, Malawi, Namibia, and Uganda coincides with the discovery of uranium in those countries," notes Michael Rubin of the American Enterprise Institute.[51] Iran is also believed to have attempted to procure yellowcake from the Central African Republic.[52]

The objectives of this outreach are clear. Iran, according to observers, sees Africa "as a critical market for uranium" to fuel its nuclear ambitions—as well as a key political and economic partner in support of its will to nuclear power.[53] Yet they also represent just one part of a larger effort on the part of the Islamic Republic to establish a beachhead on the African continent.

Iran, however, isn't the only one reaching out to Africa. Hezbollah, too, has prioritized its contacts with the continent.

TELLTALE SIGNS OF TERRORIST INFILTRATION

In May 2013, agents of Nigeria's State Security Service (SSS) and elements of the Nigerian military jointly raided a house on the outskirts of Bompai, in the country's northern Kano State. What they found there was frightening: a large underground bunker containing a massive military stash, including antitank weapons, rocket-propelled guns, and land mines.[54] Authorities would later tell reporters that the quantity of weapons seized in the bust was large enough "to sustain a civil war."[55] Three men were subsequently arrested in connection to the raid, all of them Lebanese-Nigerian nationals.

But what began as an arms bust quickly turned into something more. In subsequent interrogations, the suspects confessed to having received training from Hezbollah.[56] One of them further detailed orders from a top Hezbollah commander to surveil several targets in the Nigerian capital, including the Israeli embassy, and to obtain an aerial photo of the city for targeting purposes.[57] The revelations led Nigerian authorities and international observers to conclude that the country had just unearthed an active Hezbollah terror cell in the process of planning a major attack.

It was not the first time. Less than half a year earlier, in December 2012, Nigerian authorities had arrested three Nigerian nationals and charged them with being members of an Iranian terror cell intending to attack Israeli and American targets.[58] And in May 2013, the same month as the Kano raid, a Nigerian court sentenced an Iranian and a Nigerian to five years in prison apiece for their roles in smuggling a large shipment of weapons into West Africa. The spate of activity led experts to question whether Nigeria had turned into an operations center for Hezbollah in Africa.[59]

To be sure, Hezbollah has had an African presence for the better part of a quarter century. As long ago as the late 1980s, the U.S. intelligence community took note of indications that Hezbollah had stepped up its planning for operations beyond the Middle East—including in Africa.[60] The years that followed saw the group, operating through the continent's numerous and well-established Shia communities, transform Africa into a major base for fund-raising, both legal and illicit. For example, the group has been implicated in the continent's notorious blood-diamond trade, with instances of Hezbollah trading activity cropping up in Angola, Burkina Faso, Democratic Republic of the Congo, Liberia, and a host of other countries over the past two decades.[61] Hezbollah operatives also are known to have established a number of front companies and to use these conduits to funnel money from Africa back to the Middle East. In addition, the region has become a notable recruiting base for the group, which, working in tandem with Iran's Revolutionary Guards, has made concerted efforts to engage and enlist disaffected African Shia into its cause: resistance against Israel and the West.[62]

Even so, telltale signs in recent years indicate a broad—and troubling—trend. "Iran has stepped up its attempts to build a sphere of influence in Africa," says Israeli counterterrorism expert Ely Karmon, and as part of that effort, Hezbollah has been working "to develop bases within certain states in Africa for wider terrorist and subversion activities throughout the continent, focusing on Israeli and Jewish targets."[63]

These bases extend beyond Nigeria to a number of other regional states. Among them is Kenya, where two Iranian nationals were arrested in June 2012 on suspicion of planning attacks against Israeli, American, British, or Saudi targets. The suspects were found in possession of 15 kilograms of the explosive RDX, and 85 kilograms more were not recovered. A Kenyan court subsequently sentenced both men to life in prison.[64]

Hezbollah representatives and agents have also cropped up throughout West Africa, including in Sierra Leone, Côte d'Ivoire, and Senegal.[65] In the latter country, as J. Peter Pham of the Atlantic Council pointed out, the activities of Hezbollah-aligned Lebanese in coordination with the Iranian embassy repeatedly ran afoul of both the country's powerful Sufi brotherhoods and the Senegalese government, which, especially during the tenure of President Abdou Diouf from 1981 through 2000, accused Iranian diplomats of abusing their status to spread religious propaganda and influence the media with an eye to interfering in Senegal's internal affairs.[66]

So far, this web of activity has not elicited much by way of a regional response. Nowhere is this more apparent than in Nigeria. Just six months after they were apprehended, a federal court in Abuja acquitted two of the three suspects in the May 2013 Kano raid, dismissing all terror-related charges.[67] In its ruling, the court argued that the federal prosecution had not proved the suspects' connections to Hezbollah beyond a reasonable doubt, despite the extensive case put together by prosecutors, the confession of at least one of the suspects, and the stockpile of weapons that had been uncovered. Iran and Hezbollah, it seems, continue to have what is more or less a free hand to operate on the continent.

FUELING AFRICA'S WARS

Beginning in 2006, observers of Africa's numerous conflicts and simmering violence started noticing an unusual phenomenon. Government forces and nonstate militias were using more and more foreign-origin ammunition that bore no clear markings or manufacturer designations. This constituted a departure from regular practice, because munitions from places such as China and France—both of which have served as significant arms suppliers to Africa in the past—bore clear indications of their origin. These munitions did not, and they were spreading. Over the next several years, they cropped up in a variety of the continent's war zones, from Sudan to Darfur. And over time, it became clear that the ammo had originated thousands of miles away, in the Islamic Republic of Iran.

That was the conclusion of a six-year study by British research firm Conflict Armament Research, which found that the Islamic Republic has been a principal contributor of small-caliber munitions circulating on the African continent in the past decade. "Iranian ammunition is in service with four African governments: Côte d'Ivoire (until 2011),

Guinea, Kenya and Sudan," it noted. "Although the circumstances of acquisition are unclear, the quantities involved in the Sudan, Guinea and Kenya cases suggest direct supply by Iran."[68] That, however, is not all. "Ten additional investigations find Iranian weapons and ammunition in service with a variety of non-state entities, including foreign-backed insurgents, rebel forces, Islamist-oriented armed groups and warring civilian communities," according to the study.[69] Indeed, in late 2010, the government of The Gambia went so far as to sever diplomatic relations with Iran after a large weapons shipment, including mortars, rockets, and other military-grade arms, was intercepted as it was being smuggled into the West African country.[70]

In other words, the Islamic Republic has—either directly or indirectly—played a part in fueling the African continent's conflicts in recent years. Or, as the *New York Times* put it, "even as Iran faced intensive foreign scrutiny over its nuclear program and for supporting proxies across the Middle East, its state-manufactured ammunition was distributed through secretive networks to a long list of combatants, including in regions under United Nations arms embargoes."[71]

The revelation was significant. While its exports historically have been dwarfed by major suppliers such as Russia and China (and the United States), Iran nonetheless maintains a notable presence in the global arms market. Yet those deliveries have been localized, by and large, in the Islamic Republic's immediate periphery, taking the form of missile shipments to Hezbollah in Lebanon or Palestinian rejectionist groups in the West Bank and Gaza Strip.[72] As such, news of Iran's involvement in the provision of small-arms munitions to numerous clients in Africa indicates Iran's expanding commercial and foreign-policy horizons and its growing interest in influencing events beyond its borders.

That interest is most certainly not a thing of the past. In

recent months, Hassan Rouhani has reaffirmed that the Islamic Republic sees Africa as an important foreign-policy priority and that his administration, like that of his predecessor, is seeking closer strategic ties to the continent.[73] The message that Iran is thereby sending to Africa's leaders is unmistakable: the Islamic Republic is in Africa to stay.

A New Domain for Conflict

In October 2013, a middle-aged Iranian government func-
tionary named Mojtaba Ahmadi was found dead in a wooded
area outside the city of Karaj, located some sixty kilometers
northwest of the Iranian capital, Tehran. His death had been
a violent one; Ahmadi had been assassinated, shot twice in
the heart at close range by one or more unknown assailants.

The murder made headlines, both in Iran and abroad, and
for good reason, although not the most likely one. Ahmadi
was not an Iranian nuclear scientist, a profession that has
become comparatively high-risk amid intensifying international efforts to derail the Islamic Republic's nuclear effort.
Five nuclear scientists and one ballistic missile engineer have
died over the past decade under suspicious circumstances, in
incidents that the Iranian regime has ascribed to foreign—
specifically Israeli—"direct action." Rather, Ahmadi was a
high-ranking officer in Iran's Revolutionary Guard Corps
and a commander of its secretive Cyber War Headquarters.[1]
Ahmadi, in other words, was a "key cyber warfare commander" and quite possibly "Iran's cyber war chief."[2]

His death shed new light on a largely unexplored dimension of Iran's quest for global influence: its growing, and

increasingly aggressive, presence in cyberspace. It is an arena that is fast emerging as a new domain of conflict between Iran and the West.

STUXNET: A DOUBLE-EDGED SWORD

In the fall of 2010, the Iranian regime went public with a stunning admission. Over the preceding year, officials in Tehran grudgingly disclosed, their country had been the target of a major and sustained cyber attack—one that caused significant and at that time not yet fully understood difficulties for the Islamic Republic's nuclear program.[3]

The culprit was identified as Stuxnet, a piece of malicious software fashioned specifically to attack SCADA (supervisory control and data acquisition) systems designed by the German industrial conglomerate Siemens. This was the very type of system used by Iran to run its uranium enrichment centrifuges, leading computer experts to conclude relatively quickly that, despite related computer infections in China, Indonesia, India, and Azerbaijan, the software's principal target was the Islamic Republic's nuclear effort.[4] Iran's enrichment facility at Natanz, in many ways the public face of the regime's nuclear program, was the installation most directly affected by the attack.

The news was a bombshell. Malicious software, known as malware, is not a new phenomenon, of course. Trojan horses, worms, and other viruses are exceedingly commonplace, and risk of infection represents part of the cost of doing business on the Internet. But Stuxnet was qualitatively different, miles ahead of its predecessors in terms of both effectiveness and sophistication. It was, in the words of one leading computer expert, a "21st-century cyberweapon."[5] It was also designed for a very specific purpose: to provide false readings to SCADA operators, even as it forced the centrifuges it affected to spin out of control and break down. And, at least for a time, it raised hopes among many in Washington that a confrontation with Tehran had been avoided, and that an ingenious bit of software had done what sustained economic pressure had not been able to and successfully derailed Iran's bid for nuclear capability.

The actual effects of Stuxnet, however, turned out to be rather modest. According to the Institute for Science and International Security, a Washington-based nonproliferation think tank, from the time of its insertion into Iran's nuclear facilities in the second half of 2009 to its discovery the following fall, Stuxnet succeeded in destroying just 1,000 of the 9,000 uranium enrichment centrifuges at the Natanz facility in central Iran. What's more, the same study noted, the effect of the malware was only temporary. "Assuming Iran exercises caution, Stuxnet is unlikely to destroy more centrifuges at the Natanz plant," the institute assessed in February 2011. "Iran likely cleaned the malware from its control systems."[6]

Nor did Stuxnet succeed in substantially slowing the pace of Iran's uranium enrichment activities. The Iranians "have been able to quickly replace broken machines," one Western diplomat in the know told the *Washington Post* in the spring of 2013. "[T]he Iranians appeared to be working hard to maintain a constant, stable output" of low-enriched uranium.[7]

The U.N.'s nuclear watchdog came to similar conclusions. In a February 2011 interview with the *Washington Post*'s Lally Weymouth, International Atomic Energy Agency chief Yukiya Amano disclosed that Stuxnet had had only a temporary impact on Iran's ability to produce enriched uranium. Despite the damage it suffered from Stuxnet, Amano said, just six months later, "Iran is somehow producing uranium enriched to 3.5 percent and 20 percent" and is doing so "steadily, constantly."

Stuxnet, in other words, may have been a tactical success,

buying the international community a bit more time to formulate a plan for dealing with Iran's nuclear program. But it was a strategic failure, falling far short of meaningfully derailing the country's nuclear endeavor, as many had hoped it would.

Indeed, the malware may actually have ended up having the opposite effect. A 2013 study published in the journal of England's prestigious Royal United Services Institute concluded that Stuxnet objectively failed in attaining its goal of decreasing Iran's nuclear weapons potential.[8] "Although calculations show that Stuxnet had the *potential* to seriously damage Iranian IR-1 centrifuges, unclassified evidence of the worm's impact on uranium enrichment at Natanz is circumstantial and inconclusive," the study notes.[9] In fact, according to the study's author, Ivanka Barzashka, of King's College London, the worm was actually "of net benefit to Iran if, indeed, its government wants to build a bomb or increase its nuclear-weapons potential," making the regime "more cautious about protecting their nuclear facilities" while failing to hinder its ability to add to the number of its centrifuges.[10] It also alerted the Islamic Republic to a sobering fact: war with the West, at least on the cyber front, had been declared.

DEFENSE, AND OFFENSE

If Stuxnet woke officials in Tehran up to the fact that the West was attempting to compromise its nuclear effort, subsequent attacks on Iranian nuclear facilities and infrastructure convinced them that cyber war had the potential to be—in the words of one top leader of Iran's Revolutionary Guard Corps—"more dangerous than a physical war."[11] Their alarm was warranted. To date, at least five distinct foreign-origin cyber worms targeting the Iranian nuclear program have been identified and isolated. These include Stars, a software script targeting execution files; Duqu, a successor to Stuxnet aimed at gaining remote access to Iran's nuclear systems; Wiper, another piece of malware, which attacked internal Internet communications within the Islamic Republic; and, most recent, Flame, a cyber espionage virus developed by the United States and Israel and designed to map Iran's nuclear network.[12] Additionally, in July 2012, Iran was attacked by an indigenous cyber worm named Mahdi, suggesting the regime faces an internal cyber threat as well as an external one.

Iran mobilized in response. In July 2011, it formally launched an ambitious $1 billion governmental program to boost national cyber capabilities via the acquisition of new technologies, new investments in cyber defense, and a new cadre of cyber experts.[13] In tandem, it formed new, dedicated domestic agencies tasked with administering cyberspace. A cyber police unit had been established by the country's Ministry of Interior in 2009, in the aftermath of the Green Revolution. This was supplemented by the creation of a dedicated Cyber Defense Command in the Iranian military, as well as a Cyberspace Council within the Basij, the country's repressive domestic militia.[14]

Simultaneously, the Iranian government mobilized a cyber army of activists. While nominally independent, these patriotic hackers (also known as "hacktivists") have carried out a series of attacks on sites and entities out of favor with the Iranian regime, including the social-networking site Twitter, the Chinese search engine Baidu, and the websites of Iranian reformist elements.[15] Perhaps the most notorious hacker collective is Ashiyane, a political-criminal group identified by experts as being closely aligned with the IRGC.[16]

The U.S. intelligence community noted these developments when, in his January 2012 testimony before the Senate, Director of National Intelligence James Clapper stressed that Iran's cyber capabilities "have dramatically increased in recent years in depth and complexity."[17] Iranian officials now claim to possess the fourth-largest cyber force in the world—a broad network of quasi-official elements, as well as regime-aligned hacktivists, that engage in cyber activities broadly consistent with the Islamic Republic's interests and views.[18] The Intelligence Unit of the IRGC allegedly oversees the activities of this cyber army.[19]

Iran's moves weren't simply defensive, however. Increasingly, the Iranian regime puts its burgeoning cyber capabilities to use against Western and Western-aligned targets. Between September 2012 and January 2013, a group of hackers known as the Izz ad-Din al-Qassam Cyber Fighters carried out multiple distributed denial-of-service (DDoS) attacks against a number of U.S. financial institutions, including Bank of America, JPMorgan Chase, and Citigroup. Due to the sophistication of the attacks, U.S. officials have linked them definitively to the Iranian government.[20]

A similar attack attributed to the Iranian regime took place in August 2012, when a virus called Shamoon targeted three-quarters of the computers of Saudi Arabia's state oil corporation, Saudi Aramco. The malicious software triggered a program that replaced Aramco's corporate data with a picture of a burning American flag at a predetermined time.[21]

The Iranian regime has also distributed cyber capabilities to strategic partners. Iran reportedly provided the regime of Syrian dictator Bashar al-Assad, now locked in a protracted war against his own people, with crucial equipment and technical assistance for carrying out Internet surveillance.[22] This has helped the Assad regime to more effectively target and neutralize elements of the Syrian opposition.

But it is the United States that was, and remains, Iran's ultimate target. In late July 2011, *Kayhan*, a hard-line newspaper affiliated with Iran's Revolutionary Guards, issued a thinly veiled warning to that effect when it wrote in an editorial that America, which once saw cyber warfare as its "exclusive capability," had severely underestimated the resilience of the Islamic Republic. The paper went on to suggest that the United States should worry about "an unknown player somewhere in the world" attacking "a section of its critical infrastructure."[23]

This is not idle bluster; security professionals have taken note of Iranian efforts to probe segments of the United States' critical infrastructure, most notably the country's electrical sector.[24] Along those lines, cyber security experts have warned that, should a standoff over Iran's nuclear program precipitate a military conflict, Iran "might try to retaliate by attacking U.S. infrastructure such as the power grid, trains, airlines, refineries."[25]

This warning has proven prescient. In May 2013, U.S. officials discovered Iranian-backed hackers had conducted cyber attacks against various American energy companies. Specifically, the attacks infiltrated the control system software used by these firms, granting the hackers control over oil and gas pipelines. Although Iran has denied any involvement in the intrusions, U.S. intelligence sources are convinced that they were carried out with the backing of the Iranian government.[26]

The scope of Iran's offensive was outlined in detail in December 2014 by California-based cyber security firm Cylance.[27] "Since at least 2012, Iranian actors have directly attacked, established persistence in, and extracted highly sensitive materials from the networks of government agencies and major critical infrastructure companies in the following countries: Canada, China, England, France, Germany, India, Israel, Kuwait, Mexico, Pakistan, Qatar, Saudi Arabia, South Korea, Turkey, United Arab Emirates, and the United States," the group's eighty-six-page study said. Targets of Iranian cyber attack identified by Cylance include oil and gas firms in Kuwait, Turkey, Qatar, and France; aviation hubs in

South Korea and Pakistan; energy and utility companies in the United States and Canada; and government agencies in the United States, United Arab Emirates, and Qatar.

Moreover, the study warns, this may represent merely the tip of the iceberg. Iran's cyber capabilities, after all, are evolving rapidly, and the activities identified to date might be just a fraction of the Islamic Republic's total online presence. "As Iran's cyber warfare capabilities continue to morph . . . the probability of an attack that could impact the physical world at a national or global level is rapidly increasing," the study concludes.

For the moment, however, Iran's cyber war against the West has receded from the headlines. Experts and observers note that cyber attacks on Western targets by the Iranian regime have decreased in frequency since the start of nuclear negotiations with the P5+1 powers in November 2013.[28] The reprieve is understandable, insofar as Iran is currently obtaining significant benefits from its diplomatic engagement with the United States and its allies. But it is also potentially fleeting; in the event of a breakdown of the current talks, the world could see a further escalation of the crisis, potentially including the use of force against Iran by one or more nations. Should that happen, cyber war with Iran might become a distinct possibility.

Iran, at least, certainly believes it could. In February 2014, Supreme Leader Ayatollah Ali Khamenei issued a special message to the country's university students, in which he urged them specifically to prepare for cyber war with the West. "You are the cyber-war agents," Khamenei's message said, "get yourselves ready for such war wholeheartedly." The target of such a conflict, if or when it does take place, is abundantly clear: according to Khamenei, it is "the Dominance Power," a common Iranian euphemism for the United States.[29]

In the meantime, Iran's cyber capabilities are steadily expanding in both scope and sophistication. In October 2013, Iranian government-linked hackers penetrated unclassified computers belonging to the U.S. Navy, gaining access to its unclassified network and, potentially, to e-mail and secure communications that it hosted.[30] Subsequently, in May 2014, the cyber-intelligence firm iSIGHT Partners uncovered a complex Iranian phishing scheme dubbed Newscaster that was designed to compromise political individuals of interest through the use of social media.[31] The same month, an Iranian hacking group known as Ajax Security Team was identified as targeting U.S. defense firms in a detailed cyber-espionage campaign that utilized malicious software to gain access to target computers.[32] A recent Israeli assessment of these activities concluded that "Iran has cultivated long term cyber-related strategic objectives in recent years and . . . is becoming one of the most active players in the international cyber warfare arena."[33]

But Iran's cyber activities are not simply directed abroad. As important, if not more so, is the domestic campaign now being waged in cyberspace by the Islamic Republic. It represents a concerted, systematic effort to insulate its captive population from the Internet—and the world.

IRAN VERSUS THE WORLD WIDE WEB

In his March 2012 message to the Iranian people marking the Persian New Year, President Obama alluded to the Iranian regime's mounting domestic cyber offensive when he noted that an "electronic curtain has fallen around Iran."[34] "The Iranian people are denied the basic freedom to access the information that they want," the president said, because of "a barrier that stops the free flow of information and ideas into the country, and denies the rest of the world the benefit of interacting with the Iranian people, who have so much to offer."[35]

President Obama's description was apt. In a very real sense, the Iranian regime is erecting a digital barrier aimed at isolating its population from the World Wide Web, quelling domestic dissent, and curtailing the ability of its opponents to organize.

These efforts can be traced back to the summer of 2009, when the fraudulent reelection of Mahmoud Ahmadinejad to the Iranian presidency catalyzed a sustained groundswell of domestic opposition that became the Green Movement. From the start, Iran's various opposition elements relied extensively on the Internet and social-networking tools to organize their efforts, communicate their messages to the outside world, and rally public opinion to their side. The Iranian regime, in turn, utilized information and communication technologies extensively in its suppression of the protests. And ever since, it has invested heavily in capabilities aimed at controlling the Internet and restricting the ability of its citizens to access the World Wide Web.[36]

The Arab Spring has only reinforced this focus. Whatever their public pronouncements, officials in Tehran understand that the antiregime sentiment prevalent in the region represents a mortal threat to their corrupt, unrepresentative rule. As a result, the Iranian regime has quickened its long-running campaign against Western influence within the Islamic Republic, with cyberspace as a primary target. They have done so in a number of ways.

A Second Internet. Far and away the most ambitious effort by the Iranian regime to control cyberspace is its attempt to create a national intranet, a substitute for the global Internet. Originally slated to go online in August 2012, this "halal internet," or "second internet," represents a more sophisticated alternative to filtering systems, such as China's Great Firewall. While those simply deny users access to proscribed sites, Iran's web will reroute them to regime-approved search results, web-sites, and online content. By doing so, it will effectively sever Iran's connection to the World Wide Web and give Iranian authorities the power to create an Islamic Republic–compli-ant online reality for their citizens.

For the moment, Iran's halal internet remains something of a work in progress. As of October 2012, some 10,000 com-puters—in both private and government use—were found to be connected to this second internet.[37] Today, that figure is believed to be considerably higher, although still far from comprehensive. Nevertheless, the project is unmistakably moving forward. Experts now project that Iran's national in-tranet could come online by 2016.[38] And even before it does, its impact is already being felt. For example, in December 2012, regime authorities launched Mehr, a homegrown alter-native to YouTube that features government-approved video content designed specifically for domestic audiences.[39] And in July 2013, the Iranian government activated an indigenous e-mail service intended to serve as a substitute for Gmail, Hotmail, and Yahoo. This new feature isn't simply a benign e-mail client, however; it requires citizens to provide their names, national ID number, address, and other vital informa-tion, facilitating regime efforts to carry out surveillance on its citizenry and monitor their online behavior.[40]

Content Filtering. Simultaneously, Iran has launched a heavy-handed campaign aimed at filtering out and denying access to "immoral" content on the Internet. An August 2013 study conducted by the University of Michigan described this cen-sorship as both extensive and ambitious, extending to large amounts of content related to both pornography and politics, as well as art, society, and current events.[41] Indeed, nearly half of the world's top-500, most-visited websites are blocked in Iran.[42] And that number may soon grow: Iran's Supreme

Council of Cyberspace has recommended that all websites should be registered with the country's Ministry of Culture and Islamic Guidance, although such a step has not yet been taken.[43]

Naturally, Iranian officials have also turned their sights on social media. Iranian authorities reportedly are working on new software suites designed to better control social-networking sites, which were a hub of activity during the 2009 protests and afterward.[44] The Islamic Republic is currently one of just three countries in the world to block Facebook, YouTube, and Twitter.[45] But this prohibition is selective in the extreme; top Iranian officials, including "moderate" president Hassan Rouhani, have active social-media accounts, and even Iran's supreme leader, Ayatollah Ali Khamenei, maintains a flashy dedicated website at www. khamenei.ir. Indeed, although Rouhani has taken pains to stress freedom and human rights among Iranians since taking office in the summer of 2013, regime repression of online critics has deepened.[46]

Surveillance and Control. The Iranian regime likewise has expanded its control of domestic phone, mobile, and Internet communications. In the months after the summer 2009 protests, Iranian authorities installed a sophisticated Chinese-origin surveillance system. Since then, China's ZTE Corporation has partnered with the state-controlled Telecommunication Company of Iran (TCI) to implement advanced monitoring of the country's telecom sector.[47]

Iranian authorities have supplemented this tracking with methods intended to limit access to such media. In the spring of 2013, for example, Iranian authorities blocked most of the virtual private networks (VPNs) used by Iranians to circumvent the government's Internet filters.[48] Simultaneously, Iranian officials announced plans—since implemented—to reduce Internet speeds and increase costs of subscriptions to Internet service providers (ISPs) within the Islamic Republic.[49]

Regulation and Oversight. The foregoing restrictions and regulations are overseen by a new government agency tasked with monitoring cyberspace. Announced in early 2012, the Supreme Council of Cyberspace is led by top officials from both Iran's intelligence apparatus and the Revolutionary Guards and empowered to carry out "constant and comprehensive monitoring over the domestic and international cyberspace," with the power to issue sweeping decrees concerning the Internet that would have the full strength of law.[50] The council was formally inaugurated by Supreme Leader Ayatollah Ali Khamenei in April 2012, and now serves as a coordinating body for the Islamic Republic's domestic and international cyber policies.[51] They include new, restrictive governmental guidelines forcing Internet cafes to record the personal information of customers—including vital data, such as names, national identification numbers, and phone numbers—as well as install closed-circuit cameras to keep video logs of all customers accessing the World Wide Web.[52]

These restrictions—and, indeed, the Islamic Republic's deepening crusade against Internet freedom itself—have everything to do with well-founded official fears of the power and breadth of the Internet in Iran. Iran is currently among the most-wired nations in the region, with Internet penetration estimated at 57 percent of the population.[53] This online community, moreover, is vibrant; as of 2008, Iran was estimated to have the third-largest blogosphere in the world, after those of the United States and China, with 60,000 or more active weblogs.[54] Although a number of factors—including state repression—have seen the phenomenon of "Iran's blogestan" recede somewhat since, this has been mirrored by the rise of social-networking sites such as Facebook, which are now estimated to have upwards of four million Iranian members.[55]

All this makes the World Wide Web, which provides Iran's citizenry with access to alternative worldviews, values, and information, a mortal threat to the Iranian regime's efforts to enforce intellectual orthodoxy. The Web is also the potential hub of coordination and communication for opposition forces, the way it functioned for the Green Movement during the second half of 2009. Which is why, even as it has taken the cyber offensive abroad, the Islamic Republic has gone to extraordinary lengths to stifle Internet freedom at home.

Conclusion

The preeminent physicist and philosopher Albert Einstein once remarked that the definition of insanity is doing the same thing over and over again and expecting different results. So it is with our Iran policy. Since taking office, the Obama administration has billed its efforts to engage with the Islamic Republic as a bold new initiative designed to reverse two decades of unconstructive American policy.

In their outreach, administration officials have been animated by the belief that dialogue—however tactical at the outset—can be successfully parlayed into something substantially bigger: a true reconciliation between Washington and Tehran. Perhaps the clearest indication of this was given by Philip Gordon, the senior director of Gulf affairs in the Obama National Security Council, in the fall of 2014. "A nuclear agreement could begin a multigenerational process that could lead to a new relationship between our countries," Gordon said in a speech before the National Iranian American Council in Washington, D.C.[1]

This belief goes a long way toward explaining why the White House has gambled so heavily on the idea of détente with Iran's ayatollahs. It would be fair to say that outreach toward Iran has become the centerpiece of the Obama administration's foreign-policy agenda. "Bottom line is, this is the best opportunity we've had to resolve the Iranian issue diplomatically, certainly since President Obama came to office, and probably since the beginning of the Iraq war," Deputy National Security Advisor Ben Rhodes told a meeting of liberal activists in January 2014. "This is probably the biggest thing President Obama will do in his second term on foreign policy."[2] In fact, according to Rhodes, securing a deal with Iran is as significant as "healthcare for us"—a reference to the massive overhaul of the U.S. health-care system that became the signal achievement of the Obama administration's first term in office.[3]

In its overtures, the White House has been backed by a loose but vocal coalition of journalists, pundits, and think-tank cognoscenti from groups and media ranging from the liberal Atlantic Council on the political left to the conservative *National Interest* magazine on the political right. The particulars of their respective arguments vary, but their conclusions are very much the same: outreach toward Tehran makes good strategic sense.

The idea may be appealing, but it most definitely isn't new. Quite the opposite, in fact. For nearly a quarter-century, Western capitals have been awash in hopes that, with the proper mix of economic and diplomatic incentives, it might be possible to alter the Iranian regime's aggressive, revisionist worldview.

The effort began with the collapse of the USSR, when European nations launched a new diplomatic outreach toward the Islamic Republic. Dubbed "critical dialogue" and formally initiated at the European Council summit in Edinburgh in December 1992, that policy was an attempt to use economic carrots and "closer relations and confidence" to moderate the Islamic Republic's positions on everything from the acquisition of weapons of mass destruction to ter-

rorism.[4] Half a decade later, however, the effort fizzled when
a German court formally found Iran responsible for the 1992
assassination of four Kurdish dissidents at a Berlin restaurant
—but not before Europe infused the Islamic Republic with
much-needed cash and political legitimacy.

Europe's waning enthusiasm, however, was offset by
American eagerness. Beginning in 1997, the election of moderate cleric Mohammad Khatami to the Iranian presidency—
and his subsequent calls for a "dialogue of civilizations" with
the West[5]—fanned hopes in Washington that Tehran was
prepared to turn over a new leaf. In response, the Clinton
administration softened its diplomatic tone toward Tehran,
held some Congressional sanctions against the Islamic Republic in abeyance, and made numerous political advances
toward Iran's ayatollahs, all the while ignoring the inconve-
nient reality that the main aim of Khatami's "dialogue" was
not normalization with the West but a lessening of Iran's
global isolation.[6]

The 2000s likewise saw a slew of new initiatives aimed at
détente with Iran. Even as the Bush administration adopted
a harder line toward Iran, famously labeling it—along with
Saddam Hussein's Iraq and Kim Jong-il's North Korea—as
part of an "axis of evil," European nations redoubled their
attempts to engage with Tehran, focusing on the regime's
nuclear program as a point of reference. The first such effort, spearheaded by the E.U. 3 countries (Germany, France,
and the United Kingdom), stretched from 2003 to 2005. The
second took place in June 2008 via consultations with Iran by
the P5+1 countries (the United States, the United Kingdom,
Russia, China, France, and Germany). Nearly a dozen proposals and compromises were alternately floated by Iran and
the West before the start of the November 2013 talks in Ge-
neva.[7] But all failed to reach a substantive breakthrough with
Iran over its nuclear endeavor or blunt Iranian adventurism.

Today promises to be no different. To be sure, Iranian officials are doing their best to fan Western hopes for détente once more. Early on in his tenure, Hassan Rouhani penned an editorial in the *Washington Post* calling for "constructive engagement" between Iran and the world.[8] Since then, Iran's so-called moderate president has kept up his calls for normalization. During his fall 2014 jaunt to New York City to attend the U.N. General Assembly's annual meeting, Rouhani spoke at length about how America and Iran are now on the brink of a historic reconciliation. "[N]o doubt that the situation between the U.S. and Iran will be completely different" following the conclusion of a nuclear deal, Rouhani told reporters. Moreover, a nuclear pact, he promised, was just the beginning; there were "many potential areas of cooperation in the future" between the two countries.[9] Rouhani has made similar diplomatic overtures toward Canada, which formally severed diplomatic ties with Iran in 2011, and the United Kingdom, which serves as a core member of the Western coalition arrayed against it.

Yet a lasting reconciliation between the Islamic Republic and the West is not in the cards, and for good reason: Western culture and intellectual influence represents a mortal threat to the absolutist, activist political Islam that animates the regime in Tehran. This can be seen in repeated Iranian accusations, intoned over the past decade, that the United States and its allies are guilty of attempting to foment "velvet" revolutions within the Islamic Republic, and in regular calls from Iran's clergy to purge pernicious Western "decadence" from Iranian society.

While policy makers in Tehran may today be striking a softer tone, the idea of true rapprochement remains as toxic and dangerous to their worldview as ever. This is why Iranian president Rouhani has repeatedly skirted opportunities for an in-person tête-à-tête with President Obama since taking office in 2013, demurring again and again that the time "wasn't right" for such a summit.[10] Rouhani understands well, even if Western policy makers do not, that such a meeting would jeopardize his already-tenuous credibility within the Iranian regime and represent an ideological *casus belli* for Iran's clerical hard-liners.

Nor can the successful conclusion of a nuclear deal, if and when it does finally occur, be expected to change this calculus. "While domestic Iranian politics is famously unpredictable, there is no historic precedent nor recent evidence to suggest the Islamic Republic might abandon or modify its long-standing revolutionary principles, namely opposition to U.S. influence and Israel's existence," Iran scholar Karim Sadjadpour of the Carnegie Endowment for International Peace explained to Congress in the fall of 2014. "Throughout the last three decades these pillars of Iran's foreign policy have shown little signs of change, despite the election of moderate presidents or tremendous financial strain due to sanctions and/or low oil prices."[11]

More than three and a half decades after Khomeini's Islamic Revolution, those pillars remain intact. U.S. military documents tend to emphasize that Iran's strategy is defensive and centered around self-preservation. That impulse is indeed present in Iran's calculations. But so is an abiding ambition for regional hegemony and global prominence—and an identity defined by opposition to the West generally and the United States in particular.

As a result, when Iranian and American interests converge (as they do currently in the fight against the Islamic State terrorist group), tactical cooperation between Washington and Tehran may in fact be possible. But the Islamic Republic's founding principles, and its strategic culture, preclude a real rapprochement with the West in any meaningful, long-term fashion. In the words of Ahmad Jannati, a powerful Iranian cleric and power broker, "If pro-American tendencies come to power in Iran, we have to say goodbye to everything. After all, anti-Americanism is among the main features of our Islamic state."[12] It's a reality that policy makers in Washington have not yet internalized.

DEFINING IRAN'S DEVIANCY DOWN

During his career in Congress, Daniel Patrick Moynihan, the late Democratic senator from New York, became widely renowned as a champion for criminal justice. Among his most famous contributions to the contemporary discourse on the subject was a 1993 article in the *American Scholar*, in which Moynihan railed against growing popular acceptance of criminal behavior and the lack of strict punishment for it.[13] By allowing rising criminality to go unpunished, and by excusing it away as the product of social circumstance or a myriad of other mitigating factors, Moynihan argued, the United States was systematically "defining deviancy down," and doing so with grave consequences for civic order.

Moynihan's admonition may have been directed at America's criminal justice system, but it applies equally well to contemporary U.S. policy toward Iran. As the foregoing pages have shown, Iran's rogue behavior spans a broad spectrum of subversive activities in virtually every corner of the world. Furthermore, the Iranian leadership, in stark contrast with the rest of the country, remains revolutionary in outlook and insurgent in its behavior. As a result, Iran's regime continues to work diligently to improve its global position and export its uncompromising version of political Islam—albeit in a more subtle and sophisticated fashion than it did in the 1980s.

Yet, in its pursuit of a nuclear deal, the Obama administration has turned a blind eye to both the Iranian regime's internal deformities and its destructive behavior abroad. Worse still, the White House has become incentivized to not pay any heed to, or call attention to, what the Iranian regime truly thinks, says, and does, lest it prejudice prospects for political alignment between Washington and Tehran. The end result is an Iran policy that is predicated more upon aspiration than reality and pins its hopes on the prospect of historic reconciliation with Iran at great strategic and moral cost.

Which brings us back to the core problem. The danger emanating from Iran today is not strictly a function of its nuclear ambitions. Rather, it is a product of the Iranian regime itself. More than thirty-five years after Ayatollah Ruhollah Khomeini swept to power in Tehran, the Islamic Republic he created remains a radical expansionist and revisionist state.

As a result, any agreement struck with Iran, now or in the future, will not eliminate the strategic threat that Iran poses to America, its allies, or its global interests. This is because that threat emanates not from Iran's nuclear program, but from the Iranian regime itself. This is especially true if the deal ultimately struck between Washington and Tehran is a bad one that leaves Iran's nuclear capability largely intact, thereby granting Iran's ayatollahs the means to establish their country as a regional hegemon. Simply put, Washington will not wake up the day after a deal with Tehran to find that Iran's regime has changed its political stripes, or its ideological ones. Rather, the opposite is likely to be true; a nuclear-armed Iran, or an Iran that is a threshold nuclear power, will be more empowered than ever to promote its radical vision of global Islamic revolution.

Iranian officials, at least, certainly believe it will. Back in 2012, even as their country weathered an unprecedented economic crisis, Iran's officials were thinking big. The Islamic Republic "has broken the monopoly of the U.S. and a number of Western countries over the world management system," General Yadollah Javani, the former head of the IRGC's Politburo, told a gathering of naval forces in Bandar

Abbas that year. According to Javani, Iran "has turned into a strategic rival that can change the structure of the world's command center and become a member of it."[14] It is a view that has only strengthened of late, as America appears to undergo a process of strategic retreat in world affairs.

SENDING ALL THE WRONG SIGNALS

In December 2014, the Obama administration went public with a major change in policy toward Latin America. Speaking from the White House Cabinet Room, President Obama formally abandoned more than half a century of policy toward the Castro regime in Cuba, announcing plans to normalize diplomatic relations with Havana, sketching out plans for an embassy in the Cuban capital, and promising to formally revisit the country's designation as a State Sponsor of Terrorism.[15]

The decision was nearly two years in the making. In the fall of 2013, in a major address before the Organization of the American States, Secretary of State John Kerry announced with great fanfare that the "era of the Monroe Doctrine is over."[16] That pronouncement—intended to reassure regional powers that America's sometimes heavy-handed approach to the region was a thing of the past—touched off a year and a half of quiet diplomacy between Washington and Havana, culminating in the December 2014 opening.

Since then, more than a few Iran watchers have applauded the move, suggesting that a similar "reset" directed at Tehran would yield the same salutary results in our relationship with Iran.[17] Unfortunately, officials in Tehran appear to have drawn precisely the opposite conclusion.

As the Islamic Republic sees it, the change in U.S. policy reflects nothing less than a full-scale failure of Washington's long-standing approach to Cuba. It is also an important confirmation that continued political intransigence and anti-

Americanism can pay important strategic dividends. Or, as one spokesperson for Iran's Foreign Ministry put it, "[t]he resistance of the Cuban people and officials on their principles and the ideals of the revolution during the last 50 years showed that a policy of isolation and sanctions from domineering powers against the will and endurance of independent governments and people is ineffective and inefficient."[18]

In other words, as seen from Tehran, America's about-face on Cuba was not an enlightened attempt at outreach, as President Obama stressed in his White House announcement. Rather, it was a sign of U.S. policy collapse—and an indication that intransigence of the type practiced in both Havana and Tehran can pay concrete dividends.[19]

HARD CHOICES

Where does all this leave the United States and its allies? For much of the past decade, Western policy makers have tried to avoid making hard choices regarding Iran, preferring to defer the decisive action necessary to bring Iran's nuclear ambitions and global activism to heel. Even today, the prevailing view in Washington and European capitals appears to be that a larger political normalization will inevitably follow coming to terms with Iran over its nuclear program.

This represents a dangerous misreading of the ideology that animates the Iranian regime and of the Islamic Republic's enduring ambition for both regional hegemony and global influence. Yet those factors are more relevant than ever before. Today, perceptions of American strategic weakness, aversion to foreign entanglements, and declining appetite for global conflict have convinced Iran's leaders that they are poised for greater opportunity on the world stage than ever before.

Proving them wrong will be one of the most important and vexing challenges confronting the next American administration, whatever its political stripe.

Notes

INTRODUCTION

1. Specifically, Annex I, Section H, provides for Russian cooperation on nuclear research at the Fordow Fuel Enrichment Plant; Annex III, Section D, enumerates the extent of European aid in strengthening Iranian nuclear security; and Annex IV, Section 2, outlines the scope of international assistance in aiding Iran to master the nuclear fuel cycle through fuel fabrication.

2. See, for example, Mark Dubowitz, "Implications of a Nuclear Agreement with Iran." Testimony before the U.S. House of Representatives Committee on Foreign Affairs, July 23, 2015, http://www.defenddemocracy.org/content/uploads/documents/Dubowitz_Testimony_HFAC_Implications_of_a_Nuclear_Agreement.pdf.

3. White House, Office of the Press Secretary, "Statement by the President on the Adoption of the Joint Comprehensive Plan of Action," October 18, 2015, https://www.whitehouse.gov/the-press-office/2015/10/18/statement-president-adoption-joint-comprehensive-plan-action.

4. See, for example, Sohrab Ahmari, "The Saudis Reply to Iran's Rising Danger," *Wall Street Journal*, August 21, 2015, http://www.wsj.com/articles/the-saudis-reply-to-irans-rising-danger-1440197120.

5. "Iran GDP," Trading Economics, n.d., http://www.tradingeconomics.com/iran/gdp.

6. Nadia Bilbassy-Charters, "Ben Rhodes: Iran's New Money Post

Deal Will Go to Uplift 'Terrible Economy,'" Al Arabiya (Riyadh), July 16, 2015, http://english.alarabiya.net/en/News/middle -east/2015/07/16/Ben-Rhodes-Iran-s-extra-revenue-after-nuke -deal-will-help-uplift-terrible-economy-.html.

7. John Kerry, "Remarks at J Street's National Gala Dinner," U.S. Department of State, Washington, DC, April 18, 2016, http://www .state.gov/secretary/remarks/2016/04/255951.htm.

8. See, for example, David P. Goldman, "Fleeting Chimera: No Prosperity for Iran after Nuclear Deal," Asia Times, January 27, 2016, http://atimes.com/2016/01/no-prosperity-for-iran-after-nuclear -deal/.

9. "Iran's 2016 Budget Based on $35–40 Oil a Barrel," AzerNews, December 28, 2015, http://www.azernews.az/region/91180.html; "Next FY Budget Focuses on Foreign Capital, Non-Oil Exports," Mehr News Agency (Tehran), January 17, 2016, http:// en.mehrnews.com/news/113637/Next-FY-budget-focuses-on -foreign-capital-non-oil-exports.

10. "Iranian Banks Reconnected to SWIFT Network after Four-Year Hiatus," Reuters, February 17, 2016, http://www.reuters.com/ article/us-iran-banks-swift-idUSKCN0VQ1FD.

11. Jay Solomon, "U.S. Moves to Give Iran Limited Access to Dollars," Wall Street Journal, April 1, 2016, http://www.wsj.com/articles/u-s -moves-to-give-iran-limited-access-to-dollars-1459468597.

12. Jacob Lew, "Testimony of Treasury Secretary Jacob J. Lew before the Senate Foreign Relations Committee on the Iran Nuclear Agreement," U.S. Department of the Treasury, July 23, 2015, https:// www.treasury.gov/press-center/press-releases/Pages/jl0129.aspx.

13. National Defense Authorization Act for Fiscal Year 2012, Public Law 112-81, December 31, 2011, https://www.gpo.gov/fdsys/pkg /PLAW-112publ81/pdf/PLAW-112publ81.pdf.

14. Eric B. Lorber, "Treasury Prepares to Take Dollarized Transactions with Iran Offshore," policy brief, Foundation for Defense of Democracies, March 31, 2016, http://www.defenddemocracy .org/media-hit/eric-b-lorber-treasury-prepares-to-take-dollarized -transactions-with-iran-offshore#sthash.KJACnNL0.dpuf.

15. Jay Solomon, "U.S. to Buy Material Used in Iran Nuclear Program," Wall Street Journal, April 22, 2016, http://www.wsj.com/articles /u-s-to-buy-material-used-in-iran-nuclear-program-1461319381.

16. Najmeh Bozorgmehr and Monavar Khalaj, "IMF Calls for Iran Reforms to Attract International Investors," *Financial Times*, May 17, 2016, http://infoviewer.infodesk.com/infodisplay/item/c6a63724-f382-4932-8748-26928b6e00ee.html?CU=imf5992&APP=6.

17. Golnar Motevalli, "China, Iran Agree to Expand Trade to $600 Billion in a Decade," Bloomberg News, January 23, 2016, http://www.bloomberg.com/news/articles/2016-01-23/china-iran-agree-to-expand-trade-to-600-billion-in-a-decade.

18. "India and Iran Sign 'Historic' Chabahar Port Deal," BBC News, May 23, 2016, http://www.bbc.com/news/world-asia-india-36356163.

19. Maysam Bizaer, "EU Eyes Return as Iran's First Trade Partner," *U.S. News & World Report*, June 2, 2016, http://www.usnews.com/news/best-countries/articles/2016-06-02/eu-eyes-return-as-irans-first-trade-partner.

20. Bradley Klapper and Matthew Lee, "Boeing's Historic Deal with Iran Rests on Shaky Foundations," Associated Press, June 23, 2016, http://finance.yahoo.com/news/boeings-historic-deal-iran-rests-shaky-foundations-172206132--finance.html.

21. "World Bank Forecasts 5.8% GDP Growth for Iran in 2016," *Tehran Times*, February 6, 2016, http://www.tehrantimes.com/news/252783/World-Bank-forecasts-5-8-GDP-growth-for-Iran-in-2016.

22. See, for example, Ali Akbar Dareini and Nasser Karimi, "First Iran Vote after Nuclear Deal Gives Reformists Momentum," Associated Press, February 28, 2016, http://bigstory.ap.org/article/e4ca6f8acf64425fa6b542d21b5d4c30/iranian-reformists-set-win-all-tehran-parliamentary-seats.

23. See, for example, Shashank Bengali and Ramin Mostaghim, "Did Iran's Reformists Celebrate Too Soon? Hard-Liners Rebound after Election," *Los Angeles Times*, June 1, 2016, http://www.latimes.com/world/la-fg-iran-hardliners-20160601-snap-story.html.

24. "U.S. Wants to Restore Its Hold on Iran: Ayatollah Khamenei," Press TV (Tehran), March 20, 2016, http://www.presstv.com/Detail/2016/03/20/456734/Iran-Khamenei-Mashhad/.

25. Steve Almasy and Bijan Hosseini, "Iran Wants U.S. to Pay for 63 Years of 'Spiritual and Material Damage,'" CNN, May 18, 2016, http://edition.cnn.com/2016/05/17/middleeast/iran-us-compensation/.

CHAPTER I: IRAN'S MANIFEST DESTINY

1. Middle Eastern government official, in discussion with author, Washington, D.C., October 2014. Interview conducted in confidentiality, and name of interviewee is withheld by mutual agreement.

2. Oliver August, "The Revolution Is Over," *The Economist*, November 1, 2014, http://www.economist.com/news/special-report/21628597 -after-decades-messianic-fervour-iran-becoming-more-mature-and -modern-country.

3. Walter Russell Mead, "The Return of Geopolitics: The Revenge of the Revisionist Powers," *Foreign Affairs* (May/June 2014), http:// www.foreignaffairs.com/articles/141211/walter-russell-mead/the -return-of-geopolitics.

4. Imam Khomeini, *Islamic Government* (Tehran: The Institute for the Compilation and Publication of Imam Khomeini's Works, n.d.), http://www.google.com/url?sa=t&rct=j&q=&esrc=s&source =web&cd=7&ved=0CEgQFjAG&url=http%3A%2F%2Fkms1.isn .ethz.ch%2Fserviceengine%2FFiles%2FISN%2F125389%2Fipub licationdocument_singledocument%2Fc5044352-8f45-41a5-b670 -3fbec28b479e%2Fen%2F8006_islamic-government.pdf&ei=3t -hVOyqCYSxggTGnYP4DA&usg=AFQjCNGTiVELJgSmR5mr HS55-lqxagLk6Q&sig2=a3OEPbUdrOuy8lhYZjz6EA&bvm=bv.8 2001339,d.eXY.

5. Ruhollah Khomeini, as quoted in Robin Wright, *Sacred Rage: The Wrath of Militant Islam* (New York: Simon & Schuster, 1986), 21.

6. Constitution of Iran, adopted on October 24, 1979; amended on July 28, 1989. "Iran—Constitution," International Constitutional Law Project Information, http://www.servat.unibe.ch/icl/ir00000 _.html.

7. As quoted in Wright, *Sacred Rage*, 21.

8. Ibid., 21, 32–35.

9. See "An Open Letter: The Hizballah Program," Council on Foreign Relations, January 1, 1988, http://www.cfr.org/terrorist-organiza tions-and-networks/open-letter-hizballah-program/p30967.

10. U.S. Department of Defense, *Annual Report on Military Power of Iran, April 2010*, http://www.armscontrolwonk.com/file_download /226/2010_04_19_Unclass_Report_on_Iran_Military.pdf.

11. Richard L. Armitage, "America's Challenges in a Changed World," remarks at the United States Institute of Peace Conference, Wash-

ington, DC, September 5, 2002, http://web.archive.org/web/2002
0917202341/www.state.gov/s/d/rm/2002/13308pf.htm.

12. See, for example, Daniel Byman et al., *Iran's Security Policy in the Post-Revolutionary Era* (Santa Monica, CA: RAND, 2001), http://www.rand.org/pubs/monograph_reports/MR1320.html.

13. Edgar O'Ballance, *Islamic Fundamentalist Terrorism, 1979–95: The Iranian Connection* (New York: New York University Press, 1997), 42.

14. Julian Borger and Robert Tait, "The Financial Power of the Revolutionary Guards," *The Guardian* (London), February 15, 2010, http://www.theguardian.com/world/2010/feb/15/financial-power-revolutionary-guard.

15. Kim Murphy, "Iran's $12-Billion Enforcers," *Los Angeles Times*, August 26, 2007, http://articles.latimes.com/2007/aug/26/world/fg-guards26.

16. Babak Dehghanpisheh, "Why Sanctions Won't Hurt the Revolutionary Guards," *Newsweek*, July 10, 2010, http://www.newsweek.com/why-sanctions-wont-hurt-revolutionary-guards-74673.

17. Massimo Calabresi, "New Sanctions Target Revolutionary Guards," *Time*, June 10, 2010, http://content.time.com/time/magazine/article/0,9171,1995869,00.html.

18. Mark Gregory, "Expanding Business Empire of Iran's Revolutionary Guards," BBC News, July 26, 2010, http://www.bbc.co.uk/news/world-middle-east-10743580.

19. Iran experts, as quoted in Borger and Tait, "The Financial Power of the Revolutionary Guards."

20. Kasra Naji, *Ahmadinejad: The Secret History of Iran's Radical Leader* (London: I.B. Taurus, 2008), 33–35.

21. Ibid., 258.

22. Ali Alfoneh, "All Ahmadinejad's Men," *Middle East Quarterly* (Spring 2011): 79–84.

23. Ibid.

24. Emanuele Ottolenghi, *Pasdaran: Inside Iran's Islamic Revolutionary Guard Corps* (Washington, DC: FDD Press, 2011), 30.

25. Amir Taheri, "The Odd Guard," *New York Post*, August 29, 2007, http://nypost.com/2007/08/29/the-odd-guard/.

26. See, for example, Ali Alfoneh, *Iran Unveiled: How the Revolutionary Guards Is Transforming Iran from Theocracy to Military Dictatorship* (Washington, DC: AEI Press, 2013).

27. "U.S. Seeks to Support Iran Democratic Forces—Clinton," Reu-

ters, September 8, 2010, http://af.reuters.com/article/worldNews
/idAFTRE6874ZR20100908.

28. James R. Clapper, *Worldwide Threat Assessment of the US Intelligence Community*, Statement for the Record, Senate Select Committee on Intelligence, January 29, 2014, http://www.dni.gov/index.php /newsroom/testimonies/203-congressional-testimonies-2014/1005 -statement-for-the-record-worldwide-threat-assessment-of-the-us -intelligence-community.

29. Mohammed Mohaddessin, *Islamic Fundamentalism: The New Global Threat* (Washington, DC: Seven Locks Press, 1993), 132–36.

30. Adam C. Seitz and Anthony H. Cordesman, *Iranian Weapons of Mass Destruction: The Birth of a Regional Nuclear Arms Race?* (Santa Barbara, CA: Praeger Security International, 2009), 26.

31. Daniel Lee, *Iran's Naval Ambitions*, Iran Strategy Brief, no. 7 (American Foreign Policy Council, September 2013), 1–3.

32. Steven O'Hern, *Iran's Revolutionary Guard: The Threat That Grows While America Sleeps* (Washington, DC: Potomac Books, 2012), 8.

33. Lowell E. Jacoby, *Current and Projected National Security Threats to the United States*, Statement for the Record, Senate Select Committee on Intelligence, February 24, 2004, http://fas.org/irp/congress/2004 _hr/022404jacoby.pdf.

34. "Commander: IRGC Navy Can Sink US Warships in a Twinkling of an Eye," FARS News Agency (Tehran), May 6, 2014, http://english .farsnews.com/newstext.aspx?nn=13930215001625.

35. Mohaddessin, *Islamic Fundamentalism*, 102.

36. Greg Bruno, Jayshree Bajoria, and Jonathan Masters, "Iran's Revolutionary Guards," Council on Foreign Relations, June 14, 2013, http://www.cfr.org/iran/irans-revolutionary-guards/p14324.

37. Michael Eisenstadt, *The Strategic Culture of the Islamic Republic of Iran: Operational and Policy Implications*, MES Monographs, no. 1 (Marine Corps University, August 2011), 3, http://www.mcu.usmc.mil /MES%20Monographs/MESM%20No1,%20August%202011%20 'The%20Strategic%20Culture%20of%20the%20Islamic%20Repub lic%20of%20Iran'.pdf.

38. "Iran-Iraq War (1980–1988)," GlobalSecurity.org, n.d., http://www .globalsecurity.org/military/world/war/iran-iraq.htm.

39. Ibid.

40. United Nations, Office of the Secretary General, *Report on Iran's Reconstruction Efforts in the Wake of the Conflict between the Islamic Republic of Iran and Iraq*, December 24, 1991, 48.

41. Hooshang Amirahmadi, "Iranian Recovery from Industrial Devastation during War with Iraq," in *The Long Road to Recovery: Community Responses to Industrial Disaster*, ed. James K. Mitchell (Tokyo and New York: United Nations University Press, 1996), http://www.unu.edu/unupress/unupbooks/uu21le/uu21le00.htm#Contents.

42. See Joost Hiltermann, "Deep Traumas, Fresh Ambitions," *Middle East Report*, no. 257 (Winter 2010), http://www.merip.org/mer/mer257.

43. See, for example, Robin Wright, *In the Name of God: The Khomeini Decade* (New York: Simon & Schuster, 1990).

44. See, for example, Byman et al., *Iran's Security Policy in the Post-Revolutionary Era.*

45. *Tehran Radio*, June 25, 1989, as cited in Mohaddessin, *Islamic Fundamentalism*, 31.

46. Eisenstadt, *The Strategic Culture of the Islamic Republic of Iran*, 8.

47. U.S. Department of Defense, *Annual Report on Military Power of Iran, April 2010.*

48. U.S. Department of Defense, *Annual Report on Military Power of Iran, April 2012*, http://fas.org/man/eprint/dod-iran.pdf.

49. U.S. Department of Defense, *Annual Report on Military Power of Iran, January 2014*, http://freebeacon.com/wp-content/uploads/2014/07/Iranmilitary.pdf.

50. See, for example, David Horovitz, "For Iran's Regime, the Prime Concern Is Survival, Not Eliminating Israel, Says Stuart Eizenstat," *Times of Israel*, July 2, 2012, http://www.timesofisrael.com/for-irans-regime-the-prime-concern-is-survival-not-eliminating-israel-says-stuart-eizenstat/.

51. See Arash Karami, "Ayatollah Khamenei Urges Iran to Prepare for 'New World Order,'" *Al-Monitor*, September 5, 2014, http://www.al-monitor.com/pulse/originals/2014/09/khamenei-new-world-order.html#.

52. As cited in Hamid Algar, *Islam and Revolution Writings and Declarations of Imam Khomeini (1941–1980)* (North Haledon, NJ: Mizan Press, 1981), 286–87.

53. For a broader discussion of how Iran views its place in the Muslim World, see Vali Nasr, *The Shia Revival: How Conflicts within Islam Will Shape the Future* (New York: W.W. Norton & Company, 2007).

54. For a review of Iranian thinking in this regard, see Graham E. Fuller, *The Center of the Universe: The Geopolitics of Iran* (Boulder, CO: Westview Press, 1991).

55. "Transcript: Read Mahmoud Ahmadinejad's Speech at the U.N.

General Assembly," FoxNews.com, September 26, 2012, http://in
sider.foxnews.com/2012/09/26/transcript-read-mahmoud-ahma
dinejads-speech-at-the-u-n-general-assembly.

56. Stephen Graubard, "Lunch with the FT: Henry Kissinger," *Financial Times*, May 24/25, 2008, http://www.henryakissinger.com/inter
views/FinancialTimes240508.html.

CHAPTER II: SUBVERTING THE ARAB SPRING

1. "Lawmaker: Uprisings in Region Promising Birth of Islamic Middle-
East," FARS News Agency (Tehran), February 5, 2011, http://english
.farsnews.com/newstext.php?nn=8911161168.

2. Amir Taheri, "Iran and the Ikhwan: The Ideological Roots of a Partnership," *Asharq al-Awsat* (London), May 31, 2014, http://www.aaw
sat.net/2014/05/article55332765.

3. Casey L. Addis, *Iran: Regional Perspectives and Policies* (Congressional
Research Service, January 13, 2010), 24, http://fas.org/sgp/crs/mid
east/R40849.pdf.

4. Mehdi Khalaji, "Egypt's Muslim Brotherhood and Iran," Washington
Institute for Near East Policy, PolicyWatch 1476 (February 12, 2009),
http://www.washingtoninstitute.org/policy-analysis/view/egypts
-muslim-brotherhood-and-iran.

5. Mehdi Khalaji, "Iran on Egypt's Muslim Brotherhood," Tehran
Bureau, February 25, 2011, http://www.pbs.org/wgbh/pages/front
line/tehranbureau/2011/02/iran-on-egypts-muslim-brotherhood
.html.

6. "Egypt to Let Iranian Warships through Suez Canal," CNN.com,
February 18, 2011, http://www.cnn.com/2011/WORLD/meast/02
/18/egypt.iran.warships/index.html?_s=PM:WORLD.

7. Richard Spencer, "Egypt and Iran Forging Closer Links with Ambassadors Plan," *The Telegraph* (London), April 19, 2011, http://
www.telegraph.co.uk/news/worldnews/africaandindianocean
/egypt/8461295/Egypt-and-Iran-forging-closer-links-with-ambas
sadors-plan.html.

8. "Iran Floats Joint Atomic Work with Egypt," Global Security Newswire, July 5, 2011, http://www.nti.org/gsn/article/iran-floats-joint
-atomic-work-with-egypt/.

9. Taheri, "Iran and the Ikhwan."

10. "'Islamic Awakening': Morsi's Egypt Turns to Iran—Report," RT,
June 25, 2012, http://rt.com/news/israel-iran-egypt-morsi-686/.

11. Mostafa al-Labbad, "Morsi's Iran Speech Reasserts Egypt's Regional Role," *As-Safir* (Beirut), September 8, 2012, accessed at *Al-Monitor*, http://www.al-monitor.com/pulse/ar/politics/2012/09/political -messages-in-iran-morsi-speech.html#.

12. "Morsi Accused of Leaking State Secrets to Iran," Al Jazeera America, February 23, 2014, http://america.aljazeera.com/articles /2014/2/23/morsi-accused-ofleakingstatesecrets.html.

13. "Egypt Invites Iranian President to Sisi's Inauguration," Reuters, June 3, 2014, http://www.reuters.com/article/2014/06/03/us-iran -egypt-idUSKBN0EE1SO20140603.

14. "Russia, Egypt Seal Preliminary Deal Worth $3.5 Billion: Agency," Reuters, September 17, 2014, http://www.reuters.com/article /2014/09/17/us-russia-egypt-arms-idUSKBN0HC19T20140917.

15. "Egypt Interim Gov't Says Keen to Improve Iran Ties," Press TV (Tehran), October 7, 2013, http://presstv.com/detail/2013/10/07 /328045/egypt-eager-to-improve-ties-with-iran/.

16. "Crowd Attacks Residence of Iranian Diplomat in Egypt," Press TV (Tehran), April 6, 2013, http://presstv.com/detail/2013/04/06 /296776/crowd-attacks-iran-envoys-home-in-egypt/.

17. "Egypt Denounces Iranian Intervention within Local Affairs," *Egypt Independent*, January 8, 2014, http://www.egyptindependent.com// news/egypt-denounces-iranian-intervention-within-local-affairs.

18. See, for example, Ann Mahjar-Barducci, "Iran's Plan to Destabilize Egypt," Gatestone Institute, June 6, 2014, http://www.gatestone institute.org/4343/iran-egypt.

19. Ibid.

20. American Foreign Policy Council, *World Almanac of Islamism*, s.v. "Bahrain" (last updated August 29, 2013), http://almanac.afpc.org/Bahrain.

21. Shabnam Nourian, "Iran's Support for Bahrain Protesters Fuels Regional Tensions," Deutsche Welle, April 15, 2011, http://www .dw.de/irans-support-for-bahrain-protesters-fuels-regional-ten sions/a-6504403-1.

22. Elise Labott, "Bahrain Government Accuses Hezbollah of Aiding Opposition Groups," CNN.com, April 25, 2011, http://www.cnn .com/2011/WORLD/meast/04/25/bahrain.hezbollah/.

23. "Bahrain Jails Three for Spying for Iran: Report," Agence France-Presse, July 6, 2011, http://gulfnews.com/news/gulf/bahrain/bahrain -jails-three-for-spying-for-iran-report-1.833932.

24. "Iran Wants Bahrain as Its 'Crown Jewel,'" Agence France-Presse,

November 1, 2011, http://www.muscatdaily.com/Archive/Gcc/Iran
-wants-Bahrain-as-its-crown-jewel-minister.

25. U.S. Department of Defense, "Media Availability with Secretary Gates
from Riyadh, Saudi Arabia," News Transcript, April 6, 2011, http://
www.defense.gov/transcripts/transcript.aspx?transcriptid=4806.

26. Michael Slackman, "The Proxy Battle in Bahrain," *New York Times*,
March 19, 2011, http://www.nytimes.com/2011/03/20/weekin
review/20proxy.html?pagewanted=all&_r=0.

27. "Gulf States Send Forces to Bahrain Following Protests," BBC
News, March 14, 2011, http://www.bbc.com/news/world-middle
-east-12729786.

28. "A Talk with Peninsula Shield Force Commander Mutlaq Bin Salem
al-Azima," *Asharq al-Awsat* (London), March 28, 2011, http://www
.aawsat.net/2011/03/article55247010.

29. "Bahrain Accuses Iran of Aiding Rebels," Al Jazeera (Doha), January 3, 2014, http://www.aljazeera.com/news/middleeast/2014/01
/bahrain-accuses-iran-training-rebels-20141314404981496o.html.

30. Hakim Almasmari, "Thousands Expected to Die in 2010 in Fight
against Al-Qaeda," *Yemen Post*, April 10, 2010, http://yemenpost.net
/Detail123456789.aspx?ID=3&SubID=1749&MainCat=2.

31. "Houthis Kill 24 in North Yemen," *Yemen Post*, November 27, 2011,
http://www.yemenpost.net/Detail123456789.aspx?ID=3&SubID
=4393&MainCat=3.

32. Hakim Almasmari, "Houthi Official Denies Receiving Arms from
Iran," *The National*, March 16, 2012, http://www.thenational.ae
/news/world/middle-east/houthi-official-denies-receiving-arms
-from-iran.

33. Eric Schmitt and Robert F. Worth, "With Arms for Yemen Rebels,
Iran Seeks Wider Mideast Role," *New York Times*, March 15, 2012,
http://www.nytimes.com/2012/03/15/world/middleeast/aiding
-yemen-rebels-iran-seeks-wider-mideast-role.html.

34. Robert F. Worth and C. J. Chivers, "Seized Arms off Yemen Raise
Alarm over Iran," *New York Times*, March 2, 2013, http://www.ny
times.com/2013/03/03/world/middleeast/seized-arms-off-yemen
-raise-alarm-over-iran.html.

35. Hakim Almasmari, "Houthi Official Denies Receiving Arms from
Iran."

36. As cited in "Yemeni President Urges Iran to Stop Interference: Newspaper," Reuters, March 31, 2014, http://dailystar.com.lb/News

/Middle-East/2014/Mar-31/251780-yemen-president-urges-iran
-to-stop-interference-newspaper.ashx#axzz3DuqZzzBA.

37. Arafat Madabish, "Yemen's Houthis Advancing Close to Saudi Border: Source," *Asharq al-Awsat* (London), September 16, 2014, http://
www.aawsat.net/2014/09/article55336622.

38. Adam Baron, "Triumph of Anti-American Rebels in Yemen Raises Questions about Obama Success Claims," McClatchyDC.com, September 22, 2014, http://www.mcclatchydc.com/2014/09/22
/240647/triumph-of-anti-american-rebels.html.

39. Khaled Abdallah and Sami Aboudi, "Saudi Arabia Leads Air Strikes against Yemen's Houthi Rebels," Reuters, March 26, 2015, http://
www.reuters.com/article/2015/03/26/yemen-security-idUSL2N
0WS02B20150326.

40. "Iranian Revolutionary Guard Escalating Activities in Yemen—Diplomatic Source," *Asharq Al-Awsat* (London), July 25, 2012, http://
www.aawsat.net/2012/07/article55241229.

41. See, for example, "Iran Sends Fourth Consignment of Humanitarian Aid to Syria," Press TV (Tehran), July 28, 2013, http://www.presstv
.com/detail/2013/07/28/316055/iran-sends-humanitarian-aid-to
-syria/.

42. Andrew Parasiliti, "Iran's Foreign Minister Offers Help with Syria's Chemical Weapons," *Al-Monitor*, September 30, 2013, http://www
.al-monitor.com/pulse/originals/2013/09/foreign-minister-zarif
-seeks-iranian-role-in-syria-talks.html.

43. Luke McKenna, "Syria Is Importing Iranian Snipers to Murder Anti-Government Protesters," Business Insider, January 27, 2012, http://
www.businessinsider.com/syria-is-importing-iranian-snipers-to
-murder-anti-government-protesters-2012-1.

44. Babak Dehghanpisheh, "Elite Iranian Unit's Commander Says His Forces Are in Syria," *Washington Post*, September 16, 2012, http://
www.washingtonpost.com/world/middle_east/elite-iranian-units
-commander-says-his-forces-are-in-syria/2012/09/16/431ff096
-0028-11e2-b257-e1c2b3548a4a_story.html; Karen DeYoung and Joby Warrick, "Iran, Hezbollah Build Militia Networks in Syria in Event that Assad Falls, Officials Say," *Washington Post*, February 10, 2013, http://www.washingtonpost.com/world/national-security
/iran-hezbollah-build-militia-networks-in-syria-in-event-that
-assad-falls-officials-say/2013/02/10/257a41c8-720a-11e2-ac36
-3d8d9dcaa2e2_story.html?hpid=z2.

45. Farnaz Fassihi, "Iran Recruiting Afghan Refugees to Fight for Regime in Syria," *Wall Street Journal*, May 15, 2014, http://online.wsj .com/news/articles/SB10001424052702304908304579564161508 613846?mg=reno64-wsj&url=http%3A%2F%2Fonline.wsj.com% 2Farticle%2FSB10001424052702304908304579564161508613846 .html.

46. See, for example, Jonathan Saul and Parisa Hafezi, "Iran Boosts Military Support in Syria to Bolster Assad," Reuters, February 21, 2014, http://www.reuters.com/article/2014/02/21/us-syria-crisis-iran -idUSBREA1K09U20140221.

47. See Patrick Hilsman, "Iran's Drone War in Syria," Daily Beast, May 14, 2014, http://www.thedailybeast.com/articles/2014/05/14/iran -s-drone-war-in-syria.html.

48. "Iran, Russia, China Prop Up Syria Economy, Official Says," UPI .com, June 28, 2013, http://www.upi.com/Top_News/World-News /2013/06/28/Iran-Russia-China-prop-up-Syria-economy-official -says/78611372401000/.

49. Adam Kredo, "State Dept Confirms: Iran Now Shipping Oil to Syria," *Washington Free Beacon*, June 12, 2014, http://freebeacon.com /national-security/state-dept-confirms-iran-now-shipping-oil-to -syria/.

50. "Official: Iran Recruiting Afghans to Reduce Hizbullah Casualties in Syria," Naharnet, May 16, 2014, http://www.naharnet.com/stories /en/130818.

51. "Iranian Revolutionary Guard Corps Commander Jafari: We Support Resistance to U.S. and Israel in Syria and Elsewhere in the Region," Middle East Media Research Institute, video clip no. 4272, April 21, 2014, http://www.memritv.org/clip/en/4272.htm.

52. Simon Tisdall, "Iran and Assad Have Won in Syria, Say Top Tehran Foreign Policy Figures," *The Guardian* (London), May 12, 2014, http://www.theguardian.com/world/2014/may/11/syria-crisis -iran-assad-won-war-tehran.

53. See, for example, Dalga Khatinoglu, "Iranian Top Military Commander Killed in Syria," Trend News Agency (Baku), October 17, 2014, http://en.trend.az/iran/politics/2323112.html.

54. See, for example, Michael Young, "Hezbollah's Vietnam?" NOW Lebanon, July 6, 2013, https://now.mmedia.me/lb/en/commentary analysis/hezbollahs-vietnam.

55. "Iran's Influence Has Reached the Mediterranean," Access ADL

(blog), May 2, 2014, http://blog.adl.org/tags/supreme-leader/page/2, excerpt translated from FARS News Agency (Tehran), http://www.farsnews.com/newstext.php?nn=13930212000301.

56. Scott Peterson, "Behind Syrian Regime, a Familiar US Adversary: Iran," *Christian Science Monitor*, May 30, 2014, http://www.csmonitor.com/World/Middle-East/2014/0530/Behind-Syrian-regime-a-familiar-US-adversary-Iran.

57. As cited in "Iran Military Chief: 'We Will Support Syria to the End,'" Agence France-Presse, September 5, 2013, http://www.businessinsider.com/iranian-military-chief-we-will-support-syria-to-the-end-2013-9.

58. See, for example, Munk School of Global Affairs at the University of Toronto, "Rouhani Meter 100 Days Report," media release, November 19, 2013, http://munkschool.utoronto.ca/blog/rouhani-meter-100-days-report/.

59. Iran Human Rights Documentation Center, "IHRDC Chart of Executions by the Islamic Republic of Iran—2012," January 3, 2013, http://www.iranhrdc.org/english/publications/1000000030-ihrdc-chart-of-executions-by-the-islamic-republic-of-iran-2012.html.

60. Iran Human Rights Documentation Center," IHRDC Chart of Executions by the Islamic Republic of Iran—2013," April 9, 2014, http://www.iranhrdc.org/english/publications/1000000225-ihrdc-chart-of-executions-by-the-islamic-republic-of-iran-2013.html.

61. Iran Human Rights Documentation Center, "IHRDC Chart of Executions by the Islamic Republic of Iran—2014," January 7, 2015, http://www.iranhrdc.org/english/publications/1000000425-ihrdc-chart-of-executions-by-the-islamic-republic-of-iran-2014.html.

62. "Javad Larijani: 'Be Grateful' for Iran's High Execution Rate," International Campaign for Human Rights in Iran, March 5, 2014, http://www.iranhumanrights.org/2014/03/larijani-executions/.

63. See Alistair Sloan, "Who Are the 'Political Prisoners' in Saudi and Iran?" Middle East Monitor, April 30, 2014, https://www.middleeast-monitor.com/articles/middle-east/11203-who-are-the-political-prisoners-in-saudi-and-iran.

64. "40 Percent of Political Prisoners in Iran Are Kurds," BasNews, September 14, 2014, http://basnews.com/en/news/2014/09/14/40-percent-of-political-prisoners-in-iran-are-kurds/.

65. Colum Lynch, "Ban to Iran: Free the Journalists, Political Prisoners," *Foreign Policy*, September 19, 2014, http://thecable.foreignpolicy

.com/posts/2014/09/19/ban_to_iran_free_the_journalists_politi
cal_prisoners.

66. Michele Richinick, "Detained 'Washington Post' Journalist to Stand
Trial in Iran," MSNBC.com, January 14, 2015, http://www.msnbc
.com/msnbc/detained-washington-post-journalist-stand-trial-iran.

67. *Freedom of the Press 2013: Middle East Volatility amid Global Decline*
(Freedom House, n.d.), http://freedomhouse.org/report/freedom
-press/2013/iran#.VCIrCF4irwI.

68. Thomas Erdbrink, "Iran's Judiciary Closes a New Pro-Government
Newspaper," *New York Times*, February 20, 2014, http://www.ny
times.com/2014/02/21/world/middleeast/irans-judiciary-closes
-newspaper.html?_r=2.

69. As cited in Maha Mehrgan, "Iran's Liberal Media Continue Decline
under Rouhani," *Asharq al-Awsat* (London), May 14, 2014, http://
www.aawsat.net/2014/05/article55332248.

CHAPTER III: IRAN'S OWN "WAR ON TERROR"

1. Susan Crabtree, "FLASHBACK: Obama: Al Qaeda Is on 'a Path to
Defeat'; Calls for Resetting Terror Policy," *Washington Times*, May
23, 2013, http://www.washingtontimes.com/news/2013/may/23
/obama-al-qaeda-is-on-a-path-to-defeat/?page=all.

2. Jessica D. Lewis, *Al-Qaeda in Iraq Resurgent: The Breaking the Walls
Campaign, Part 1*, Middle East Security Report 14 (Institute for the
Study of War, September 2013), http://www.understandingwar.org
/report/al-qaeda-iraq-resurgent.

3. Bassem Mroue, "Syria and Iraq Al Qaeda Merger Annulment Announced by Ayman al Zawahiri," Associated Press, June 10, 2013.

4. "Expert: ISIS' Declaration of Islamic State 'Poses a Huge Threat to
Al Qaeda,'" CBS DC, June 30, 2014, http://washington.cbslocal
.com/2014/06/30/expert-isis-declaration-of-islamic-state-poses-a
-huge-threat-to-al-qaeda/.

5. See "Sunni Rebels Declare New 'Islamic Caliphate,'" Al Jazeera
(Doha), June 30, 2014, http://www.aljazeera.com/news/middleeast
/2014/06/isil-declares-new-islamic-caliphate-2014629173266
69749.html.

6. See J. M. Berger, "The Islamic State vs. Al Qaeda," *Foreign Policy*, September 2, 2014, http://www.foreignpolicy.com/articles/2014/09/02
/islamic_state_vs_al_qaeda_next_jihadi_super_power.

7. Spencer Ackerman, "'Apocalyptic' ISIS beyond Anything We've

Seen, Say US Defence Chiefs," *The Guardian* (London), August 22, 2014, http://www.theguardian.com/world/2014/aug/21/isis-us-military-iraq-strikes-threat-apocalyptic.

8. Jim Sciutto, Jamie Crawford, and Chelsea J. Carter, "ISIS Can 'Muster' between 20,000 and 31,500 Fighters, CIA Says," CNN.com, September 12, 2014, http://www.cnn.com/2014/09/11/world/meast/isis-syria-iraq/.

9. U.S. Department of State, Bureau of Counterterrorism, "Foreign Terrorist Organizations," in *Country Reports on Terrorism 2013*, April 2014, http://www.state.gov/j/ct/rls/crt/2013/224829.htm.

10. Martin Chulov, "How an Arrest in Iraq Revealed Isis's $2bn Jihadist Network," *The Guardian* (London), June 15, 2014, http://www.theguardian.com/world/2014/jun/15/iraq-isis-arrest-jihadists-wealth-power.

11. Ian Johnston, "The Rise of Isis: Terror Group Now Controls an Area the Size of Britain, Expert Says," *The Independent* (London), September 3, 2014, http://www.independent.co.uk/news/world/middle-east/the-rise-of-isis-terror-group-now-controls-an-area-the-size-of-britain-expert-claims-9710198.html.

12. Arash Karami, "Iran Interior Minister Says Advisers Sent to Iraqi Kurdistan," *Al-Monitor*, August 26, 2014, http://www.al-monitor.com/pulse/originals/2014/08/iran-sends-advisers-kurdistan-region-iraq.html#ixzz3CTppCln9.

13. Babak Dehghanpisheh, "Iran's Elite Guards Fighting in Iraq to Push Back Islamic State," Reuters, August 3, 2014, http://www.reuters.com/article/2014/08/03/us-iraq-security-iran-insight-idUSKBN0G30GE20140803.

14. "Iran 'Backs US Military Contacts' to Fight Islamic State," BBC News, September 5, 2014, http://www.bbc.com/news/world-middle-east-29079052.

15. Jesse Byrnes, "Secy. Kerry Says Iran Can Help Defeat ISIS," *The Hill*, September 19, 2014, http://thehill.com/blogs/blog-briefing-room/news/218391-iran-can-help-defeat-isis-kerry-says.

16. Jay Solomon and Carol E. Lee, "Obama Wrote Secret Letter to Iran's Khamenei about Fighting Islamic State," *Wall Street Journal*, November 6, 2014, http://www.wsj.com/articles/obama-wrote-secret-letter-to-irans-khamenei-about-fighting-islamic-state-1415295291.

17. Michael Doran and Max Boot, "The United States Should Not Cooperate with Iran on Iraq," *Washington Post*, June 17, 2014, http://

www.washingtonpost.com/opinions/the-united-states-should-not
-cooperate-with-iran-on-iraq/2014/06/17/f3144b9c-f63e-11e3
-a3a5-42be35962a52_story.html.

18. For a detailed overview of Iran's terror infrastructure, see Ilan Berman, *Tehran Rising: Iran's Challenge to the United States* (Lanham, MD: Rowman & Littlefield, 2005), 3–30.

19. See, for example, Robert Baer, *See No Evil: The True Story of a Ground Soldier in the CIA's War on Terrorism* (New York: Crown Publishers, 2002).

20. Scott Modell and David Asher, *Pushback: Countering the Iran Action Network* (Washington, DC: Center for a New American Security, September 2013), 8, http://www.cnas.org/files/documents/publica tions/CNAS_Pushback_ModellAsher_0.pdf.

21. U.S. Department of State, Bureau of Counterterrorism, "State Sponsors of Terrorism Overview," in *Country Reports on Terrorism 2013*, April 2014, http://www.state.gov/j/ct/rls/crt/2013/224826.htm.

22. Modell and Asher, *Pushback*, 28.

23. For more, see Kayhan Barzegar, "Iran's Foreign Policy in Post-Taliban Afghanistan," *The Washington Quarterly* 37, no. 2 (2014), https://twq.elliott.gwu.edu/sites/twq.elliott.gwu.edu/files/down loads/Barzegar_PDF.pdf.

24. *Iranian Influence in the Levant, Egypt, Iraq, and Afghanistan* (American Enterprise Institute and the Institute for the Study of War, 2012), 79, https://www.understandingwar.org/sites/default/files/IranianInflu enceLevantEgyptIraqAfghanistan.pdf.

25. Joshua Hersh, "Afghanistan Trade Deal with Iran Complicates U.S. Aims," *Huffington Post*, May 9, 2012, http://www.huffingtonpost .com/2012/05/09/afghanistan-trade-deal-iran_n_1504062.html.

26. *Iranian Influence in the Levant, Egypt, Iraq, and Afghanistan*, 79.

27. "Afghan-Iran Trade Volume Hits $5b," *Afghanistan Times*, December 30, 2014, http://www.afghanistantimes.af/news_details.php?id=40 11&&cid=1.

28. Alireza Nader et al., *Iran's Influence in Afghanistan: Implications for the U.S. Drawdown* (Santa Monica, CA: RAND, 2014), 9, http://www.rand .org/content/dam/rand/pubs/research_reports/RR600/RR616 /RAND_RR616.pdf.

29. *Iranian Influence in the Levant, Egypt, Iraq, and Afghanistan*, 85.

30. Ibid.

31. See, for example, Sanjay Kumar, "Tehran's Designs on Afghanistan,"

The Diplomat, May 23, 2013, http://thediplomat.com/2013/05/teh
rans-designs-on-afghanistan/.

32. Jawed Ziarayjal, "Herat Police Chief Blames Iran for Insecurity,"
Tolo News, August 3, 2014, http://www.tolonews.com/en
/afghanistan/15814-herat-police-chief-blames-iran-for-insecurity.

33. U.S. Department of State, Office of the Coordinator for Counterterrorism, "State Sponsors of Terrorism Overview," in *Country Reports on Terrorism 2012*, May 2013, http://www.state.gov/j/ct/rls/crt
/2012/209985.htm.

34. Lara Setrakian, "Petraeus Accuses Iran of Aiding Afghan Taliban,"
ABC News, December 16, 2009, http://abcnews.go.com/Politics
/Afghanistan/gen-petraeus-iran-backing-iraq-militias-afghan
-taliban/story?id=9346173.

35. Maria Abi-Habib, "Iranians Build Up Afghan Clout," *Wall Street
Journal*, October 26, 2012, http://online.wsj.com/articles/SB100014
24052970204076204578078564022815472.

36. Ibid.

37. Sumitha Narayanan Kutty, "Iran's Continuing Interests in Afghanistan," *Washington Quarterly* 37, no. 2 (2014): 142, https://twq.elliott
.gwu.edu/sites/twq.elliott.gwu.edu/files/downloads/Kutty_PDF
.pdf.

38. Islamic Republic of Afghanistan, Office of the President, "Dr. Ashraf
Ghani Ahmadzai Meets Iran's Vice President," September 30, 2014,
http://president.gov.af/en/news/36978.

39. Interviews with Israeli officials, in discussion with the author, Jerusalem and Tel Aviv, Israel, September 2014. Interviews conducted in
confidentiality, and names of interviewees are withheld by mutual
agreement.

40. Adam Ciralsky, "Did Israel Avert a Hamas Massacre?" *Vanity Fair*,
October 21, 2014, http://www.vanityfair.com/politics/2014/10
/gaza-tunnel-plot-israeli-intelligence.

41. Robert Tait, "Iran Cuts Funding for Hamas over Syria," *The Telegraph*
(London), May 31, 2013, http://www.telegraph.co.uk/news/world
news/middleeast/palestinianauthority/10091629/Iran-cuts-Hamas
-funding-over-Syria.html.

42. Fares Akram and Jodi Rudoren, "Qatar Offers Cash to Pay Some
Staff in Gaza Strip," *New York Times*, October 28, 2014, http://www
.nytimes.com/2014/10/29/world/middleeast/some-hamas-govern
ment-workers-in-gaza-to-get-salaries.html?_r=0.

43. Adnan Abu Amer, "Iran Resumes Monetary Aid to Hamas," *Al-Monitor*, March 24, 2014, http://www.al-monitor.com/pulse/originals/2014 /03/iran-hamas-finance-economy-resistance-axis-gaza.html.

44. Kay Armin Serjoie, "One Result of Gaza Conflict: Iran and Hamas Are Back Together," *Time*, August 19, 2014, http://time.com/3138 366/iran-and-hamas-alliance-after-gaza-war/.

45. Israeli officials, in discussion with the author, Jerusalem and Tel Aviv, Israel, September 2014. Interviews conducted in confidentiality, and names of interviewees are withheld by mutual agreement.

46. Elie Rekhess, "The Terrorist Connection—Iran, the Islamic Jihad and Hamas," *Justice* 5 (May 1995).

47. Ibid.

48. Brigitte Dusseau, "US Renews Calls for Dialogue with Iran to Address Terrorism Concerns," Agence France-Presse, March 11, 1998.

49. Ehud Ya'ari, "Iran Out of Control," *Jerusalem Report*, September 6, 2004.

50. Anton La Guardia, "Iran 'in Control of Terrorism in Israel,'" *The Telegraph* (London), October 15, 2004.

51. See, for example, "Khamenei: Keep Arming Palestinians until Israel Is Destroyed," *Times of Israel*, July 25, 2014, http://www.timesofisrael .com/khamenei-keep-arming-palestinians-until-israel-is-destroyed/.

52. See Matthew Levitt, *Hamas: Politics, Charity, and Terrorism in the Service of Jihad* (New Haven: Yale University Press, 2006), 172–73.

53. Avi Jorisch, "Hamas' Benefactors: A Network of Terror." Testimony before the U.S. House of Representatives Committee on Foreign Affairs Subcommittee on the Middle East and North Africa and Subcommittee on Terrorism, Non-Proliferation, and Trade, September 9, 2014, http://www.avijorisch.com/11003/hamas-benefac tors-a-network-of-terror.

54. Jeffrey Heller, "Israel Seizes Ship with Iran Arms for Gaza-Netanyahu," Reuters, March 15, 2011, http://www.reuters.com/article /2011/03/15/us-israel-ship-idUSTRE72E2RR20110315; Yaakov Lappin, "Iranian Arms Vessel Captured by IDF Docks in Eilat," *Jerusalem Post*, March 8, 2014, http://www.jpost.com/Defense/Iranian -arms-vessel-captured-by-IDF-to-dock-in-Eilat-344702.

55. Israeli officials, in discussion with the author, Jerusalem and Tel Aviv, Israel, September 2014. Interviews conducted in confidentiality, and names of interviewees are withheld by mutual agreement.

56. Nazila Fathi, "Wipe Israel 'Off the Map' Iranian Says," *New York Times*,

October 27, 2005, http://www.nytimes.com/2005/10/26/world/africa/26iht-iran.html?_r=0.

57. See, for example, Camelia Entekhabi-Fard, "Commander Qassem Suleimani, Iran's Worst Kept Secret?" Al Arabiya, November 3, 2014, http://english.alarabiya.net/en/views/news/middle-east/2014/11/03/Commander-Qassem-Suleimani-Iran-s-worst-kept-secret-.html.

58. U.S. Department of Defense, *Unclassified Report on Military Power of Iran, April 2010*, http://www.iranwatch.org/sites/default/files/us-dod-reportmiliarypoweriran-0410.pdf.

59. Dexter Filkins, "The Shadow Commander," *New Yorker*, September 30, 2013, http://www.newyorker.com/magazine/2013/09/30/the-shadow-commander.

60. Ibid.

61. Kimberly Kagan, "Iran's Proxy War against the United States and the Iraqi Government," *Iraq Report* (Institute for the Study of War and WeeklyStandard.com, May 2006–August 20, 2007), https://www.understandingwar.org/sites/default/files/reports/IraqReport6.pdf.

62. Joseph Felter and Brian Fishman, *Iranian Strategy in Iraq: Politics and "Other Means,"* occasional paper (Combating Terrorism Center at West Point, October 13, 2008), http://reap2-ws1.stanford.edu/publications/iranian_strategy_in_iraq_politics_and_other_means/.

63. Mehdi Khalaji, presentation at the AIPAC National Policy Forum, Chicago, Illinois, October 28, 2008.

64. Robert Fisk, "The Silent Cleric Who Holds the Key to Iran's Future," *The Independent* (London), December 29, 2009, http://www.independent.co.uk/voices/commentators/fisk/robert-fisk-the-silent-cleric-who-holds-the-key-to-irans-future-1852108.html.

65. Vali Nasr, *The Shia Revival: How Conflicts within Islam Will Shape the Future* (New York: W.W. Norton, 2007), 71–72; see also Phillip Smyth, "The Battle for the Soul of Shi'ism," *Middle East Review of International Affairs* 16, no. 3 (2012), http://www.gloria-center.org/2012/11/the-battle-for-the-soul-of-shi'ism/.

CHAPTER IV: IRAN'S EUROPEAN ENABLERS

1. Benjamin Weinthal, "Holland Votes to Put Iran's RGC on EU-Terror List," *Jerusalem Post*, November 27, 2009, http://www.jpost.com/International/Holland-votes-to-put-Irans-RGC-on-EU-terror-list.

2. "Sanctions Committee Implementation Assistance Notice—24 July 2009," *The Telegraph* (London), February 2, 2011, http://www.tele graph.co.uk/news/wikileaks-files/iran-wikileaks/8299124/SANC TIONS-COMMITTEE-IMPLEMENTATION-ASSISTANCE -NOTICE-24-JULY-2009.html.

3. Interviews with author, Berlin, Germany, November 2009.

4. Ibid.

5. Justyna Pawlak, "Insight—How European Courts Are Dismantling Sanctions on Iran," Reuters, July 15, 2013, http://uk.reuters .com/article/2013/07/15/uk-iran-nuclear-courts-insight-idUK BRE96E0M920130715.

6. Ibid.

7. Najmeh Bozorgmehr and Geoff Dyer, "China Overtakes EU as Iran's Top Trade Partner," *Financial Times*, February 8, 2010, http:// www.ft.com/intl/cms/s/0/f220dfac-14d4-11df-8f1d-00144feab49a .html#axzz3OU6XSupz.

8. Juergen Baetz, "European Businesses Rushing to Find Iran Bonanza," Associated Press, January 22, 2014, http://news.yahoo.com/european -businesses-rushing-iran-bonanza-170338509--finance.html.

9. Benoît Faucon, "Iran Deal Opens Door for Businesses," *Wall Street Journal*, December 1, 2013, http://www.wsj.com/news/articles/SB 10001424052702304579404579232131395661284?mod=WSJ_busi ness_LeadStoryRotator&autologin=y.

10. "Foreign Carmakers Jostle for Position in Iran," *Guardian* (London), December 13, 2013, http://www.theguardian.com/world/iran-blog /2013/dec/13/iran-carmakers-market.

11. Susanne Koebl, "'Chance of a Century': International Investors Flock to Tehran," *Der Spiegel* (Hamburg), January 2, 2014, http:// www.spiegel.de/international/world/geneva-deal-sparks-new-in ternational-investor-interest-in-iran-a-940629.html.

12. "Iran to Attract $100bn under New Contracts: Officials," Press TV (Tehran), February 26, 2014, http://presstv.com/detail/2014/02 /26/352354/iran-to-attract-100bn-under-new-deals/.

13. A brochure from the event, including a list of the conference's featured speakers, is available at http://de.stopthebomb.net/fileadmin/ed itors_de/The_First_Europe-Iran_Forum_Brochure-MD__2_.pdf.

14. Benjamin Weinthal, "Germany, Inc. Heads to Tehran," *Foreign Policy*, January 31, 2014, http://foreignpolicy.com/2014/01/31/germany-inc -heads-to-tehran/.

15. See, for example, Andrea Thomas, "German Business Looks to Renew Iran Contacts," *Wall Street Journal*, August 3, 2014, http://www.wsj.com/articles/german-businesses-warm-to-iran-1407099835.

16. Koebl, "'Chance of a Century.'"

17. Weinthal, "Germany, Inc. Heads to Tehran."

18. John J. Lumpkin, "Iran's Nuclear Program Growing at Secret Sites, Rebel Group Alleges," Associated Press, August 14, 2002; "Iran Said to Have Secret Nuclear Facilities," *Deutsche Presse-Agentur*, August 14, 2002.

19. David Rennie, "Alarm as Iran Takes Another Step towards Nuclear Weapons," *The Telegraph* (London), March 10, 2003, http://www.telegraph.co.uk/news/worldnews/middleeast/israel/1424228/Alarm-as-Iran-takes-another-step-towards-nuclear-weapons.html.

20. Dan De Luce, "Iran in Nuclear Climbdown," *The Guardian* (London), October 21, 2003, http://www.theguardian.com/world/2003/oct/22/iran.politics.

21. Stephen Fidler, "Iran Centrifuge Plan Dashes Hopes of a Nuclear Deal," *Financial Times* (London), June 25, 2004.

22. See Arms Control Association, "History of Official Proposals on the Iranian Nuclear Issue," January 2014, http://www.armscontrol.org/factsheets/Iran_Nuclear_Proposals.

23. As cited in Elaine Sciolino, "Showdown at U.N.? Iran Seems Calm," *New York Times*, March 14, 2006, http://www.nytimes.com/2006/03/14/international/middleeast/14iran.html?_r=0.

24. *Conference on Security and Co-operation in Europe Final Act*, Helsinki, Finland, August 1, 1975, 6, http://www.osce.org/mc/39501?download=true.

25. Organization for Security and Cooperation in Europe, "Signing of the Helsinki Final Act," n.d., http://www.osce.org/who/43960.

26. *Report of the Secretary-General on the Situation of Human Rights in the Islamic Republic of Iran*, UNWatch.org, March 11, 2014, http://blog.unwatch.org/index.php/2014/03/18/report-of-the-secretary-general-on-the-situation-of-human-rights-in-the-islamic-republic-of-iran-march-2014/.

27. See, for example, Sam Brownback, "Activating the Human Rights Dimension," in *Taking on Tehran: Strategies for Confronting the Islamic Republic*, ed. Ilan Berman (Lanham, MD: Lexington Books, 2007).

28. Abbas Rezai, "EU Parliament to Visit Iran without Preconditions," UPI, December 9, 2013, http://www.upi.com/Top_News/Analysis

/Outside-View/2013/12/09/Outside-View-EU-Parliament-to
-visit-Iran-without-preconditions/82581386565380/.

29. Ibid.

30. As cited in Eli Lake, "State Dept. Declares 2012 the Year of Iranian
Terror," Daily Beast, May 30, 2013, http://www.thedailybeast.com
/articles/2013/05/30/state-dept-declares-2012-the-year-of-iranian
-terror.html.

31. U.S. Department of State, Office of the Coordinator for Counterterrorism, "State Sponsors of Terrorism Overview," in *Country Reports on Terrorism 2012*, May 2013, http://www.state.gov/j/ct/rls/crt
/2012/209985.htm.

32. "Israel Blames Iran in Deadly Bulgaria Bus Blast," Associated Press,
July 18, 2012, http://www.cbsnews.com/news/israel-blames-iran
-in-deadly-bulgaria-bus-blast/.

33. "Bulgaria Says Hezbollah behind Burgas Bombing," Reuters, February 5, 2013, http://www.reuters.com/article/2013/02/05/us
-bulgaria-bombing-idUSBRE9140O020130205.

34. Matthew Levitt, "Hezbollah's European Enablers," *National Post*,
March 11, 2013, http://fullcomment.nationalpost.com/2013/03/11
/matthew-levitt-hezbollahs-european-enablers/#__federated=1.

35. Matthew Levitt, "Islamic Extremism in Europe: Beyond al-Qaeda—
Hamas and Hezbollah in Europe." Testimony before the Joint Hear-
ing of the U.S. House of Representatives Committee on International Relations and Subcommittee on Europe and Emerging
Threats, April 27, 2005, http://www.washingtoninstitute.org/policy
-analysis/view/islamic-extremism-in-europe-beyond-al-qaeda
hamas-and-hezbollah-in-europe.

36. Nicholas Kulish, "Despite Alarm by U.S., Europe Lets Hezbollah
Operate Openly," *New York Times*, August 12, 2012, http://www
.nytimes.com/2012/08/16/world/europe/hezbollah-banned-in
-us-operates-in-europes-public-eye.html?pagewanted=all&_r=0
#commentsContainer.

37. "Hezbollah Planning Berlin Headquarters," *Der Spiegel* (Hamburg),
June 24, 2002; "Hezbollah Plans to Settle in Berlin," *Die Welt* (Berlin), June 26, 2002.

38. Bruno Schirra, "Extremism—Tehran's Secret Fighters—The Shiite
Terror Organization Hizballah Also Has Adherents in Germany,"
Welt am Sonntag (Berlin), July 23, 2006.

39. Justyna Pawlak and Adrian Croft, "EU Adds Hezbollah's Mili-

tary Wing to Terrorism List," Reuters, July 22, 2013, http://www
.reuters.com/article/2013/07/22/us-eu-hezbollah-idUSBRE96K
0DA20130722.

40. Ulrike Putz, "EU Terror List: Hezbollah Unlikely to Feel Sanctions,"
Der Spiegel (Hamburg), July 22, 2013, http://www.spiegel.de/inter
national/world/eu-terrorist-group-designation-to-have-little-im
pact-on-hezbollah-a-912448.html.

41. Ibid.

42. Julian Pecquet, "Europeans Raise Concerns with Hezbollah Sanctions Bill," *Al-Monitor*, October 30, 2014, http://www.al-monitor
.com/pulse/originals/2014/10/hezbollah-sanctions-bill-european
-concerns.html.

43. See Ari Kattan, "Fact Sheet: Iran Sanctions," Center for Arms Control
and Non-Proliferation, March 2013, http://armscontrolcenter.org
/publications/factsheets/fact_sheet_iran_sanctions/.

44. European Commission, Directorate-General for Trade, "Russia:
Main Indicators," n.d., http://trade.ec.europa.eu/doclib/docs/2006
/september/tradoc_111720.pdf.

45. "Russia in the European Energy Sector," *Wikipedia*, n.d., http://
en.wikipedia.org/wiki/Russia_in_the_European_energy_sector
#cite_note-gas_security_directive-3.

46. Ibid.

47. Daniel Gross, "Russia Is Europe's Gas Station," Slate.com, July 24,
2014, http://www.slate.com/articles/business/the_juice/2014/07
/putin_economic_sanctions_he_has_nothing_to_fear_because_russia
_is_europe.html.

48. See, for example, Keith Smith, "A Bear at the Door," *Journal of International Security Affairs*, no. 17 (Fall 2009).

49. See, for example, Jason Czerwiec, "Emerging from Russia's Energy
Shadow," *U.S. News & World Report*, November 4, 2014, http://www
.usnews.com/opinion/blogs/world-report/2014/11/04/lithuania
-embraces-energy-independence-from-russia.

50. Charles Recknagel, "Iran Says Ready to Supply Natural Gas to Europe," Radio Free Europe/Radio Liberty, May 15, 2014, http://
www.rferl.mobi/a/iran-says-ready-to-supply-natural-gas-to-europe
-/25386226.html.

51. Ibid.

52. Ibid.

53. Samaneh Nazerian and M. A. Saki, "Iran, EU Can Be Allies in Trade,

Campaign against Terrorism: Danish FM," *Tehran Times*, September 10, 2014, http://www.tehrantimes.com/component/content /article/94-headline/118304-iran-eu-can-be-allies-in-trade-cam paign-against-terrorism-danish-fm-.

CHAPTER V: EURASIA CALLING

1. These principles are encapsulated in the organization's charter. Shanghai Cooperation Organization, "Charter of the Shanghai Cooperation Organization," May 7, 2009, http://www.sectsco.org/EN123 /show.asp?id=69.
2. Oliver August, "Iran in Talks to Join Alliance against West," *Times of London*, June 16, 2006, http://www.timesonline.co.uk/article/0,,13 509-2228233,00.html.
3. Michael Mainville, "Central Asian Bloc Considering Iran for Membership," *Washington Times*, June 5, 2006, http://www.washington times.com/world/20060604-103052-2402r.htm.
4. "The Limits of the Shanghai Cooperation Organization," Radio Free Europe/Radio Liberty, August 7, 2006, http://www.rferl.org/con tent/pressrelease/1105890.html.
5. "Sanctions against Iran 'Unacceptable'—Russia, China and Other SCO Nations," RT, September 13, 2013, http://rt.com/news /nuclear-iran-sco-summit-833/.
6. Shannon Tiezzi, "The New, Improved Shanghai Cooperation Organization," *The Diplomat*, September 13, 2014, http://thediplomat .com/2014/09/the-new-improved-shanghai-cooperation-organiza tion/.
7. "Studio Interview: SCO Leaders Seek Further Development through Expansion," CCTV (Beijing), September 12, 2014, http://english .cntv.cn/2014/09/12/VIDE1410497046260218.shtml; Li Li, "Commentary: Deeper SCO Cooperation Promises Regional Peace, Development," Xinhuanet (Beijing), September 11, 2014, http://news .xinhuanet.com/english/china/2014-09/11/c_133636179.htm.
8. "Iranian Diplomat: Tehran Seeks Full Shanghai Cooperation Organization Membership," RIA Novosti (Sputnik International), September 10, 2014, http://sputniknews.com/world/20140910/1928033 69/Iranian-Diplomat-Tehran-Seeks-Full-Shanghai-Cooperation .html; "SCO Seeks Enhanced Ties with Iran: President Rouhani," Press TV (Tehran), September 13, 2014, http://www.presstv.com /detail/2014/09/13/378567/sco-seeks-enhanced-ties-with-iran/.

9. "Iran's Bid to Join SCO Cannot Be Considered at the Moment—MFA," Kazinform, September 16, 2014, http://www.turkishweekly.net/news/172084/iran-39-s-bid-to-join-sco-cannot-be-considered-at-the-moment-mfa.html.

10. Tweet by Sputnik News on November 19, 2014, archived at https://twitter.com/SputnikInt/status/534988877669613568. See also "Russia Says Iran's Joining SCO Becoming More Relevant," Trend News Agency (Baku), November 19, 2014, http://en.trend.az/iran/politics/2334734.html.

11. "Sanctioned Russia and Iran Sign 5-Yr Deal to Ease Western Pressure," RT, August 6, 2014, http://rt.com/business/178316-russia-iran-oil-deal-sanctions/.

12. Mark Katz, "Russia and Iran: Who Is Strong-Arming Whom?" *Radio Free Europe/Radio Liberty Newsline* 8, no. 131 (2004).

13. See, for example, Bruce Clark and Anatol Lieven, "U.S., Turkey and Iran Chase Power in Central Asia," *Times of London*, February 17, 1992.

14. Brenda Shaffer, *Partners in Need: The Strategic Relationship of Russia and Iran* (Washington, DC: Washington Institute for Near East Policy, 2001), 11–12, 71.

15. Ibid.

16. Vladimir Isachenkov, "Russia to Build More Nuclear Reactors in Iran," Associated Press, November 11, 2014, http://bigstory.ap.org/article/b1282dd da1f447d794058304ac7eae38/russia-build-more-nuclear-reactors-iran.

17. Ibid.

18. Oxana Antonenko, "Russia's Military Involvement in the Middle East," *Middle Eastern Review of International Affairs* 5, no. 1 (March 2001), http://www.rubincenter.org/2001/03/antonenko-2001-03-03/.

19. For a full description of this effort, see Ilan Berman, *Tehran Rising: Iran's Challenge to the United States* (Lanham, MD: Rowman & Littlefield, 2005).

20. Polina Garaev, "Report: Russia to Offer Iran S-300 Missiles, New Reactor," Ynetnews.com, September 11, 2013, http://www.ynetnews.com/articles/0,7340,L-4428465,00.html.

21. Anders Fogh Rasmussen and Philip M. Breedlove, "A NATO for a Dangerous World," *Wall Street Journal*, August 17, 2014, http://online.wsj.com/articles/anders-fogh-rasmussen-and-philip-m-breedlove-a-nato-for-a-dangerous-world-1408317653.

22. See, for example, Edward Lucas, "Russia's New Cold War," *Wall Street Journal*, February 19, 2014, http://www.wsj.com/articles/SB1 0001424052702304675504579388913610934806.
23. Roger Cohen, "The Iran-Ukraine Affair," *New York Times*, November 10, 2014, http://www.nytimes.com/2014/11/11/opinion/roger-cohen-the-iran-ukraine-affair.html?_r=0.
24. "Iran Says No Deal with U.S. to Ship Enriched Uranium to Russia," Reuters, January 3, 2015, http://mobile.reuters.com/article/idUSKBN0KC06W20150103?irpc=932.
25. Michele Kelemen, "Bush Sends Rice, Aid to Show Support for Georgia," NPR.org, August 13, 2008, http://www.npr.org/templates/story/story.php?storyId=93575217.
26. Emanuele Ottolenghi, "How Iran Is Skirting Sanctions in the South Caucasus," *National Interest*, December 15, 2014, http://defenddemocracy.org/media-hit/emanuele-ottolenghi-how-iran-is-skirting-sanctions-in-the-southern-caucasus/.
27. Ibid.
28. Claude Moniquet and William Racimora, eds., *The Armenia-Iran Relationship: Strategic Implications for Security in the South Caucasus Region* (European Strategic Intelligence and Security Center, January 17, 2013), 4, http://www.esisc.org/upload/publications/analyses/the-armenian-iran-relationship/Armenian-Iran%20relationship.pdf.
29. Ze'ev Wolfson, *Armenian "Traces" in the Proliferation of Russian Weapons in Iran*, ACPR Policy Paper, no. 143 (Ariel Center for Policy Research, December 2002), 25.
30. Central Intelligence Agency, *The World Factbook*, s.v. "Iran" (last updated June 22, 2014), https://www.cia.gov/library/publications/the-world-factbook/geos/ir.html.
31. See, for example, "Azerbaijani Foreign Minister Urges Iran to End Broadcasts into Southern Azerbaijan," *Radio Free Europe/Radio Liberty Newsline* 7, no. 204 (October 27, 2003).
32. Emanuele Ottolenghi, "Iran's Armenian Connection," *Weekly Standard*, April 16, 2012, http://www.weeklystandard.com/blogs/irans-armenian-connection_637088.html.
33. "Iran-Armenia Ties Strengthening to Counter Turkey-Azerbaijan Alliance," *Today's Zaman* (Istanbul), March 31, 2013, http://www.todayszaman.com/diplomacy_iran-armenia-ties-strengthening-to-counter-turkey-azerbaijan-alliance_311218.html.
34. Vladimir Socor, "Iran-Armenia Gas Pipeline: Far More than Meets

the Eye," *Eurasia Daily Monitor* 4, no. 56 (Jamestown Foundation, March 21, 2007), http://www.jamestown.org/single/?no_cache =1&tx_ttnews%5Btt_news%5D=32607#.VJjhaAH88.

35. Moniquet and Racimora, eds., "The Armenia-Iran Relationship."

36. Central Intelligence Agency, *The World Factbook*, s.v. "Armenia" (last updated June 23, 2014), https://www.cia.gov/library/publications /the-world-factbook/geos/am.html.

37. See, for example, "Iranian, Armenian Defence Ministers Discuss Regional Security Issues," IRNA, March 5, 2002; "Armenia, Iran Sign Military Cooperation Accord," ARMInfo Independent News Agency (Yerevan), March 5, 2002.

38. Joshua Kucera, "Rouhani Visits Baku as Azerbaijan-Iran Conflicts Fade into Past," Eurasianet.org, November 16, 2014, http://www .eurasianet.org/node/70946.

39. Mubariz Aslanov, "Azerbaijani-Iranian Joint Declaration on Friend-ship and Cooperation Approved," APA (Baku), December 30, 2014, http://en.apa.az/xeber_azerbaijani-iranian_joint_declaration_on _221100.html.

40. U.S. Department of the Treasury, "Treasury Targets Network At-tempting to Evade Iran Sanctions," April 11, 2013, http://www .treasury.gov/press-center/press-releases/Pages/jl1893.aspx.

41. "Tajikistan: Where Money Takes a Bath?" Eurasianet.org, August 21, 2013, http://www.eurasianet.org/node/67417.

42. Ibid.

43. Maya Lester, "2 More Iranian Bank Listings Annulled—Sorinet and Zanjani," *European Sanctions* (blog), July 5, 2014, http://europeansanc tions.com/2014/07/05/2-more-iranian-bank-listings-annulled -sorinet-and-zanjani/.

44. Basel Institute on Governance, "Basel Institute on Governance Pub-lishes the 2013 Edition of the Basel AML Index," n.d., https://www .baselgovernance.org/news/basel-institute-governance-publishes -2013-edition-basel-aml-index.

45. Mohiaddin Mesbahi, "Iran and Tajikistan," in *Regional Power Rival-ries in the New Eurasia: Russia, Turkey, and Iran*, ed. Alvin Z. Rubin-stein and Oles M. Smolansky (Armonk: M.E. Sharpe, 1995), 120.

46. Ibid.

47. Fozi Mashrab, "Tajikistan Wary of Iranians Bearing Gifts," Asia Times Online, March 30, 2012, http://www.atimes.com/atimes/Middle _East/NC30Ak03.html.

48. "Iran Strategic Partner for Tajikistan: Tajik Foreign Minister," Press TV (Tehran), July 18, 2013, http://www.presstv.com/detail /2013/07/18/314375/iran-strategic-partner-for-tajikistan/.

49. See Irina Zviagelskaya, "In Search of Support Points: Iran in Central Asia," Russian International Affairs Council, November 18, 2014, http://russiancouncil.ru/en/inner/?id_4=4782#top.

50. Sébastien Peyrouse and Sadykzhan Ibraimov, "Iran's Central Asia Temptations," *Current Trends in Islamist Ideology* 10 (Hudson Institute, April 2010), http://www.hudson.org/content/researchattachments /attachment/1290/peyrouse_ibraimov.pdf.

51. Ibid.

52. Sébastien Peyrouse, "Iran's Growing Role in Central Asia? Geopolitical, Economic and Political Profit and Loss Account," Al Jazeera (Doha), April 6, 2014, http://studies.aljazeera.net/en/dossiers/2014 /04/2014416940377354.html.

53. "Iran-Tajikistan Cooperation Reduces Impact of International Sanctions," *New Europe*, April 22, 2012, http://www.neurope.eu/article /iran-tajikistan-cooperation-reduces-impact-international-sanctions.

54. Peyrouse, "Iran's Growing Role in Central Asia?"

CHAPTER VI: IRAN'S ASIAN LIFELINE

1. Colin Clark, "JSF Survives, Global Hawk Dies, Global Strike Revives; Panetta's Budget," *Breaking Defense*, January 26, 2012, http:// breakingdefense.com/2012/01/jsf-survives-global-hawk-dies -global-strike-revives-panetta-r/.

2. U.S. Department of Defense, *Sustaining U.S. Global Leadership: Priorities for 21st Century Defense*, January 2012, www.defense.gov/news /Defense_Strategic_Guidance.pdf.

3. Gal Luft, "Fueling the Dragon: China's Race into the Oil Market," *IAGS Journal of Energy Security* (n.d.), http://www.iags.org/china .htm.

4. Wood Mackenzie, "China on Track to Spend US$500bn on Crude Oil Imports by 2020, Surpassing US Import Requirements," August 20, 2013, http://www.woodmacresearch.com/cgi-bin/wmprod/portal /corp/corpPressDetail.jsp?oid=11495385.

5. See, for example, Kang Wu, "Energy Security in China: Role of Oil and Gas in the Global Context," June 2013, http://www.esi.nus .edu.sg/docs/event/kang-wu-presentation-at-esi-june-2013.pdf ?sfvrsn=0.

6. Robin Wright, "Iran's New Alliance with China Could Cost U.S. Leverage," *Washington Post*, November 17, 2004.

7. Gal Luft, "China's Future Energy Development and Strategies." Statement before U.S.-China Economic and Security Review Commission, July 21, 2005, http://www.uscc.gov/sites/default/files/7.21 -22.05luft_gal_wrts_0.pdf.

8. Islamic Republic of Iran, National Iranian Oil Corporation, "China Increases Oil Imports from Iran," August 24, 2011, http://www.nioc .ir/Portal/Home/ShowPage.aspx?Object=NEWS&ID=325ad576 -bc0d-40cf-a86a-cd861a39d255&LayoutID=a48e86dd-dd07-4c23 -b5c1-4ee5da821796&CategoryID=9d32c839-2930-4ee6-9321-78 2d4ac9484a.

9. "China Oil Imports from Iran Hit a Record High," Press TV (Tehran), July 22, 2014, http://www.presstv.com/detail/2014/07/22/372302 /china-oil-imports-from-iran-hit-record/.

10. As cited in Zachary Keck, "Asia Is Purchasing Nearly All of Iran's Oil," *The Diplomat*, January 5, 2013, http://thediplomat.com/2013/01/asia -is-purchasing-nearly-all-of-irans-oil/.

11. Comprehensive Iran Sanctions, Accountability, and Divestment Act of 2010, Public Law 111-195, July 1, 2010, http://www.treasury.gov /resource-center/sanctions/Documents/hr2194.pdf.

12. Wayne Ma, "China Imports Record Amount of Iranian Crude," *Wall Street Journal*, July 21, 2014, http://online.wsj.com/articles/china -imports-record-amount-of-iranian-crude-1405946504.

13. U.S. Department of Defense, Office of the Secretary of Defense, *Proliferation: Threat and Response 1996* (1996), 14.

14. Richard F. Grimmett, *Conventional Arms Transfers to Developing Nations, 1993–2000* (Congressional Research Service, August 16, 2001), 28.

15. Louis Charbonneau, Jonathan Saul, and James Pomfret, "Exclusive: Iran Uses China Bank to Transfer Funds to Quds-Linked Companies —Report," Reuters, November 18, 2014, http://news.yahoo.com/ex clusive-iran-uses-china-bank-transfer-funds-quds-051934779.html.

16. "China, Iran Defense Officials Pledge Closer Ties," Associated Press, October 23, 2014, http://bigstory.ap.org/article/864c06776bc740ce a5262bce2efc9ffc/china-iran-defense-officials-pledge-closer-ties.

17. Brian Murphy, "Iran and China Deepen a 'Blue Water' Friendship," *Washington Post*, October 28, 2014, http://www.washingtonpost .com/blogs/worldviews/wp/2014/10/28/iran-and-china-deepen -a-blue-water-friendship/.

18. Scott Harold and Alireza Nader, *China and Iran: Economic, Political, and Military Relations*, occasional paper (Santa Monica, CA: RAND, 2012), 1–2, http://www.rand.org/content/dam/rand/pubs/occasional_papers/2012/RAND_OP351.pdf.

19. Chad O'Carroll, "Iran Builds Pyongyang's First Mosque," NKNEWS.org., January 22, 2013, http://www.nknews.org/2013/01/iran-buillds-pyongyangs-first-mosque/.

20. Christina Y. Lin, "China, Iran, and North Korea: A Triangular Strategic Alliance," *Middle East Review of International Affairs* 14, no. 1 (March 2010), http://www.gloria-center.org/2010/03/lin-2010-03-05/.

21. Ibid.

22. Ibid.

23. Mark E. Manyin, *North Korea: Back on the Terrorism List?* (Congressional Research Service, June 29, 2010), http://www.fas.org/sgp/crs/row/RL30613.pdf.

24. See Stephanie Griffith, "Iran Present at North Korean Missile Launch Says U.S.," Agence France-Presse, July 20, 2006, http://www.spacewar.com/reports/Iran_Present_At_North_Korea_Missile_Launch_Says_US_999.html; see also "Reports: Iran Experts Aiding North Korea Rocket Launch," FoxNews.com, March 29, 2009, http://www.foxnews.com/story/2009/03/29/reports-iran-experts-aiding-north-korea-rocket-launch/.

25. Bill Gertz, "Iran, North Korea Secretly Developing New Long-Range Rocket Booster for ICBMs," *Washington Free Beacon*, November 26, 2013, http://freebeacon.com/national-security/iran-north-korea-secretly-developing-new-long-range-rocket-booster-for-icbms/.

26. See "Secret Nuclear Sites Detailed," *Iran Brief*, November 6, 1995.

27. "Source: Hundreds of NK Nuclear and Missile Experts Working in Iran," *Korea Times* (Seoul), November 13, 2011, http://www.koreatimes.co.kr/www/news/nation/2011/11/113_98613.html; Madeline Chambers, "North Korea Supplied Nuclear Software to Iran: German Report," Reuters, August 24, 2011, http://www.reuters.com/article/2011/08/24/us-nuclear-northkorea-iran-idUSTRE77N2FZ20110824.

28. "Iran 'Paid Millions for Ringside Seat at N. Korean Nuke Test,'" *Chosun Ilbo* (Seoul), February 18, 2013, http://english.chosun.com/site/data/html_dir/2013/02/18/2013021801176.html.

29. See, for example, David P. Goldman, "Did Iran Test a Nuclear Bomb

in North Korea in 2010?" PJ Media, March 4, 2012, http://pjmedia
.com/spengler/2012/03/04/did-iran-test-a-nuclear-bomb-in
-north-korea-in-2010/.

30. Claudia Rosett, "Iran Follows in North Korea's Nuclear Shoes," *Asian
Wall Street Journal*, November 19, 2013, http://online.wsj.com/news
/articles/SB10001424052702304439804579207422182734460.

31. Ileana Ros-Lehtinen, "North Korea's Support for Terrorist Groups
and State Sponsors of Terrorism," internal memo to House Repub-
licans, May 8, 2008, http://freekorea.us/2008/05/09/leaked-to-ofk
-internal-house-memo-on-n-koreas-support-for-terrorism/.

32. Victor Cha and Gabriel Scheinmann, "North Korea's Hamas Connection: 'Below' the Surface?" *National Interest*, September 4, 2014,
http://nationalinterest.org/feature/north-koreas-hamas-connection
-below-the-surface-11195.

33. "Iranian Defector Tipped Syrian Nuke Plans," Associated Press, March
19, 2009, http://www.ynetnews.com/articles/0,7340,L-3689320,00
.html.

34. Robin Wright and Joby Warrick, "Syrians Disassembling Ruins at
Site Bombed by Israel, Officials Say," *Washington Post*, October 19,
2007.

35. Jay Solomon, "Iran–North Korea Pact Draws Concern," *Wall Street
Journal*, March 8, 2013, http://online.wsj.com/news/articles/SB100
01424127887323628804578348640295282274.

36. Ibid.

37. See, for example, Heather Saul, "Kim Jong-un 'Purge': Six North
Korea Officials Missing for Weeks 'May Have Been Executed,'" *The
Independent* (London), October 23, 2014, http://www.independent
.co.uk/news/world/asia/kim-jongun-purge-north-korean-officials
-missing-for-weeks-may-have-been-executed-9812616.html.

38. "North Korea Submarine: Nuclear Missile Launch Tests Being
Overseen by Kim Jong Un," Inquisitr.com, November 4, 2014, http://
www.inquisitr.com/1584335/north-korea-submarine-nuclear
-missile-launch-tests-being-overseen-by-kim-jong-un/.

39. James R. Clapper, *Worldwide Threat Assessment of the US Intelligence
Community*, Statement for the Record, Senate Select Committee
on Intelligence, January 29, 2014, http://www.dni.gov/index.php
/newsroom/testimonies/203-congressional-testimonies-2014/1005
-statement-for-the-record-worldwide-threat-assessment-of-the-us
-intelligence-community.

40. Josh Rogin and Eli Lake, "Iran and North Korea: The Nuclear 'Axis of Resistance,'" Daily Beast, January 31, 2014, http://www.thedailybeast.com/articles/2014/01/31/iran-and-north-korea-the-nuclear-axis-of-resistance.html.

41. "Hezbollah Planned to Attack Israeli Tourists," Daily Star (Lebanon), April 19, 2014, http://www.dailystar.com.lb/News/Lebanon-News/2014/Apr-19/253847-hezbollah-planned-to-attack-israeli-tourists.ashx.

42. See Haroon Siddique and agencies, "Thailand Arrests Hezbollah Suspect after Terror Tipoff," The Guardian (London), January 13, 2012, http://www.theguardian.com/world/2012/jan/13/thailand-arrests-hezbollah-suspect-terror-tipoff.

43. Ibid.

44. Joel Greenberg and Simon Denyer, "Israel Blames Iran for India and Georgia Bombings; Tehran Denies Role," Washington Post, February 13, 2012, http://www.washingtonpost.com/world/bombs-target-israeli-diplomats-in-india-georgia-2-injured/2012/02/13/gIQA2kDlAR_story.html.

45. As cited in "Delhi Car Blast: Has Hizbollah Found Supporters in India?" Rediff.com, February 14, 2012, http://www.rediff.com/news/slide-show/slide-show-1-delhi-car-blast-has-hizbollah-found-supporters-in-india/20120214.htm.

46. Matthew Levitt, Hezbollah: The Global Footprint of Lebanon's Party of God (Washington, DC: Georgetown University Press, 2013), 122.

47. Ibid., 117–39.

48. See, for example, U.S. Department of State, Office of the Spokesperson, "Additional Treasury and State Designations Targeting Networks Linked to Iranian WMD Proliferation and Sanctions Evasion," media note, December 12, 2013, http://www.state.gov/r/pa/prs/ps/2013/218637.htm.

49. Louis Charbonneau, "Exclusive: Iran's Illicit Procurement Appears to Slow Amid Nuclear Talks—U.N. Experts," Reuters, May 11, 2014, http://www.reuters.com/article/2014/05/11/us-iran-nuclear-sanctions-idUSBREA4A05820140511.

50. David Albright, Daniel Schnur, and Andrea Stricker, Iran Admits Illegally Acquiring Goods for Its Nuclear Program, ISIS Report (Institute for Science and International Security, September 10, 2014), http://isis-online.org/isis-reports/detail/iran-admits-illegally-acquiring-goods-for-its-nuclear-programs/.

51. "Iran Elite Group Suspected of Keeping Secret Funds in Asia," Kyodo

News International, May 4, 2014, http://www.globalpost.com /dispatch/news/kyodo-news-international/140504/iran-elite -group-suspected-keeping-secret-funds-asia.

52. Ibid.

53. Farhan Bokhari, "Pakistan to Build $1.5bn Iran Pipeline," *Financial Times*, January 31, 2013, http://www.ft.com/intl/cms/s/0/3a2abb18 -6bbe-11e2-a700-00144feab49a.html#axzz2JfYA3fbG.

54. "Iran Cancels Pakistan's Gas Pipeline Loan," Associated Press, December 14, 2014, http://www.washingtonpost.com/world/asia_pacific /iran-cancels-pakistan-gas-pipeline-loan/2013/12/14/8ff1078e -64bd-11e3-afod-4bb80d704888_story.html.

55. Ibid.

56. "Pakistan Owes Iran $100m for Electricity Imports," Press TV (Tehran), September 27, 2014, http://presstv.com/detail/2014/09 /27/380221/pakistan-owes-iran-100m-for-electricity/.

57. Gal Luft, "Iran-Pakistan Pipeline: Iran's New Economic Lifeline," *IAGS Journal of Energy Security* (June 18, 2009), http://ensec.org /index.php?view=article&catid=96%3Acontent&id=199%3Airan -pakistan-pipeline-irans-new-economic-lifeline&tmpl=component &print=1&page=&option=com_content&Itemid=345.

58. See, for example, "Iran, Afghanistan and India to Sign Pact, Official Says," Haaretz.com (Tel Aviv), March 30, 2014, http://www.haaretz .com/news/world/1.582805.

CHAPTER VII: A FOOTHOLD IN LATIN AMERICA

1. Joel Hirst, "The ALBA: Iran's Gateway," in *Iran's Strategic Penetration of Latin America*, ed. Joseph M. Humire and Ilan Berman (Lanham, MD: Lexington Books, 2014), 22–23.

2. Adrian Oliva, "A Bolivian Base for Iran's Military Advisors," in *Iran's Strategic Penetration of Latin America*, ed. Joseph M. Humire and Ilan Berman, 71.

3. Ibid., 71–73.

4. Ibid.

5. Luis Fleischman, "Venezuela: Anatomy of a Dictator," *Journal of International Security Affairs*, no. 11 (Fall 2006).

6. "Hugo Chávez de Visita en Irán hasta el Lunes," *El Universal* (Caracas), May 18, 2001, http://buscador.eluniversal.com/2001/05/18 /eco_art_18202GG.shtml.

7. As cited in "Venezuela e Irán en Camino Hacia una 'Alianza Estraté-

gica,'" *El Universal* (Caracas), May 21, 2001, http://www.eluniversal.com/2001/05/21/eco_art_21204AA.

8. Sean Goforth, *Axis of Unity: Venezuela, Iran and the Threat to America* (Washington, DC: Potomac Books, 2012), 31.

9. Victor Flores, "Venezuela-Iranian Anti-Washington Alliance," Agence France-Presse, September 17, 2006.

10. Parisa Hafezi, "Iran, Venezuela in 'Axis of Unity' against U.S.," Reuters, July 2, 2007, http://www.reuters.com/article/2007/07/02/us-iran-venezuela-idUSDAH23660020070702.

11. Norman A. Bailey, *Iran's Venezuelan Gateway*, Iran Strategy Brief, no. 5 (American Foreign Policy Council, February 2012), 2.

12. See Martin Rodil, "A Venezuelan Platform for Iran's Military Ambitions," in *Iran's Strategic Penetration of Latin America*, ed. Joseph M. Humire and Ilan Berman.

13. See, for example, "Venezuela Aids Iranian Missile Sales to Syria, Intelligence Agencies Say," Global Security Newswire, December 22, 2008, http://www.nti.org/gsn/article/venezuela-aids-iranian-missile-sales-to-syria-intelligence-agencies-say/.

14. Joana Paraszczuk, "Iran Admits Exporting Drone Tech to Venezuela," *Jerusalem Post*, December 12, 2012, http://www.jpost.com/Iranian-Threat/News/Iran-admits-exporting-drone-tech-to-Venezuela.

15. U.S. Department of Defense, *Unclassified Report on Military Power of Iran, April 2010*, http://www.iranwatch.org/sites/default/files/us-dod-reportmiliarypoweriran-0410.pdf.

16. "Kuwaitis among Trainees in 'Guards' Latin Camp," *Arab Times*, April 28, 2011, http://www.arabtimesonline.com/NewsDetails/tabid/96/smid/414/ArticleID/168534/reftab/36/Default.aspx.

17. Ibid.

18. Martin Arostegui, "U.S. Ties Caracas to Hezbollah Aid," *Washington Times*, July 7, 2008, http://www.washingtontimes.com/news/2008/jul/07/us-ties-caracas-to-hezbollah-aid/?page=1.

19. Julio A. Cirino, Silvana L. Elizondo, and Geoffrey Wawro, "Latin America's Lawless Areas and Failed States: An Analysis of New Threats," in *Latin American Security Challenges: A Collaborative Inquiry from North to South* (Newport, RI: Naval War College, 2004), 22–23.

20. Ely Karmon, "Iran and Its Proxy Hezbollah: Strategic Penetration in Latin America," Real Instituto Elcano, April 8, 2009, http://www.realinstitutoelcano.org/wps/portal/web/rielcano_en/conten

ido?WCM_GLOBAL_CONTEXT=/elcano/elcano_in/zonas_in
/international+terrorism/dt18-2009#.VRHb9Sjy-lc; Alan Levine,
"Hugo's Hezbollah," FrontPageMag.com, December 11, 2008,
http://archive.frontpagemag.com/readArticle.aspx?ARTID=33373.

21. Bailey, *Iran's Venezuelan Gateway.*

22. Figures derived from the International Monetary Fund's Direction of
Trade Statistics database (compilation in author's collection).

23. "Obama Signs Law against Iran's Influence in Latin America," Agence
France-Presse, December 29, 2012, http://www.dailynewsegypt
.com/2012/12/29/obama-signs-law-against-irans-influence-in
-latin-america.

24. Hugh Tomlinson, "Tehran Opens 24-Hour News TV," *Times of London*,
February 1, 2012, http://www.thetimes.co.uk/tto/news/world
/middleeast/article3304624.ece.

25. See "Irán Se Escuchará en Español con el Canal Hispan TV," *Correo
de Orinoco* (Caracas), July 18, 2011, http://www.correodelorinoco
.gob.ve/multipolaridad/iran-se-escuchara-espanol-canal-hispan-tv/.
A list of countries where HispanTV is broadcast is available online at
http://hispantv.com/Distribucion.aspx. Notably, the United States
is among those countries where cable providers accept and distribute
the Iranian channel.

26. Ian Black, "Iran to Launch Spanish-Language Television Channel,"
The Guardian (London), September 30, 2010, http://www.guardian
.co.uk/world/2010/sep/30/iran-spanish-language-television; "Iran
Launches Spanish TV Channel," Associated Press, January 31, 2012,
http://www.guardian.co.uk/world/2012/jan/31/iran-launches
-spanish-tv-channel.

27. Regional experts and journalists, in discussion with the author,
Quito, Ecuador, May 2012. Interviews conducted in confidentiality.

28. Joseph Humire, "Iran's Informal Ambassadors to Latin America,"
Latino.FoxNews.com, February 18, 2012, http://latino.foxnews
.com/latino/politics/2012/02/18/joseph-humire-irans-informal
-ambassadors-to-latin-america/.

29. U.S. Department of Defense, *Unclassified Report on Military Power of
Iran, April 2010.*

30. Kaveh L. Afrasiabi, "Iran and the Left in Latin America," Asia Times
Online, September 4, 2008, http://www.atimes.com/atimes/Mid
dle_East/JI04Ak01.html.

31. "Bolivia Moving Mideast Embassy to Iran from Egypt," Associated

Press, September 5, 2008, http://usatoday30.usatoday.com/news
/world/2008-09-05-3373415607_x.htm.

32. Journalists, activists, and opposition politicians, in discussion with the author, La Paz and Santa Cruz, Bolivia, January–February 2012. Interviews conducted in confidentiality.

33. "Iran 'Partner' in the Industrialization of Bolivia's Lithium Reserves," MercoPress, October 30, 2010, http://en.mercopress.com /2010/10/30/iran-partner-in-the-industrialization-of-bolivia-s -lithium-reserves.

34. Opposition politicians and government officials, in discussion with the author, Chile, Bolivia, and Argentina, January–February 2012. Interviews conducted in confidentiality.

35. "Gobierno Boliviano Rectifica Hallazgo de Uranio en La Paz," *El Tiempo* (Bogota), August 29, 2012, http://www.eltiempo.com/archi vo/documento/CMS-12174392.

36. Government officials and private-sector experts, in discussion with the author, Santiago, Chile, January 2012. Interviews conducted in confidentiality.

37. "Iran Loans Bolivia 280 Million USD to Develop Industry and Energy Sector," MercoPress, July 31, 2009, http://en.mercopress .com/2009/07/30/iran-loans-bolivia-280-million-usd-to-develop -industry-and-energy-sector.

38. "Bolivia to Buy Warplanes, Helicopters from Iran," *Latin American Herald Tribune*, n.d., http://www.laht.com/article.asp?ArticleId=374 965&CategoryId=14919.

39. "Iranian President Meets with Bolivia's Morales Reinforce Cooperation Deals," MercoPress, June 20, 2012, http://en.mercopress .com/2012/06/20/iranian-president-meets-with-bolivia-s-morales -reinforce-cooperation-deals.

40. As of 2012, bilateral trade between Iran and Ecuador totaled merely $16.8 million. See "Latin America: Iran Trade Triples," Latinvex .com, October 16, 2012, http://www.latinvex.com/app/article.aspx ?id=303.

41. Journalists and experts, in discussion with the author, Quito, Ecuador, April–May 2012. Interviews conducted in confidentiality.

42. See Alex Perez, "Sanctions Busting Schemes in Ecuador," in *Iran's Strategic Penetration of Latin America*, ed. Joseph M. Humire and Ilan Berman.

43. "Terroristas de Medio Oriente en Ecuador," *Vistazo* (Quito), April 7, 2011.

44. "Brazil Doesn't Recognize Unilateral Sanctions on Iran," *Tehran Times*, November 10, 2008.

45. "Brazil Is Iran's Most Important Trading Partner, Followed by Argentina," *Santiago Times*, December 7, 2009, http://www.santiagotimes.cl/index.php?option=com_content&view=article&id=17784:iran-triples-latin-american-trade-to-us29-billion&catid=48:other&Itemid=122.

46. As cited in Joe Leahy, "New Brazil Creates Some Distance from Iran," *Financial Times*, January 23, 2012, http://www.ft.com/intl/cms/s/0/881b4494-45e7-11e1-9592-00144feabdc0.html#axzz3LhnFw9a5.

47. Statistics derived from Brazil's Ministério do Desenvolvimento, Indústria e Comércio Exterior. Online at http://www.mdic.gov.br//sitio/interna/interna.php?area=5&menu=576.

48. Journalist, in discussion with the author, São Paulo, Brazil, April–May 2012. Interview conducted in confidentiality.

49. Ibid.

50. "Foreign Guests Arriving in Tehran to Attend Rouhani's Swearing-In Ceremony," Tasnim News Agency (Tehran), August 3, 2013.

51. Marcelo Martinez Burgos and Alberto Nisman, "Office of Criminal Investigations: AMIA Case," Investigations Unit of the Office of the Attorney General (report; request for arrests), 2006, http://www.peaceandtolerance.org/docs/nismanindict.pdf.

52. "Don't Lie to Me, Argentina," *The Economist*, February 25, 2012, http://www.economist.com/node/21548242.

53. Julian M. Obiglio and Diego C. Naveira, "Rewriting History in Argentina," in *Iran's Strategic Penetration of Latin America*, ed. Joseph M. Humire and Ilan Berman, 82.

54. Diego Melamed, "Meeting of Argentina and Iran Ministers Rankles Israel, U.S.," JTA.org, September 30, 2012, http://www.jta.org/2012/09/30/news-opinion/united-states/meeting-of-argentina-and-iran-ministers-rankles-israel-u-s.

55. "Argentina and Iran Create 'Truth Commission,'" Al Jazeera (Doha), January 28, 2013, http://www.aljazeera.com/news/americas/2013/01/20131272055398688.html.

56. Figures derived from the International Monetary Fund's Direction of Trade Statistics database (compilation in author's collection).

57. "Argentine Court Strikes Down 'Truth Commission' Deal with Iran on 1994 Bombing," Reuters, May 16, 2014, http://www.haaretz.com/jewish-world/jewish-world-news/1.591028.

58. Obiglio and Naveira, "Rewriting History in Argentina," 82.

59. Nonproliferation consultant for the U.S. government, in discussion with the author, Washington, D.C., July 2013. Interview conducted in confidentiality.

60. See Cynthia J. Arnson, Haleh Esfandiari, and Adam Stubits, eds., *Iran in Latin America: Threat or 'Axis of Annoyance'?* Woodrow Wilson Center Reports on the Americas, no. 23 (July 2008), http://www.wilson center.org/sites/default/files/Iran_in_LA.pdf.

61. "Israel: Ties to South America Aiding Iran's Nuclear Program," Ynetnews.com, May 25, 2009, http://www.ynetnews.com/articles /0,7340,L-3721335,00.html.

62. U.S. Department of Defense, *Annual Report on Military Power of Iran, April 2012*, http://www.fas.org/man/eprint/dod-iran.pdf.

63. Roman Ortiz, "Ayatollahs Cast Growing Shadow in Latin America," *Atlanta Journal-Constitution*, September 9, 2009, http://www.ajc.com /opinion/ayattolahs-cast-growing-shadow-135031.html.

64. See, for example, "Iran Firm to Boost Ties with Latin America: Rouhani," Press TV (Tehran), February 10, 2014, http://www.presstv .com/detail/2014/02/10/350081/iran-vows-close-ties-with-latam -mexico/.

65. "Iranian MPs Leave Tehran for Tour of Latin America," FARS News Agency (Tehran), May 26, 2014, http://english.farsnews.com/news text.aspx?nn=13930305001318.

66. "Iran Triples Trade Envoys Abroad to Boost Commerce," Associated Press, May 5, 2014, http://bigstory.ap.org/article/iran-triples-trade -envoys-abroad-boost-commerce.

67. "Iran Set Up Terrorist Network in Latin America," Reuters, May 30, 2013, http://www.jpost.com/Iranian-Threat/News/Prosecutor -Iran-set-up-terrorist-networks-in-Latin-America-314793.

68. Federal Bureau of Investigation, New York Field Office, "Abdul Kadir Sentenced to Life in Prison for Conspiring to Commit Terrorist Attack at JFK Airport," December 15, 2010, http://www.fbi.gov /newyork/press-releases/2010/nyfo121510a.htm.

69. Charles Savage and Scott Shane, "Iranians Accused of a Plot to Kill Saudis' U.S. Envoy," *New York Times*, October 11, 2011, http://www .nytimes.com/2011/10/12/us/us-accuses-iranians-of-plotting-to -kill-saudi-envoy.html?pagewanted=all.

70. "La Amenaza Iraní," Univision, December 9, 2011, http://noticias .univision.com/article/786870/2011-12-09/documentales/la-ame naza-irani/la-amenaza-irani.

71. "U.S. Expels Venezuelan Diplomat in Miami," CNN, January 9, 2014, http://www.cnn.com/2012/01/08/us/venezuela-consul/.

72. Countering Iran in the Western Hemisphere Act of 2012, H.R. 3783, 112th Congress, 2011–2013, Second Session, https://www.govtrack .us/congress/bills/112/hr3783/text.

73. Ibid.

74. United States Government Accountability Office, *Combating Terrorism: Strategy to Counter Iran in the Western Hemisphere Has Gaps That State Department Should Address*, September 2014, http://www.gao .gov/assets/670/666202.pdf.

75. Josh Rogin, "State Department Ordered Review of Iranian Terror Activity in Latin America," Daily Beast, August 5, 2013, http://www .thedailybeast.com/articles/2013/08/05/state-department-ordered -review-of-iranian-terror-activity-in-latin-america.html.

76. Joseph M. Humire, "Anticipating Iran's Next Moves," in *Iran's Strategic Penetration of Latin America*, ed. Humire and Ilan Berman, 100.

CHAPTER VIII: INROADS IN AFRICA

1. Secretary of State, "Iran and Syria Nonproliferation Act—Notification of Sanctions against Three Sudanese Entities," December 28, 2006, https://cablegatesearch.wikileaks.org/cable.php?id=06STATE 203861&q=sudan%20yarmouk.

2. Amos Harel and Avi Issacharoff, "Sudan Opposition: Bombed Arms Factory Belongs to Iran's Revolutionary Guard," Haaretz.com (Tel Aviv), October 24, 2012, http://www.haaretz.com/news/middle -east/sudan-opposition-bombed-arms-factory-belongs-to-iran-s -revolutionary-guard.premium-1.472090.

3. Ibid.

4. Sheera Frenkel, "Israeli Operations in Sudan Aimed at Disrupting Gaza Arms Trade, Officials Say," McClatchyDC.com, October 25, 2012, http://www.mcclatchy.com/2012/10/25/172602_israeli-opera tions-in-sudan-aimed.html?rh=1.

5. As cited in Lee Smith, "Smugglers Galore," *Weekly Standard* 18, no. 16 (December 31, 2012), http://www.weeklystandard.com/articles /smugglers-galore_690839.html.

6. Jonathan Schanzer, "A Deadly Love Triangle," *Weekly Standard*, August 6, 2008, https://www.weeklystandard.com/Content/Public /Articles/000/000/015/401vcvba.asp.

7. Ibid.

8. Steven O'Hern, *Iran's Revolutionary Guard: The Threat That Grows while America Sleeps* (Washington, DC: Potomac Books, 2012), 79–80.

9. Ibid.

10. Amir Taheri, "Sudan: An Expanding Civil War with an Iran Connection," *New York Times*, April 9, 1997, http://www.nytimes.com /1997/04/09/opinion/09iht-edamir.t.html.

11. O'Hern, *Iran's Revolutionary Guard*, 80.

12. Human Rights First, *Arms Transfers to Sudan, 2004–2006*, n.d., http:// www.humanrightsfirst.org/wp-content/uploads/pdf/CAH-081001 -arms-table.pdf.

13. "Tehran Opposes Al-Bashir Arrest," FARS News Agency (Tehran), September 8, 2008, http://eurasia.ro/?p=16676.

14. "West Sanctions on Iran, Sudan Politically-Motivated: Larijani," Press TV (Tehran), October 1, 2012, http://www.presstv.ir/detail /2012/10/01/264471/west-bans-on-iran-sudan-political/.

15. J. Peter Pham, "Shi'a in Senegal: Iran's Growing Reach into Africa," WorldDefenseReview.com, February 18, 2010, http://world defensereview.com/pham021810.shtml.

16. "Iran 'Could Share Nuclear Skills,'" BBC News, April 25, 2006, http://news.bbc.co.uk/2/hi/middle_east/4943782.stm.

17. As cited in Eric Reeves, "Sudan Embraces Genocide, Terrorism—and Iran," *Washington Post*, November 30, 2014, http://www.washington post.com/opinions/sudan-embraces-genocide-terrorism--iran/2014 /11/30/2ed603ae-75bb-11e4-a755-e32227229e7b_story.html.

18. Armin Rosen, "Desperate for Allies and Secret Assets, Iran Penetrates Africa," *The Tower*, no. 5, August 2013, http://www.thetower.org/ article/desperate-for-allies-and-secret-assets-iran-penetrates-africa/.

19. For more, see Ilan Berman, "Iran's Mullahs Blame Mahmoud," *Wall Street Journal Europe*, October 11, 2012, http://www.wsj.com/news /articles/SB10000872396390444799904578048500234241748?mg=r eno64-wsj.

20. See, for example, Geneive Abdo, "Iran: Ahmadinejad vs Khamenei," Al Jazeera (Doha), July 6, 2011, http://www.aljazeera.com/indepth /opinion/2011/06/201162994514399969.html.

21. Rana Rahimpour, "Ahmadinejad's Last Africa Tour Tries to Cement Ties," BBC News, April 15, 2013, http://www.bbc.com/news /world-middle-east-22150235.

22. Michael Rubin, "'Forgotten' Africa Turns to Iran as a Result of Western Neglect," *Public Service Europe*, May 7, 2013, accessed at Ameri-

can Enterprise Institute, https://www.aei.org/publication/forgotten-africa-turns-to-iran-as-a-result-of-western-neglect/.

23. "List of Diplomatic Missions of Iran," *Wikipedia*, n.d., http://en.wikipedia.org/wiki/List_of_diplomatic_missions_of_Iran; Argaw Ashwine, "Iran to Open Four New Embassies in Africa," AfricaReview.com, January 31, 2012, http://www.africareview.com/News/-/979180/1317204/-/gnv98pz/-/index.html.

24. Michael Rubin, *Africa: Iran's Final Frontier?* Middle Eastern Outlook, no. 2 (American Enterprise Institute, April 2013), https://www.aei.org/wp-content/uploads/2013/04/-africa-irans-final-frontier_145228692703.pdf.

25. "Iran Telecoms: MTN Plans Mobile-Phone Roll-Out," Economic Intelligence Unit, July 21, 2006.

26. Rubin, *Africa: Iran's Final Frontier?*

27. "SA-Iran Strengthen Ties," Fin24.com, October 31, 2013, http://www.fin24.com/Economy/South-Africa/SA-Iran-strengthen-ties-20131031.

28. Fredrik Dahl, "South Africa Throws UN Nuclear Meeting on Iran into Disarray," Reuters, September 13, 2012, http://www.reuters.com/article/2012/09/13/us-nuclear-iran-iaea-idUSBRE88C0I620120913.

29. "MTN 'Set Up Arms Meetings with Iran,'" *City Press* (Johannesburg), June 9, 2012, http://www.citypress.co.za/business/mtn-set-up-arms-meetings-with-iran-20120609/; Steve Stecklow, "Special Report: Documents Detail How MTN Funneled U.S. Technology to Iran," Reuters, August 30, 2012, http://www.reuters.com/article/2012/08/30/us-mtn-iran-documents-idUSBRE87T05R20120830.

30. Avi Jorisch, "MTN Has No Business Aiding Terror in Iran," *Sunday Times* (South Africa), March 25, 2012, http://www.avijorisch.com/10974/mtn-has-no-business-aiding-terror-in-iran.

31. Bill Meyer, "Morocco's King Mohammed VI Challenges Muslim World's Holocaust Denial," *Cleveland Plain Dealer*, July 25, 2009, http://www.cleveland.com/world/index.ssf/2009/07/moroccos_king_mohammed_vi_chal.html; "Morocco Severs Relations with Iran," Al Jazeera (Doha), March 8, 2009, http://www.aljazeera.com/news/africa/2009/03/2009370303221419.html.

32. See, for example, El Houssaine Naaim, "Morocco to Name New Ambassador to Iran, Resume Diplomatic Relations," MoroccoWorldNews.com, December 22, 2014, http://www.moroccoworld

news.com/2014/12/147751/morocco-to-name-new-ambassador
-to-iran-resume-diplomatic-relations/.

33. Jeff Lefebvre, "Iran in the Horn of Africa: Outflanking U.S. Allies,"
Middle East Policy Journal XIX, no. 2 (Summer 2012), http://www
.mepc.org/journal/middle-east-policy-archives/iran-horn-africa
-outflanking-us-allies.

34. Ibid.

35. Rubin, "'Forgotten' Africa Turns to Iran as a Result of Western
Neglect."

36. Lefebvre, "Iran in the Horn of Africa."

37. George Jahn, "Iran Hunts for Uranium Supplies, Finds Scrutiny,"
Associated Press, February 24, 2011, http://www.salon.com/news
/feature/2011/02/24/iran_nuclear_capacity_zimbabwe.

38. Vivienne Walt, "Is Iran Running Out of Uranium?" *Time*, April 27,
2010, http://www.time.com/time/world/article/0,8599,1984657
,00.html.

39. Ali Vaez and Karim Sadjadpour, *Iran's Nuclear Odyssey: Costs and
Risks* (Washington, DC: CEIP, 2013), http://carnegieendowment
.org/2013/04/02/iran-s-nuclear-odyssey-costs-and-risks#.

40. "Report: Iran Seeking to Smuggle Raw Uranium," Associated Press,
December 29, 2009, http://www.msnbc.msn.com/id/34622227/ns
/world_news-mideast/n_africa/.

41. Jahn, "Iran Hunts for Uranium Supplies, Finds Scrutiny."

42. "List of Countries by Uranium Reserves," *Wikipedia*, n.d., http://
en.wikipedia.org/wiki/List_of_countries_by_uranium_reserves.

43. Ibid.

44. "Why Iran Wants to Beef Up Zimbabwe's Military," *Christian Science
Monitor*, March 12, 2012, http://www.csmonitor.com/World/Africa
/2012/0315/Why-Iran-wants-to-beef-up-Zimbabwe-s-military.

45. "Zimbabwe Strikes Deal to Sell Uranium to Iran, According to Report," *Telegraph* (London), August 10, 2013, http://www.telegraph
.co.uk/news/10234749/Zimbabwe-strikes-deal-to-sell-uranium-to
-Iran-according-to-report.html.

46. "US Warns Zim against Iran Uranium Deal," News24, August 12,
2013, http://m.news24.com/nigeria/Africa/News/US-warns-Zim
-against-Iran-Uranium-deal-20130812-2.

47. Jon Swain, David Leppard, and Brian Johnson-Thomas, "Iran's
Plot to Mine Uranium in Africa," *Sunday Times* (London), August 5,
2006, http://www.freerepublic.com/focus/f-news/1678482/posts.

48. Kevin Kelley, "Uranium Being Smuggled via EA to Iran—WikiLeaks," *East African* (Nairobi), January 8, 2011, http://www.theeastafrican .co.ke/news/Uranium-being-smuggled-via-EA-to-Iran-WikiLeaks /-/2558/1082236/-/view/printVersion/-/9bpcac/-/index.html.

49. Abdoulaye Massalatchi, "Iran's Ahmadinejad Visits Uranium-Producing Niger," Reuters, April 15, 2013, http://www.reuters.com /article/2013/04/15/us-iran-niger-idUSBRE93E0RL20130415.

50. "Iran-Guinea Trade Exchanges Up by 140%," FARS News Agency (Tehran), May 1, 2010, http://english2.farsnews.com/newstext.php ?nn=8902111538.

51. Rubin, *Africa: Iran's Final Frontier?*

52. Ibid.

53. Jason Warner, "How Africa Plays into Iran's Nuclear Ambitions," CNN.com, January 17, 2012, http://globalpublicsquare.blogs.cnn .com/2012/01/17/how-africa-plays-into-irans-nuclear-ambitions/.

54. "JTF Uncovers Lebanese Terror Cell in Kano . . . Mustapha Fawaz, Co-Owner of Popular Amigo Supermarket Arrested," Xclusive Nigeria, May 31, 2013, http://www.exclusivenigeria.com/index.php /politics/item/698-jtf-uncovers-lebanese-terror-cell-in-kanomusta pha-fawaz-co-owner-of-popular-amigo-supermarket-arrested.

55. Benjamin Weinthal, "Analysis: The Rise of Hezbollah in Africa," *Jerusalem Post*, July 11, 2013, http://www.jpost.com/International/The -rise-of-Hezbollah-in-Africa-319512.

56. "JTF Uncovers Lebanese Terror Cell in Kano."

57. Ikechukwu Nnochiri, "Hezbolla: I Got Order to Survey Israeli Embassy in Nigeria—FAWAZ," *Vanguard* (Abuja), August 1, 2013, http://www.vanguardngr.com/2013/08/hezbolla-i-got-order-to -survey-israeli-embassy-in-nigeria-fawaz/.

58. Camillus Eboh, "Nigeria Says Arrests Iran-Linked Cell Targeting U.S., Israel," Reuters, February 21, 2013, http://www.reuters.com /article/2013/02/21/us-nigeria-iran-idUSBRE91K09420130221.

59. Ely Karmon, "Out of Iran, into Africa: Hezbollah's Scramble for Africa," Haaretz.com (Tel Aviv), June 17, 2013, http://www.haaretz .com/news/features/.premium-1.530327.

60. Matthew Levitt, *Hezbollah: The Global Footprint of Lebanon's Party of God* (Washington, DC: Georgetown University Press, 2013), 253.

61. Ibid., 261.

62. Ibid., 265.

63. Karmon, "Out of Iran, into Africa."

64. Tom Odula, "Kenyan Court Sentences 2 Iranians to Life in Jail," Associated Press, May 6, 2013, http://bigstory.ap.org/article/kenyan -court-sentences-2-iranians-life-jail.

65. Karmon, "Out of Iran, into Africa."

66. Pham, "Shi'a in Senegal."

67. Ikechukwu Nnochiri, "Kano Arms Cache: Court Frees 2 Lebanese Suspects," *Vanguard* (Lagos), November 30, 2013, http://www.van guardngr.com/2013/11/kano-arms-cache-court-frees-2-lebanese -suspects/.

68. Conflict Armament Research, "The Distribution of Iranian Ammunition in Africa: Results From a Nine-Country Investigation," December 2012, http://www.conflictarm.com/wp-content/uploads /2014/09/Iranian_Ammunition_Distribution_in_Africa.pdf.

69. Ibid.

70. See J. Peter Pham, "Behind Iran's Foiled Gambian Gambit," World-DefenseReview.com, December 2, 2010, http://worlddefensereview .com/pham120210.shtml.

71. C. J. Chivers, "A Trail of Bullet Casings Leads from Africa's Wars Back to Iran," *New York Times*, January 11, 2013, http://www.nytimes .com/2013/01/12/world/africa/a-trail-of-bullet-casings-leads -from-africas-wars-to-iran.html?pagewanted=all&_r=0.

72. Ibid.

73. "Iran Seeks Closer Ties with African States: Rouhani," Press TV (Tehran), February 24, 2014, http://www.presstv.com/detail/2014 /02/24/352108/iran-keen-to-expand-ties-with-africa/.

CHAPTER IX: A NEW DOMAIN FOR CONFLICT

1. Damien McElroy and Ahmad Vahdat, "Iran Cyber Warfare Commander Shot Dead in Suspected Assassination," *The Telegraph* (London), October 2, 2013, http://www.telegraph.co.uk/news/world news/middleeast/iran/10350285/Iranian-cyber-warfare-command er-shot-dead-in-suspected-assassination.html.

2. Kevjn Lim, "Iran's Cyber Posture," OpenBriefing.org, November 18, 2013, http://www.openbriefing.org/regionaldesks/middleeast /irans-cyber-posture/.

3. "Iran's Nuclear Agency Trying to Stop Computer Worm," Associated Press, September 25, 2010, http://www.webcitation.org/5t1vbet.

4. Gregg Keizer, "New Stuxnet Clues Suggest Sabotage of Iran's Uranium Enrichment Program," *Computerworld*, November 15, 2010,

http://www.computerworld.com/article/2514314/security0/new
-stuxnet-clues-suggest-sabotage-of-iran-s-uranium-enrichment
-program.html.

5. Ralph Langner, "Cracking Stuxnet, a 21st-Century Cyber Weapon,"
   TED Talk, March 2011, http://www.ted.com/talks/ralph_langner
   _cracking_stuxnet_a_21st_century_cyberweapon?language=en.

6. David Albright, Paul Brannan, and Christina Walrond, *Stuxnet Malware and Natanz: Update of ISIS December 22, 2010 Report*, ISIS Report
   (Institute for Science and International Security, February 15, 2011),
   http://isis-online.org/uploads/isis-reports/documents/stuxnet
   _update_15Feb2011.pdf.

7. As cited in Joby Warrick, "Iran's Natanz Nuclear Facility Recovered
   Quickly from Stuxnet Cyberattack," *Washington Post*, February 16,
   2011, http://www.washingtonpost.com/wp-dyn/content/article/2011
   /02/15/AR2011021505395.html.

8. Ivanka Barzashka, "Are Cyber-Weapons Effective? Assessing Stuxnet's Impact on the Iranian Nuclear Programme," *RUSI Journal* 148,
   no. 2 (2013): 48–56, http://www.tandfonline.com/doi/pdf/10.1080
   /03071847.2013.787735.

9. Ibid., 48.

10. "Study: Stuxnet Strengthened Iranian Nuclear Program," Ynetnews
    .com (Tel Aviv), May 16, 2013, http://www.ynetnews.com/articles
    /0,7340,L-4380512,00.html.

11. "Iran Sees Cyber Attacks as Greater Threat than Actual War," Reu-
    ters, September 25, 2012, http://www.reuters.com/article/2012/09/
    25/net-us-iran-military-idUSBRE88O0MY20120925.

12. Ellen Nakashima, Greg Miller, and Julie Tate, "U.S., Israel Developed
    Flame Computer Virus to Slow Iranian Nuclear Efforts, Officials Say,"
    Washington Post, June 19, 2012, http://www.washingtonpost.com
    /world/national-security/us-israel-developed-computer-virus-to
    -slow-iranian-nuclear-efforts-officials-say/2012/06/19/gJQA6xB
    PoV_story.html.

13. Yaakov Katz, "Iran Embarks On $1b. Cyber-Warfare Program,"
    Jerusalem Post, December 18, 2011, http://www.jpost.com/Defense
    /Article.aspx?id=249864http://www.jpost.com/Defense/Article
    .aspx?id=249864.

14. See, for example, Kevjn Lim, "Iran's Cyber Posture," OpenBriefing
    .org, November 18, 2013, http://www.openbriefing.org/regional
    desks/middleeast/irans-cyber-posture/.

15. Farvartish Rezvaniyeh, "Pulling the Strings of the Net: Iran's Cyber Army," PBS *Frontline*, February 26, 2010, http://www.pbs.org /wgbh/pages/frontline/tehranbureau/2010/02/pulling-the-strings -of-the-net-irans-cyber-army.html; Alex Lukich, "The Iranian Cyber Army," Center for Strategic & International Studies, July 12, 2011, http://csis.org/blog/iranian-cyber-army.

16. Frank J. Cilluffo, "The Iranian Cyber Threat to the United States." Testimony before the U.S. House of Representatives Committee on Homeland Security; Subcommittee on Counterterrorism and Intelligence; and Subcommittee on Cybersecurity, Infrastructure Protection, and Security Technologies, April 26, 2012, http://homeland .house.gov/sites/homeland.house.gov/files/Testimony%20-%20 Cilluffo.pdf.

17. James R. Clapper, *Worldwide Threat Assessment of the US Intelligence Community*, Statement for the Record, Senate Select Committee on Intelligence, January 29, 2014, http://www.dni.gov/index.php /newsroom/testimonies/203-congressional-testimonies-2014/1005 -statement-for-the-record-worldwide-threat-assessment-of-the-us -intelligence-community.

18. "Iran Enjoys 4th Biggest Cyber Army in World," FARS News Agency (Tehran), February 2, 2013, http://abna.ir/data.asp?lang =3&Id=387239.

19. University of Pennsylvania Iran Media Program, "Mapping Internet Censorship in Iran," n.d., http://hyperakt.com/items/iran-censorship -infographic/.

20. Nicole Perlroth and Quentin Hardy, "Bank Hacking Was the Work of Iranians, Officials Say," *New York Times*, January 8, 2013, http://www .nytimes.com/2013/01/09/technology/online-banking-attacks -were-work-of-iran-us-officials-say.html?pagewanted=1&_r=0.

21. Nicole Perlroth, "In Cyberattack on Saudi Firm, U.S. Sees Iran Firing Back," *New York Times*, October 23, 2012, http://www.ny times.com/2012/10/24/business/global/cyberattack-on-saudi-oil -firm-disquiets-us.html?pagewanted=all.

22. Ellen Nakashima, "Iran Aids Syria in Tracking Opposition via Electronic Surveillance, U.S. Officials Say," *Washington Post*, October 9, 2012, http://articles.washingtonpost.com/2012-10-09/world /35500619_1_surveillance-software-syrians-president-bashar.

23. "STUXNET Has Returned Home," *Kayhan* (Iran), July 27, 2011 (author's collection).

24. Author's confidential e-mail communications with infrastructure security expert, August 17, 2011.

25. Brian Ross, "What Will Happen to the US If Israel Attacks Iran?" ABC News, March 5, 2012, http://abcnews.go.com/Blotter/israel-attacks-iran-gas-prices-cyberwar-terror-threat/story?id=15848522#.T4g5tqvY9Ll.

26. Siobhan Gorman and Danny Yadron, "Iran Hacks Energy Firms, U.S. Says," *Wall Street Journal*, May 23, 2013, http://online.wsj.com/news/articles/SB10001424127887323336104578501601108021968.

27. Cylance, *Operation Cleaver*, December 2, 2014, http://www.cylance.com/assets/Cleaver/Cylance_Operation_Cleaver_Report.pdf.

28. Author's confidential e-mail communication with cybersecurity experts, summer 2014. Names of correspondents withheld by mutual agreement.

29. As cited in Joshua Levitt, "Iran Supreme Leader Khamenei Tells Students to Get Ready for Cyber War," Algemeiner.com, February 12, 2014, http://www.algemeiner.com/2014/02/12/iran-supreme-leader-khamenei-tells-students-to-get-ready-for-cyber-war/.

30. Julian Barnes and Siobhan Gorman, "U.S. Says Iran Hacked Navy Computers," *Wall Street Journal*, September 27, 2013, http://online.wsj.com/article/SB10001424052702304526204579101602356751772.html.

31. Mike Lennon, "Iranian Hackers Targeted US Officials in Elaborate Social Media Attack Operation," SecurityWeek.com, May 29, 2014, http://www.securityweek.com/iranian-hackers-targeted-us-officials-elaborate-social-media-attack-operation.

32. Dune Lawrence, "Iranian Hackers, Getting More Sophisticated, Target U.S. Defense Companies," *BusinessWeek*, May 14, 2014, http://www.businessweek.com/articles/2014-05-14/iranian-hackers-getting-more-sophisticated-target-u-dot-s-dot-defense-companies.

33. Gabi Siboni and Sami Kronenfeld, "Iranian Cyber Espionage: A Troubling New Escalation," INSS Insight No. 561, Institute for National Strategic Studies, June 16, 2014, http://www.inss.org.il/index.aspx?id=4538&articleid=7091.

34. White House, Office of the Press Secretary, "Remarks of President Obama Marking Nowruz," March 20, 2012, http://www.whitehouse.gov/the-press-office/2012/03/20/remarks-president-obama-marking-nowruz.

35. Ibid.

36. See, for example, Saeid Golkar, "Liberation or Suppression Technologies? The Internet, the Green Movement and the Regime in Iran," *International Journal of Emerging Technologies and Society* 9, no. 1 (2011): 50–70, http://www.swinburne.edu.au/hosting/ijets/journal/V9N1/pdf/Article%204%20Golkar.pdf.

37. Sara Reardon, "First Evidence for Iran's Parallel Halal Internet," *New Scientist*, no. 2886, October 10, 2012, http://www.newscientist.com/article/mg21628865.700-first-evidence-for-irans-parallel-halal-internet.html.

38. Tom Risen, "Iran's Dubious Digital Revolution," *U.S. News & World Report*, May 30, 2014, http://www.usnews.com/news/articles/2014/05/30/hassan-rouhani-youtube-and-irans-dubious-internet-revolution.

39. David Murphy, "Iran Launches 'Mehr,' Its Own YouTube-Like Video Hub," *PC Magazine*, December 9, 2012, http://www.pcmag.com/article2/0,2817,2413014,00.asp.

40. Majid Rafizadeh, "Iran's 'Halal' Version of the Internet," Al Arabiya, July 12, 2013, http://english.alarabiya.net/en/views/business/media/2013/07/12/Iran-s-Halal-version-of-the-Internet-.html.

41. Timothy B. Lee, "Here's How Iran Censors the Internet," *Washington Post*, August 15, 2013, http://www.washingtonpost.com/blogs/the-switch/wp/2013/08/15/heres-how-iran-censors-the-internet/.

42. National Council of Resistance of Iran, "Iran: Sale and Use of VPNs to Be a Crime in Latest Internet Clampdown," May 13, 2014, http://www.ncr-iran.org/en/news/human-rights/16521-iran-sale-and-use-of-vpns-to-be-a-crime-in-latest-internet-clampdown.

43. Charlie Warzel, "How Iran Uses Wikipedia to Censor the Internet," BuzzFeed.com, November 12, 2013, http://www.buzzfeed.com/charliewarzel/how-iran-uses-wikipedia-to-censor-the-internet.

44. Golnaz Esfandiari, "Iran Developing 'Smart Control' Software for Social-Networking Sites," Radio Free Europe/Radio Liberty, January 5, 2013, http://www.rferl.org/content/iran-developing-smart-control-software-for-social-networking-sites/24816054.html.

45. National Council of Resistance of Iran, "Iran: Sale and Use of VPNs to Be a Crime in Latest Internet Clampdown."

46. "Pres. Rouhani Underlines Vital Role of Cyber Security," IRIB World Service, February 3, 2014, http://english.irib.ir/news/iran1/item/177545-pres-rouhani-underlines-vital-role-of-cyber-security.

47. Steve Stecklow, "Special Report: Chinese Firm Helps Iran Spy on

Citizens," Reuters, March 22, 2012, http://www.reuters.com/article
/2012/03/22/us-iran-telecoms-idUSBRE82L0B820120322.

48. "Iran Blocks Use of Tool to Get around Internet Filter," Reuters,
March 10, 2013, http://www.reuters.com/article/2013/03/10/us
-iran-internet-idUSBRE9290CV20130310.

49. Reporters Without Borders, "Iran," in "Surveillance," special edition,
The Enemies of Internet (March 12, 2013), http://surveillance.rsf.org
/en/iran/.

50. Ramin Mostaghim and Emily Alpert, "Iran's Supreme Leader Calls
for New Internet Oversight Council," *Los Angeles Times*, March 7,
2012, http://latimesblogs.latimes.com/world_now/2012/03/iran-in
ternet-council-khamenei.html.

51. University of Pennsylvania Iran Media Program, "Internet Censorship in Iran."

52. Golnaz Esfandiari, "Iran Announces New Restrictions for Internet
Cafes," Radio Free Europe/Radio Liberty, January 4, 2012, http://
www.rferl.org/content/iran_announces_new_internet_restric
tions/24442396.html.

53. "Middle East," Internet World Stats, accessed May 29, 2015, http://
www.internetworldstats.com/middle.htm.

54. See, for example, John Kelly and Bruce Etling, "Mapping Iran's
Online Public: Politics and Culture in the Persian Blogosphere,"
Harvard University, Berkman Center for Internet & Society, April
5, 2008, http://cyber.law.harvard.edu/sites/cyber.law.harvard.edu
/files/Kelly&Etling_Mapping_Irans_Online_Public_2008.pdf.

55. Fred Petrossian, Arash Abadpour, and Mahsa Alimardani, "The Decline of Iran's Blogestan," *Washington Post*, April 11, 2014, http://
www.washingtonpost.com/blogs/monkey-cage/wp/2014/04/11
/the-decline-of-irans-blogestan/.

CONCLUSION

1. "White House Official: Nuclear Deal Could Portend Iran Ties," JTA,
September 28, 2014, http://www.jta.org/2014/09/28/news-opin
ion/united-states/white-house-official-nuclear-deal-could-portend
-iran-ties#ixzz3Euy24qYh.

2. As cited in Matthew Continetti, "The Coming Détente with Iran,"
Washington Free Beacon, October 31, 2014, http://freebeacon.com
/columns/the-coming-detente-with-iran/.

3. Ibid.

4. Johannes Reissner, "Europe and Iran: Critical Dialogue," in *Honey and Vinegar: Incentives, Sanctions, and Foreign Policy*, ed. Richard N. Haass and Meghan L. O'Sullivan (Washington, DC: Brookings Institution Press, 2000), 42; see also Geoffrey Kemp, "The United States, Europe & Iran: The Ingredients for U.S.-European Policy," in *The Iranian Dilemma: Challenges for German and American Foreign Policy*, conference report, American Institute for Contemporary German Studies and Johns Hopkins University, Washington, DC, April 21, 1997.

5. "Transcript of Interview with Iranian President Mohammed Khatami," CNN.com, January 7, 1998, http://www.cnn.com/WORLD/9801/07/iran/interview.html.

6. See Reuel Marc Gerecht, "Iran: Fundamentalism and Reform," in *Present Dangers: Crisis and Opportunity in American Foreign and Defense Policy*, ed. Robert Kagan and William Kristol (San Francisco: Encounter Books, 2000), 111–45.

7. For a good summary, see "History of Official Proposals on the Iranian Nuclear Issue," Arms Control Association, January 2014, http://www.armscontrol.org/factsheets/Iran_Nuclear_Proposals.

8. Hassan Rouhani, "President of Iran Hassan Rouhani: Time to Engage," *Washington Post*, September 19, 2013, http://www.washingtonpost.com/opinions/president-of-iran-hassan-rouhani-time-to-engage/2013/09/19/4d2da564-213e-11e3-966c-9c4293c47ebe_story.html.

9. As cited in "Rohani's Outstretched Hand," *The Economist*, October 4, 2014, http://www.economist.com/printedition/2014-10-04.

10. Julian Borger, "Iranian President Gives Qualified Support for Western Action against Isis," *The Guardian* (London), September 26, 2014, http://www.theguardian.com/world/2014/sep/27/iranian-qualified-support-western-action-isis.

11. Karim Sadjadpour, "Examining What a Nuclear Iran Deal Means for Global Security." Testimony before the U.S. House of Representatives Committee on Foreign Affairs Subcommittee on the Middle East and North Africa, November 20, 2014, http://docs.house.gov/meetings/FA/FA13/20141120/102758/HHRG-113-FA13-Wstate-SadjadpourK-20141120.pdf.

12. Ibid.

13. Daniel Patrick Moynihan, "Defining Deviancy Down," *American Scholar* 62, no. 1 (Winter 1993): 17–30, http://www.utexas.edu/law

/journals/tlr/sources/Volume%2092/Issue%206/Koppelman /Koppelman.fn051.Moynihan.DefiningDeviancy.pdf.

14. "Former IRGC Politburo Chief: Iran Is 'Strategic Rival' of West," IranDailyBrief.com, October 23, 2012, http://www.irandailybrief .com/2012/10/23/former-irgc-politburo-chief-iran-is-strategic -rival-of-west/.

15. White House, Office of the Press Secretary, "Statement by the President on Cuba Policy Changes," December 17, 2014, http://www .whitehouse.gov/the-press-office/2014/12/17/statement-president -cuba-policy-changes.

16. Keith Johnson, "Kerry Makes It Official: 'Era of Monroe Doctrine Is Over,'" *Wall Street Journal*, November 18, 2013, http://blogs .wsj.com/washwire/2013/11/18/kerry-makes-it-official-era-of -monroe-doctrine-is-over/.

17. See, for example, Ryan Costello and Trita Parsi, "If It's True on Cuba, It's True on Iran," National Iranian American Council, December 17, 2014, http://www.niacouncil.org/true-cuba-true-iran/; see also Barbara Slavin, "Cuba Shift Could Help Break Iran Deadlock," Voice of America, December 23, 2014, http://www.voanews.com/content /slavin-cuba-shift-could-help-/2570501.html.

18. Arash Karami, "Iran Sees Failure of US Sanctions in Cuba Decision," *Al-Monitor*, December 23, 2014, http://www.al-monitor.com/pulse /originals/2014/12/iran-us-cuba-rapprochement-sanctions-failure .html.

19. For a further discussion, see Behnam Ben Taleblu, "Reading Washington's New Cuba Policy in Tehran," policy brief, Foundation for Defense of Democracies, December 26, 2014, http://defenddemoc racy.org/media-hit/behnam-ben-taleblu-reading-washingtons-new -cuba-policy-in-tehran/.

Index

Abbas, Mahmoud, 55
Abedini, Saeed, 43
Abuja (Nigeria), 144
Afghanistan, 50–54, 60–61, 80–81, 106, 107
Afghanistan-Iran Strategic Cooperation Agreement, 53
Afghanistan War, 50, 52, 53, 60, 80, 111
Afghan refugees, 39–40
Africa, Iranian involvement in: diplomatic outreach, 134–36, 137; economic arrangements, 23, 50, 136; Hezbollah and, 141–44; Iranian nuclear program and, 135–36, 138–41; Iranian strategies, 134; security arrangements, 23, 50, 131–33, 137–38; in South Africa, 136–37; in Sudan, 131–34; trade, 136, 141
Agence France Presse, 41
Ahmadi, Mojtaba, 147–48
Ahmadinejad, Mahmoud:

Africa-Iran relations and, 134–35, 137, 140; Chávez and, 111–12; elected to Iranian presidency, 16, 111; as Holocaust denier, 137; IRGC and, 16–17; on Israel's elimination, 59; Khamenei vs., 134–35; Latin America–Iran relations and, 111–12, 116, 117, 120–21, 126–27; North Korea–Iran relations and, 102; Pakistan-Iran pipeline project approved by, 106; reelection of, 28, 63, 156; SCO appearance of, 80; spiritual teacher of, 61; Tajikistan-Iran relations and, 91; U.N. speech of, 24, 123
Ajax Security Team, 155
Akil, Ibrahim, 101
ALBA. *See* Bolivarian Alliance of the Americas
Aliyev, Ilham, 89
Amano, Yukiya, 149